TREE HUGGERS

Victory, Defeat & Renewal
in the Northwest Ancient Forest Campaign

FOR THE FOREST

"These are the shrines saved from all the land that was once known and lived on by the original people, the little bits left as they were, the last little places where intrinsic nature totally wails, blooms, nests, glints away."

—GARY SNYDER, *"The Etiquette of Freedom,"* 1990

TREE HUGGERS

Victory, Defeat & Renewal
in the Northwest Ancient Forest Campaign

KATHIE DURBIN

THE
MOUNTAINEERS

Published by
The Mountaineers
1001 SW Klickitat Way
Seattle, WA 98134

0 9 8 7 6
5 4 3 2 1

Published simultaneously in Canada by Douglas & McIntyre, Ltd., 1615 Venables Street, Vancouver, B.C. V5L 2H1

Published simultaneously in Great Britain by Cordee, 3a DeMontfort Street, Leicester, England, LE1 7HD

Manufactured in the United States of America

Editor: Mary Anne Stewart
Copyeditor: Dana Fos
Map design and photo layout: Gray Mouse Graphics
Cover design: Pat Lanfear and Helen Cherullo
Book design and layout: Ani Rucki

Cover photographs: *Hundreds of old growth trees at Honeytree are victims of the cut and run salvage rider* (Photo: Sky Shiviah). Inset: *Hundreds rally in Portland during the 1993 Northwest Forest Conference* (Photo: Elizabeth Feryl/Environmental Images)

Library of Congress Cataloging-in-Publication Data
Durbin, Kathie.
    Tree huggers : victory, defeat & renewal in the Northwest ancient forest
campaign / Kathie Durbin.
        p.   cm.
    Includes bibliographical references.
    ISBN 0-89886-488-7
    1. Old growth forests—Oregon. 2. Old growth forests—Northwest,
Pacific. 3. Logging—Oregon. 4. Logging—Northwest, Pacific. 5. Old
growth forest conservation—Oregon. 6. Old growth forest conservation—
Northwest, Pacific. 7. Forest policy—United States. I. Title.
SD387.043D87   1996
333.75'17'09795—dc20   96–9757
                                                                          CIP

Contents

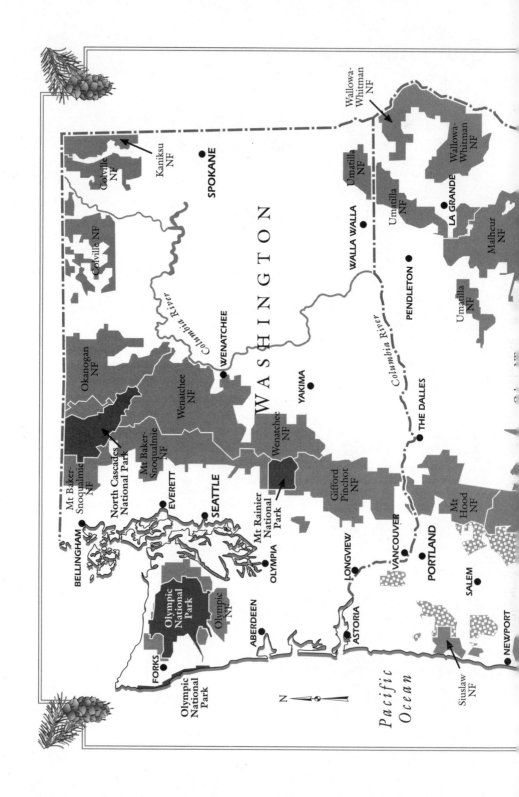

WASHINGTON

SPOKANE

Kaniksu
NF

Colville
NF

Colville NF

Wallowa-
Whitman
NF

Wallowa-
Whitman
NF

Umatilla
NF

LA GRANDE

Malheur
NF

Umatilla
NF

WALLA WALLA

PENDLETON

Umatilla
NF

Columbia River

Okanogan
NF

Wenatchee
NF

WENATCHEE

Columbia River

THE DALLES

YAKIMA

Mt Baker-
Snoqualmie
NF

North Cascades
National Park

Mt Baker-
Snoqualmie
NF

Wenatchee
NF

Gifford
Pinchot
NF

Mt
Hood
NF

BELLINGHAM

EVERETT

SEATTLE

Mt Rainier
National Park

OLYMPIA

LONGVIEW

VANCOUVER

PORTLAND

SALEM

Olympic National
Park

Olympic
NF

ABERDEEN

ASTORIA

NEWPORT

FORKS

Olympic
National
Park

N

Pacific
Ocean

Siuslaw
NF

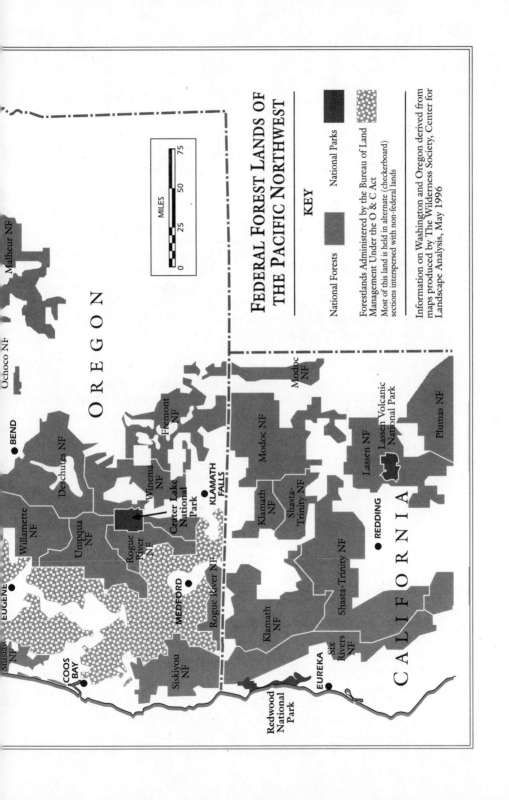

FEDERAL FOREST LANDS OF THE PACIFIC NORTHWEST

KEY

National Forests

National Parks

Forestlands Administered by the Bureau of Land Management Under the O & C Act
Most of this land is held in alternate (checkerboard) sections interspersed with non-federal lands

Information on Washington and Oregon derived from maps produced by The Wilderness Society, Center for Landscape Analysis, May 1996

MILES

0   25   50   75

OREGON

Malheur NF
Ochoco NF
• BEND
Deschutes NF
Willamette NF
Umpqua NF
Winema NF
Fremont NF
Rogue River NF
Crater Lake National Park
KLAMATH FALLS
• Siuslaw NF
• EUGENE
COOS BAY
Siskiyou NF
MEDFORD
Rogue River NF

CALIFORNIA

Modoc NF
Klamath NF
Shasta-Trinity NF
Lassen NF
Lassen Volcanic National Park
Plumas NF
• REDDING
Shasta-Trinity NF
Klamath NF
Six Rivers NF
EUREKA
Redwood National Park

Foreword

I remember so vividly the fall of 1975, when I moved to the deep green Northwest to teach law at the University of Oregon. Chapin Clark, my dean, had assigned me to teach Public Land Law. It was a logical decision, for I had credentials. Although I'd never taught Public Land Law for a minute or written a syllable about it, I had the necessary intellectual drive: I loved to fish and hike in the national forests. "Don't worry," Chapin told me, about being new to the field. "Look, for all practical purposes this is a new area. Work hard and you'll be all right." Then he added: "My guess is that you're really going to have some fun with this. It looks to me as though the national forests are in for some big changes. And everything in the Pacific Northwest turns on timber."

Chapin had it exactly right, and it turned out to be one of my life's joys to teach and write about these fascinating events, to see them up close, more or less from the beginning. It was an extraordinarily dynamic time in the Pacific Northwest, near the beginning of an era when you could see history being made right in front of you, day by day, year by year. The *Monongahela* decision, enjoining clearcutting on national forest lands in West Virginia, came down in 1975 and within months a federal judge had applied it in Alaska. Everywhere the question was asked: how would the law and politics of clearcutting play out in the Pacific Northwest?

The struggle over clearcutting made front-page news regularly, and inevitably so. These were some of the most commercially valuable stands of timber on earth. Oregon was the nation's top timber-producing state. Region Six of the Forest Service, covering Oregon and Washington, put out between 4.5 and 5 billion board feet of timber every year, nearly half of the cut from the entire national forest system. If a public body were eligible for the Fortune 500, Region Six would be highly ranked. *The Oregonian* once compared the Regional Forester, officed in Portland, to the governorship of Oregon in terms of actual political power.

The ancient forests also called out to the deepest parts of our humanity. Rains and storms blew in off the Pacific, and the low coastal ranges and high Cascades welcomed and held the moisture, creating a land of ferns, moss, and great trees, of grubs, elk, and salmon, of mist, fog, and dripping, of secrecy, solitude, and mystery. These green cathedrals, as much as the ocean and broad rivers, defined the Pacific Northwest.

A great and complex public debate usually takes at least a generation before its resolution begins to take form. Almost always, the terms of the debate will change over such a long time, and that surely took place in the Northwest. Twenty years ago, in the mid-1970s, the furor in the national forests focused quite specifically on clearcutting and its effect on trees. The idea of biodiversity—the web of life in a living forest—had not yet become part of the public discourse. The Endangered Species Act would not be given teeth until the 1978 decision in *Tennessee Valley Authority* v. *Hill* and would not reach the Northwest forests until a decade after that. Battle raged over the Pacific salmon, but the issue was Indian fishing rights, not the very survival of the fast, silvery species. Although another animal had become the subject of scientific inquiry during the 1970s, to my knowledge not a single northern spotted owl contacted the Sierra Club Legal Defense Fund to sign up as a plaintiff in federal court litigation until the late 1980s.

After the passage of nearly a quarter of a century, we can begin to appreciate the full significance of these events. We finally are grasping the immensity of the post–World War II boom in the American West. To meet the region's explosion from 16 million to 57 million people, we savaged the lands and rivers and creatures that drew so many here, that made the place sacred. We can mark down the postwar era, along with the California Gold Rush, as one of the West's two most fundamentally defining eras. The fury in the national forests—every bit as much as the conflicts over the big dams, the power plants, and the build-up of the metropolises—lies at the center of it.

This is, then, an epic series of events that Kathie Durbin explores in her remarkable book, *Tree Huggers*. It is a compelling, arresting story that encompasses a broad landscape of people, events, and places—and a story that has accelerated in the past few years. Durbin, one of the country's finest environmental journalists, does it justice in every way.

Readers will applaud the authenticity of *Tree Huggers*. In a sense, the heart of this struggle has been the story of people trapped: activists defending their homelands against encroaching fronts of Caterpillar tractors and chainsaws; Forest Service employees caught in their agency's mythology and budget numbers; politicians who have lost their options to big-money campaign donations; people in the timber industry facing the inevitability of the Northwest's changing values and economy. Over the years, I've been fortunate to know most of the people of whom Durbin writes. Her accounts are unerring, both as to the public personalities of the participants and as to the motivations that drive them.

Durbin also rings true when she takes us into the woods, which are a main character in this book. It was the old forests that inspired such deep passions and that drove so many people to become tree huggers and to act so fiercely for so long. Durbin's book is rooted where it should be, in the rich, wet forest floors.

This generation-long epic has brought considerable reform. The cut has come down. Harvesting practices better protect the life in the national forests. We have a far better understanding of the consequences of our actions. Nevertheless, much remains to be done, both on the public lands and on the private timber lands that are, after all, part of the same webbing. One of the world's most magnificent natural systems still hangs in the balance. The question left open in *Tree Huggers* is whether the impressive public resolve that has welled up in the Pacific Northwest since the early 1970s will finally implant itself deeply enough and soon enough to keep the forests both sanctuary to us and homeland for the intertwined lives that dwell within.

—*Charles F. Wilkinson*

Preface and Acknowledgments

I grew up in the heart of timber country: Lane County, Oregon. My grandfather, George Monteith, logged the giants of Grays Harbor County, Washington, on the Olympic Peninsula. Trees formed the contours of my childhood. But I did not begin to learn the forest until I began to explore my world as a woman. And I did not begin to understand the politics of timber until I began to write about the conflict surrounding the fate of the Northwest's old-growth forests as a journalist, in 1989.

In his book *The Klamath Knot,* David Rains Wallace equates the experience of being in an evergreen forest with the long life stage known as maturity: "There are no horizons in the forest. Beginnings and endings seem far away among the trees, and one feels caught in the fabric of life." Ancient forests, and the story of the campaign to save them, have become woven into the fabric of my life these past seven years.

A word about the title of this book: "Tree huggers" is a term often hurled at forest activists as a dismissive epithet. However, the term has quite different connotations in other cultures. Indian environmental activist Sunderlal Bahaguna, a follower of Ghandi and a spiritual leader, spends his days trekking through the Himalayas, speaking with villagers and schoolchildren and stopping to hug scrawny oaks from which limbs have been lopped to provide scarce firewood. He is the driving force behind a grassroots movement called Chipko—Hindi for "to embrace, or hug"—that hopes to halt deforestation in the Himalayas. In the Pacific Northwest, grassroots activists have wrapped metaphorical arms around ancient forests—the arms of passion, of law, of political persuasion, and of a growing ecological awareness.

The job of covering the most significant environmental conflict of the late 20th century fortunately fell to a cadre of dedicated local, regional, and national journalists who knew they were recording conservation history in the making. I am indebted to my colleagues on the beat who contributed to the common pool of information: Rocky Barker, Jeff Barnard, Joel Connelly, Bill Dietrich, Sandi Doughton, Tim Egan, Paul Fattig, Tom Kenworthy, Dick Manning, Eric Pryne, Lance Robertson, Scott Sonner, Rob Taylor, Julie Titone, Roberta Ulrich, David Whitney, and in particular Paul Koberstein, the publisher of

Cascadia Times and my colleague on the environmental team at *The Oregonian* during four critical years of this saga.

I am grateful to scores of scientists, environmental activists, Forest Service and Bureau of Land Management employees, and others who took time to show me the forest. I regret that I could not mention each one by name in this book and that so many stories of courage and dedication had to go untold. I am indebted to photographers Elizabeth Feryl, Trygve Steen, Sky Shiviah, and Gary Braasch who gave generously of their work, and to editor Mary Anne Stewart, who helped me to shape a finished book from a rough manuscript on an impossibly short timeline. I wish to thank Margaret Foster of The Mountaineers Books, who stood by this project, and my agent, Jane Dystel, who believed in it from the first. A warm thank-you, also, to Cottages at Hedgebrook, and to Nancy Nordhoff, for giving me sanctuary in the forest when I needed it most.

My family and friends kept me going when the task ahead seemed hopeless. Stefanie and Casey opened their home to me in Washington, D.C.; Audrey, David and Brenda offered moral support at crucial moments. My parents were steadfast cheerleaders.

Finally, without the encouragement and faith of my husband, Doug Babb, this book would not have come to fruition.

Kathie Durbin
June 1996

Prologue

The immense Douglas-firs on Grayback Mountain began falling in early September of 1995. All summer, forest activists from nearby southwestern Oregon communities had held prayer vigils on the mountain, hoping to win these forests a reprieve. On September 9, as loggers cut the first openings in the unbroken forest canopy, locked gates and armed guards kept protesters at a distance.

High in the Oregon Cascades, on a logging road overlooking a valley carved by clearcuts, a small band of forest defenders dug in on that same September week to block the logging of blackened timber in an old-growth forest torched four years earlier by arsonists.

In early October, 33-year-old Tim Ream began a 75-day fast outside the federal courthouse in Eugene, Oregon, to draw attention to a law passed by Congress and signed by President Clinton that required the logging of ancient forests regardless of the consequences for fish and wildlife, soils and streams.

Over the next nine months, across the Pacific Northwest, these forests continued to fall. But they did not fall unnoticed. Each forest doomed to destruction had a name, and each name became a kind of lament: Sugarloaf. Roman Dunn. Warner Creek. Rocky. Yellow Creek. Honeytree. Hoxie Griffin. Caracao Cat. First. Last. Tobe West. Enola Hill.

On the other side of the Cascades, in the pine and mixed-conifer forests of eastern Oregon and Washington, Idaho, and western Montana, the Forest Service prepared to push roads into some of the last large unprotected wilderness areas in the Intermountain West under the guise of restoring the forests to health.

Environmentalists accustomed to working through the system and activists on the radical fringe of the forest preservation movement united to fight the leveling of these forests. They rallied, trespassed on logging roads, wrote letters to Congress and the White House, and sent their lawyers to argue fruitlessly in federal court that these trees, these mountainsides, these watersheds should not be logged.

In February of 1996, balmy temperatures melted the mountain snowpack in the Cascade Mountains and a storm front dropped curtains of rain on the Pacific Northwest, filling rivers and reservoirs to overflowing and unleashing the most devastating floods since 1964. Rain pummeled the clearcut mountainsides and saturated the logging roads of the high country, setting off landslides and sending torrents downstream to rip away bridges and houses and roads. Still the logging continued.

13

This was not the way it was supposed to be.

For a quarter-century, a scattered tribe of forest defenders battled the timber industry and the political establishment to save remnants of the Pacific Northwest's virgin forests. They used law, science, and a growing public awareness of the ecological value of these forests to make the case for protection. In 1993, they won a fragile, incomplete victory. In 1995, Congress and the Clinton administration took that victory away.

The passionate protests that flared across the region in the fall, winter, and spring of 1995–96 marked a tragic setback, and a critical turning point, in the Northwest ancient forest campaign.

The forests at stake in this campaign hold within them the complex wisdom of many thousands of years of evolution. They are fragments of the great conifer forest that once cloaked the mountain ranges at the western edge of North America, from Southeast Alaska to Monterey Bay and inland to the Continental Divide.

The green cloak, now tattered nearly beyond repair after a century of forest liquidation, is a weave of many conifer species: Sitka spruce in the narrow band of coastal rainforest stretching north to Alaska; Douglas-fir, western redcedar, and western hemlock in the coastal mountains and on the western slopes of the Cascades; incense cedar, sugar pine, and rare Brewer's spruce in the Siskiyous; ponderosa pine and western larch in the open forests east of the Cascades. All grow larger in the Pacific Northwest than anywhere else on Earth; some grow only in this region of wet winters and dry summers. The conifer forest with its intricate web of plant and animal life evolved over millennia, shaped by climate and altitude, latitude and terrain, wind and fire—natural forces unique to a time and a place on this planet that we will not see again.

The moral argument for saving some of this natural legacy is powerful. But from the beginning, the odds against success were high. The great forests of the Pacific slope held untapped wealth for an expanding young nation. Accessible forests along the lower reaches of coastal rivers began falling in the mid-19th century. Over a century, logging progressed steadily into the foothills and climbed steep slopes into the headwaters where salmon spawned.

The American conservation movement, born in the waning years of the 19th century, heightened awareness of the vast western wilderness and won early protection for such treasures as Mount Rainier, an alpine paradise of glaciers and meadows in the Washington Cascades, and Oregon's Crater Lake, a blue jewel within the caldera of ancient Mount Mazama.

In 1892 John Muir, the Scottish-born patron saint of wilderness, co-founded the Sierra Club to create a broader constituency for preserving wild places. The Sierra Club drew affluent hikers and mountaineers who valued wilderness for its recreational and esthetic qualities. Over a century Congress conferred permanent protection on many scenic gems of the public domain by including them in the national park system.

In 1905, President Teddy Roosevelt established the national forest system to protect some of this forested domain from the lumberman's ax. By then, loggers had leveled virgin forests on the Olympic Peninsula and on the islands of Puget Sound, along the Lower Columbia River, in the vast Douglas-fir trove of Oregon's Coos Bay watershed, and in the misty coastal redwood region along the northern California coast.

Through the efforts of visionary foresters Aldo Leopold and Bob Marshall, in the 1930s the Forest Service designated some of its remote backcountry as primitive areas. But because these areas had no statutory protection, they were soon opened to logging, one pristine watershed after another. In 1935, Marshall and Leopold founded the Wilderness Society to work for wilderness preservation on federal lands.

In 1938, over vehement opposition from timber companies, Congress carved Olympic National Park out of a shrinking national forest reserve. The park was the first in the Pacific Northwest to remove large swaths of commercial forests from timber production.

Howard Zahniser, a longtime conservationist and former employee of the federal government's National Biological Survey, became executive secretary of the Wilderness Society in 1945. He formed a powerful alliance with David Brower, the legendary executive director of the Sierra Club, to work for wilderness preservation and fight dams on western rivers.

In 1964, when Congress passed the Wilderness Act, it created a framework for conferring permanent protection on wild forests. Yet most of the 9.1 million acres that won instant protection under the act was calendar-art wilderness: snow-capped mountain peaks and alpine meadows, not land forested with commercially valuable timber. In the late 1960s, when the modern forest preservation campaign was born, the last wild forest strongholds were going fast.

The wilderness campaigns of the 1970s and early 1980s, led by the Sierra Club and the Wilderness Society, introduced new people to these wild forests. But the 1984 bills left many millions of acres unprotected. After 1984, when the wilderness wars had played out, grassroots activists committed to saving unprotected wildlands were left to fight on alone during years of accelerated logging. By the late 1980s, a century after industrial logging commenced in the Northwest, no more than 15 percent of the original forest canopy remained; much of that survived as islands surrounded by logged-over land.

This book tells a story rooted in Oregon, where the stakes were high as the new era of forest activism dawned. Oregon was the nation's top timber-producing state. Virtually all of the state's public and private forest lands were scheduled to be logged. The political power of the timber industry went largely unchallenged. Though Oregon had a reputation as an environmentally progressive state, there was a strange disconnect between that image and the reality of its scarred mountainsides and ruined streams. The timber industry was to Oregon as coal was to West Virginia.

Thick-skinned and determined adversaries were required to challenge the state's political and economic establishment. Oregon's young forest activists were desperate and foolhardy enough to embrace the challenge. With forest and wildlife research centered at Oregon State University in Corvallis, and environmental activism concentrated 40 miles to the south on the University of Oregon campus in Eugene, the Corvallis–Eugene axis became a conduit for a powerful information exchange between scientists and activists.

Environmentalists used the results of scientific research conducted in the 1970s and 1980s to argue in the courts, in Congress, and in the news media that the ancient forests must be saved for their wildlife and salmon, for the pure drinking water that flowed from their headwater streams, for their trees that anchored soil and streambanks, for their irreplaceable genetic legacy.

Over nearly two decades, activists in Oregon, Washington, and California worked separately on their separate campaigns. That changed in 1989. The northern spotted owl, which ranged across the forests of all three states, brought these natural allies together. The wild salmon of the Columbia River Basin knitted together the fate of forests east and west of the Cascades. The marbled murrelet, a diminutive seabird that nested in coastal old growth, linked the Northwest with British Columbia and Southeast Alaska. (These campaigns are touched upon only lightly here. Each deserves its own book.)

In the early 1990s, national conservation groups and foundations joined the grassroots forest protection campaign, contributing money and access. The success of the campaign was remarkable. Before long, a great many people far from the Pacific Northwest knew the story of the ancient forests.

As the destruction of tropical rainforests became a planetary issue, and as timber companies searched the globe for untapped forests, the campaign to protect native forests accelerated in the radiata pine forests of Chile and the hardwood forests of Malaysia and the boreal forests of the Russian Far East. The battle for the ancient forests of the Northwest helped to inspire and mobilize similar efforts around the globe.

In 1993, when Bill Clinton became president, he promised to resolve the bitter impasse over forest management in a way that would follow where science led and comply with the nation's environmental laws. It seemed possible that the United States might become the only industrialized nation to preserve a significant remnant of its virgin forests for future generations.

What happened next—the betrayal of that promise, the fracturing of the forest preservation movement over tactics and philosophy, the environmental backlash unleashed by the Republican-led 104th Congress on behalf of its corporate constituents, the passage of a law that ordered logging to proceed in the most vital forest sanctuaries, the anguish and anger that drove forest activists back to protest and direct action in the woods—is a tale of tenuous victory and crushing defeat.

It is the saga of fiercely independent activists who suddenly found themselves playing in the big leagues, of the painful adjustments they had to endure and the hard political lessons they learned on the way to maturity.

And it is much more.

The ancient forest campaign demonstrates the transitory nature of political victory in a democratic system. It shows both the power and the limitations of science in resolving contentious issues of public policy. It proves how difficult it is to change the entrenched culture of a captive agency. It reveals, once again, the corrupting influence of political power.

With all of that, the ancient forest campaign remains an American success story. Its sustaining vision has ushered in a change in public consciousness about the value of forests. It has promoted a new ecological awareness. And it has slowed, if not entirely stopped, the destruction of an irreplaceable national legacy: forests older than the United States of America, older than the history of European settlement in the New World.

Logging within the Shelton Unit, on Washington's Olympic Peninsula, trans-formed the landscape and became a paradigm for national forest management after World War II. The ecological effects of logging practices here and on steep slopes across the Pacific Northwest will take centuries to repair.

PART ONE

GETTING OUT THE CUT

1946–78

“In Europe people talk a great deal of the wilds of America, but the Americans themselves never think about them; they are insensible to the wonders of inanimate nature and they may be said not to perceive the mighty forests that surround them until they fall beneath the hatchet.”

—ALEXIS DE TOCQUEVILLE,
Democracy in America, 1835

“It was the intoxicating profusion of the American continent which induced a state of mind that made waste and plunder inevitable.”

—STEWART L. UDALL, *The Quiet Crisis, 1963*

“For more than 150 years, the lumber and forest products industry has provided a prime example of migrating capital, rapid liquidation of resources, and boom-and-bust cycles for towns dependent on the forest bounty.”

—WILLIAM ROBBINS, *Hard Times in Paradise, 1988*

ON EARTH DAY 1970, WHEN the modern environmental movement made its debut, loggers had been at the task of leveling the Pacific Northwest's virgin forests for a century. By the end of World

War II the timber industry had liquidated most of its own timber hold-ings and was turning to the federal government to help supply its mills. Congress and the U.S. Forest Service complied by opening the national forests to commercial logging. The rate of logging increased steadily over the next quarter-century.

The grassroots environmental groups that sprouted in the aftermath of Earth Day to fight for protection of wilderness on the national forests faced formidable odds. Environmentalists' early lawsuits and appeals slowed the leveling of old-growth forests, while organizing by national conservation groups built a network of support for saving some of the roadless wilderness.

Chapter One

The Glory Days of Logging

Drive along stream corridors shaded by elegant fronds of western redcedar. Climb a wide gravel washboard road leading into the high country on the east side of Washington's Olympic Peninsula. The vista begins to open as soon as you enter the national forest lands. But wait. To get the full effect, you must press on to the high ridge road above Lebar Creek.

At Lebar Creek, an entire roaded and logged watershed yawns before you. Roads cut 65-degree slopes near the ridgelines, at midslope, and near the valley bottom. Above the roadcuts, the slopes are unraveling. Roads built to haul thick logs off the mountains for 40 years now bleed dirt into unnamed tributary streams. The clearcuts staggered across the slopes between the roadcuts are geometric: diamonds, trapezoids, triangles. At first glance they seem nearly continuous. But a closer look reveals subtle differences in the greens that gradually overtake the browns as conifer seedlings take hold and grow.

This is the infamous Shelton Sustained Yield Unit. In 1946, the Forest Service signed a 99-year contract with Simpson Timber Company giving the Washington company exclusive cutting rights on the entire forested southeast quadrant of the Olympic National Forest. Under this arrangement, the only one of its kind in the national forest system, Simpson combined 250,000 acres of its own cutover land with 110,000 acres of publicly owned virgin public forests. Simpson won the right to cut trees from national forest lands at a rate far exceeding the ability of those lands to regenerate. In exchange, Simpson agreed to process the logs from the national forests—and, in time, from its own second-growth lands—at its mills in Shelton and McCleary, Washington.

The Forest Service held the Shelton Unit exempt from the laws and rules that Congress passed to guide management on the rest of the national forest lands. For 40 years, the unit was roaded and logged like no place else in the national forest system. Many roads were built on loose soil dug from the mountainsides. After logging, workers burned the slash, leaving bare soil open to erosion. Slash burns frequently got away from overworked timber sale administrators.

Today the naked-shouldered mountains of the Shelton Unit, and the landslides that scar its slopes, bear witness to the glory days of logging.

AN OCEAN OF FIR

As a monopoly blessed by Congress for the benefit of a single company, the Shelton Unit is unique. But as a paradigm for the history of logging on the national forests of the Pacific Northwest from the end of World War II until the late 1980s, it is instructive. To the Forest Service, timber barons, and their benefactors in Congress, the great unlogged national forests of the Pacific slope were vast, faceless, and seemingly inexhaustible oceans of massive conifers waiting to be mapped and measured and roaded and clearcut to provide wood for the nation, profits for mill-owners, and jobs for the small timber towns scattered at the forest's edge.

Many of the same entrepreneurs who cleared the forests of the Great Lakes between 1860 and 1890 came west in the latter decades of the 19th century to stake their claim to the great Pacific forests. They bought up vast tracts of virgin timberland granted to the railroads by the federal government to encourage homesteading, often acquiring the land by fraudulent means.

As they set about leveling the virgin forests, loggers were limited at first by the sheer size of the conifers, the remoteness of the region, and the primitive logging technology of the times. They nibbled away at the formidable green wall of trees, working close to coastal rivers near natural harbors: Grays Harbor in Washington, Coos Bay in Oregon, Humboldt Bay in California. They built primitive railroads into the heart of wilderness to haul the behemoths out and floated them down rivers to waiting ships or sawmills. When diesel-powered log trucks supplanted railroad logging, the higher-elevation forests became accessible and an orgy of overcutting and mill construction began. By 1916, Washington had half again as many sawmills as the woods could supply.

This overproduction drove prices down, eroded corporate profits, and played havoc with the economies of small timber towns. By the 1930s, abandoned timber communities were a ubiquitous part of the Northwest landscape. Towns thrown up to log and roughly mill the logs lost their purpose once the forests surrounding them were gone.

Between 1926 and 1960, government-subsidized logging roads would penetrate nearly 35 million acres of virgin forest in the Northwest. As early as 1937, Forestry Dean Hugo Winkenwerder of the University of Washington warned, "We are cutting our timber three and one half times faster than we are replacing it by reforestation. It is evident that only a disastrous result can be the outcome of this practice."

By the end of World War II, the major timberland owners of the Northwest had logged most of their accessible old growth. Nearly gone were giant conifer stands on the west end of the Olympic Peninsula, in southwest Washington's Willapa Hills, on the west slopes of the Oregon Coast Range, and in California's coastal redwood zone.

But the promise of the national forests, which lay higher in the Olympics, the Cascades, the Oregon Coast Range and the Klamath Mountains, remained largely untapped. Much of this high country was still unroaded and inaccessible to the public. It was terra incognita.

THE TIMBER TRIANGLE

In the late 1940s the Forest Service launched a commercial timber sale program on the national forests. For the next 40 years, the timber industry, Northwest lawmakers, and federal forest managers worked together in a powerful timber triangle, steadily leveling the great, biologically diverse natural forests and converting them to plantations of young Douglas-fir. The region's entire political and academic apparatus, from colleges of forestry to state forestry boards to local communities kept alive by timber receipts, supported this arrangement.

With passage of the 1897 Forest Management Act, Congress had clearly stated that the purpose of the nation's newly created forest reserves—its future national forests—would be "to furnish a continuous supply of timber for the use and necessities of citizens of the United States." In 1944, with the Sustained Yield Forest Management Act, Congress formalized the responsibility of the Forest Service to sustain rural timber communities. In the postwar period, old-growth timber from the federal lands became the federal pork that Northwest congressmen brought home for their constituents.

The "timber triangle" worked this way: Wealthy timber executives and timber industry associations donated to the campaigns of U.S. senators and representatives from the Northwest and lobbied the Forest Service chief directly. Congress, through House and Senate Appropriations Subcommittees, set annual timber sale targets. Seats on those subcommittees were earmarked for Northwest members. The Forest Service and Bureau of Land Management were judged by how well they met the targets. This imperative to cut timber was communicated down the line to district rangers in rural communities, who formed natural alliances with timber companies.

Though the national forests belonged to all the American people, the decision to liquidate the old growth on these public lands was made largely without public scrutiny, debate, or an understanding of the ecological consequences or the scope of the conversion already underway on the industry's own lands.

The rate of logging on the national forests climbed slowly at first, as private companies accelerated cutting on their own lands to meet the postwar housing construction boom. In Oregon, total timber harvests peaked in 1954, when the volume cut soared to 8.9 billion board feet—a level that has never been surpassed.

THE SCIENCE OF FORESTRY

Forestry in the postwar era followed an industrial model. Forestry research at Oregon State University in Corvallis focused on efficient ways of clearcutting commercially valuable Douglas-fir, which regenerates best in the open.

"Virtually all the biological research was funded by the timber industry," said John Beuter, a forest economist and longtime member of the Oregon State University College of Forestry faculty. "It was research on Douglas-fir, Douglas-fir, Douglas-fir—and some ponderosa pine. A research advisory committee was dominated by industry. They made their preferences known."

Future foresters learned techniques for burning the slash left after logging, poisoning the shrubby plants and hardwoods that colonized the logged-over land, and using fertilizers to enhance the growth of Douglas-fir plantations.

"People were driven by budgets and regulations to do things that they wouldn't do if it were their own forests," Beuter said. "Where are the incentives? Follow the money."

The goal from the 1940s until well into the 1980s was to liquidate the old growth and replace it with what foresters referred to as a "fully regulated forest." "Their mindset didn't include keeping any old growth," Beuter said. "That wasn't a flaw in their thinking. In the 1930s there was more old growth than anyone thought could be used up."

The 1964 Wilderness Act, passed after an eight-year battle by the Wilderness Society and the Sierra Club, declared the intent of Congress to set aside wilderness areas "where the earth and its community of life are untrammeled by man, where man himself is a visitor who does not remain." It required the Forest Service, the National Park Service, and the Fish and Wildlife Service to conduct inventories of their roadless areas and determine which ones warranted protection as wilderness. But the Forest Service actively opposed designating wilderness in areas that contained commercially valuable timber. It had no incentive to do so; the agency's budget and sense of mission came from selling timber.

In 1966, Oregon voters elected Mark Hatfield, a moderate Republican and two-term Oregon governor, to the U.S. Senate. Hatfield's allegiance to the timber industry, and his assignment to the powerful Senate Appropriations Committee, assured that the cozy arrangement among the industry, federal forest managers, and Congress would continue.

FILLING THE GAP

In the 1960s, only a few naturalists, hikers, and mountain climbers glimpsed the full import of what was occurring in the mountains of the Pacific Northwest.

By the early 1970s, however, the frenetic pace of logging in the national forests no longer could be ignored on Sunday trips to the mountains. Mills in the Northwest operated around the clock, employing tens of thousands of workers. Timber jobs continued to be the mainstay of the rural Northwest economy. But because most companies had not reforested their lands, they faced a gap of several decades before their second-growth plantations would be ready for harvest.

In 1974, Eric Allen, the respected editor of the Medford, Oregon, *Mail Tribune*, wrote an editorial warning that forest regeneration in Oregon was not keeping up with logging. Oregon Governor Tom McCall, a popular Republican, read it and demanded to know from the Oregon Board of Forestry whether it was true.

Soon after, Forestry Dean Carl Stoltenberg, who chaired the Board of Forestry, asked John Beuter to conduct a study that would answer the question: "Is logging in Oregon sustainable at the current rate?"

Beuter cajoled timber companies into providing closely guarded proprietary information about the age of their timber. The Beuter Report, released in 1976, concluded that a timber supply gap of at least 20 years loomed beginning in the early 1990s, because companies had depleted their older stands and their second-growth plantations would not be of harvestable age for decades. In the meantime, the report concluded, the only timber available to fill the gap was on federal land.

"The industry operated on the assumption that if the national forests could sustain them, they would not have to worry about cutting their own timber too fast," recalls George Leonard, retired associate chief of the Forest Service. "It was not an outlandish assumption at the time."

The Forest Service, the timber industry, and the Northwest congressional delegation embraced the Beuter Report. Federal timber harvests began ratcheting up soon after.

PAYING THE PRICE

Over 30 or 40 years, the massive stumps that anchored the steep mountainsides of the Shelton Unit gradually rotted and lost their grip on the soil. When the rains came, landslides accelerated. Roads washed out. Streams ran muddy. With 800 miles of logging roads, the Shelton Unit is the most densely roaded tract in the national forest system. At least 15,000 road failures have occurred on its scarred slopes.

The extent of the damage is hard to fathom. Start with this: Lebar Creek is but one of many tributaries of the South Fork of Skokomish River. The South Fork is but one of four major rivers draining the Shelton Unit. Each of those has several tributaries, several Lebar Creeks. Multiply the vista at Lebar Creek many times over and you begin to comprehend the magnitude of what was done here.

It was the early 1990s before the Forest Service faced the full environmental consequences of this deal consummated in an era of undisguised timber mining. "In the Shelton Unit, we went way over what the landscape can tolerate," said Jan Henderson, a U.S. Forest Service ecologist.

In 1994, President Bill Clinton closed the door on future clearcutting of the Shelton Unit. Under his Northwest Forest Plan, only selective thinning of younger trees is allowed. Congress gave the Olympic National Forest $2 million for watershed restoration. That allowed work on Lebar Creek to begin.

Workers using heavy equipment pulled up unanchored dirt, laid down coconut fiber matting, and planted natural grasses. They built "cribs" of live willow to catch the soil from upslope slides. Though much of this work was experimental, it seemed to help stem the erosion.

But to fix just a few of the worst road sections in the Lebar Creek drainage cost $750,000. David Craig, the district ranger who oversaw the Shelton Unit in the mid-1990s, calculated that it would take $100 million to repair all of the unit's unraveling roads.

In 300 years, if they are left alone, the mountainsides of the Shelton Unit may be blanketed with old forest again—not the original forest, which can never be replaced or restored, but trees large enough to hold the soil, and shade the streams, and reweave the fabric of life here.

There is hope that time may heal even the Shelton Unit. Hope, but no guarantee.

Chapter Two

Stopping the Juggernaut

In the late 1960s, as logging was accelerating in the Northwest's virgin forests, Brock Evans, an Ohio native newly graduated from the University of Michigan Law School, arrived in Seattle. Evans joined the Mountaineers, a hiking and mountaineering club, so he could learn the new country at his back door. As he hiked in the Washington Cascades, he noticed that logging roads and clearcuts were obliterating his favorite trails. "Gradually it dawned on me," he said, "that they were going to destroy it all."

Evans became a citizen activist. And in March of 1967 David Brower, executive director of the Sierra Club, hired him as the club's Seattle-based Northwest representative, to oversee Washington, Oregon, Idaho, and Montana.

Evans quickly deduced that Oregon's reputation as an environmentally progressive state was not entirely deserved. "Oregon did the easy things, like recycling, but when the gut industries like timber were at stake it was the worst of the four states," he said. The timber industry dominated Oregon politically, economically, even culturally. As he traveled around the region, trying to set up meetings with local Sierra Club members, Evans found the atmosphere so hostile in some Oregon timber towns that activists did not want to be seen with him in public.

SAVE FRENCH PETE

Still, Evans found one group of battle-weary warriors who did want his help. In late 1967 he visited Eugene, met with them, and took a hike in a valley called French Pete.

Eugene and the neighboring mill town of Springfield sat at the edge of some of the world's most productive tree-growing country. To the west lay the fast-growing forests of the Oregon Coast Range. To the east and south, the Willamette National Forest, big as New Jersey, stretched for 110 miles along the western slope of the Cascades. Within the Willamette's boundaries six high Cascade peaks rise, alpine basins cradle clear lakes, and fast cold trout streams course through valleys forested with giant Douglas-fir. Hikers, campers, fishermen, wildflower gatherers, river-runners, rock collectors, and mountain climbers loved the Willamette. And because it yielded far more timber annually than any other national forest, scores of mills depended on it for a steady flow of timber. The Willamette was a forest ripe for conflict.

The battle lines had been drawn there in Oregon's first big battle over old-growth forests. The disputed turf was the narrow, 30,000-acre watershed of French Pete Creek, a low-lying valley 40 miles east of Eugene that bloomed with wildflowers in spring and offered year-round hiking. Once, western Oregon had been graced with many valleys like French Pete. But because these low-elevation forests had the biggest trees and the gentlest terrain, by the 1960s nearly all of them had been logged.

In the 1930s, the Forest Service included French Pete and the surrounding watersheds in the Three Sisters Primitive Area. But in 1953 the U.S. secretary of agriculture withdrew protection for 53,000 acres, including French Pete. The regional forester justified the decision by explaining that the area contained no unique flora and that harvesting some of its 1.5 billion board feet of timber would help to prevent mill closures. Local environmentalists appealed, but the agriculture secretary upheld the decision. By the late 1960s, French Pete was all that remained of the former primitive area.

Wilderness had a small but vocal constituency within the Many Rivers Group of the Sierra Club and the Oregon Cascades Conservation Council, but the early efforts of these groups were no match for the state's politically powerful timber industry.

In the fall of 1967, Evans met with two dozen activists who wanted to protect French Pete. "They had tried everything," he said. "I told them, 'We can do this.'" As he recalls it, "There was a magic turning point in that meeting, where one of these old warriors said, 'Okay, Brock, if you say so, we can save it.'"

Soon after, Willamette National Forest Supervisor David Gibney announced a timber sale in French Pete. The locals petitioned for withdrawal of the sale, but Gibney formed a hand-picked citizens' committee that endorsed his proposal. Armed with this expression of the public will, he denied the petition.

"I said, 'We need a hook,'" Evans recalled. "What was most striking to me was the space of French Pete. In Washington there were lots of big intact valleys left to hike in." But he suspected that was not the case in Oregon. So he spent three days in January of 1968 poring over maps of the national forests in western Oregon. He counted 70 valleys 10 miles or more in length. Only three, including French Pete, remained unlogged.

This revelation of how much had been lost and how little remained struck a nerve. Local conservationists formed the Save French Pete Committee. In November of 1969, 1,500 protesters gathered outside the Federal Building in Eugene to demand that French Pete be saved. The protest drew the attention of the national conservation groups. Michael McCloskey, executive director of the Sierra Club, said that if environmentalists could win protection for French Pete, they could win anywhere.

A NATIONAL HERITAGE

If Oregon's forests were a national sacrifice zone, Washington's—at least some of them—were recognized as a national heritage. The filtered green light of the Olympic rainforest, the austere beauty of the sheer-faced North Cascades, the soft grandeur of Mount Rainier, visible from downtown Seattle on clear days, were recognized early as gems worthy of showcasing in the national park system.

It didn't take Evans long to discern that Washington was different from Oregon both culturally and politically. "Portland was dominated by the regional offices of the Forest Service and other federal agencies. Seattle had Boeing, a tradition of saving places, a much more urban culture and more educated people." Seattle also was the Northwest base of operations for the Sierra Club and the Wilderness Society. Though timber giant Weyerhaeuser Company wielded immense political power, timber did not dominate Washington's economy as it did Oregon's. The Washington congressional delegation reflected the state's more evolved conservation ethic as well.

The establishment of Mount Rainier National Park in 1899, Olympic National Park in 1938, and North Cascades National Park in 1968 protected the crowning peaks of the Washington Cascades and the Olympics. The boundaries of these parks were drawn to include as little commercial forest land as possible. Still, Evans once calculated that the creation of Olympic National Park alone saved 100 billion board feet of fine old-growth forest with one stroke, more by far than had been saved in all of Oregon at that time.

SACRIFICE ZONES

Yet Washington had its sacrifice areas as well. The most dramatic and visible was the west side of the Olympic Peninsula, which in the 1960s was a virtual timber colony, thinly populated and remote from the commerce and culture of Puget Sound. On private lands in the "west end," some of the Northwest's most egregious logging practices were given free rein. Timber companies logged 60,000 acres of old-growth western redcedar on the Quinault Reservation between 1950 and 1980, leaving only stumps and defiled salmon streams. Private lands bordering the Strait of Juan de Fuca on the peninsula's northern shore were cut with no regard for fish, wildlife, scenery, or recreational values.

In the early 1970s, Tim McNulty and Jerry Gorsline were partners in Olympic Reforestation, a company that planted burned-over clearcuts on private, state, and federal lands, including the Shelton Unit. "We were seeing units the spring after the loggers pulled out," McNulty said. "The roots holding these slopes together were charred, and the tributary streams choked with slash and debris."

This on-the-ground exposure gave them a clear-eyed view of what was in store for unprotected forests on the peninsula. It also gave them a chance to see the beauty of what remained. In the winter, when he wasn't planting trees, McNulty wrote articles advocating wilderness preservation and poetry about the material poverty of a tree-planter's life.

The Gifford Pinchot National Forest in southwestern Washington was a timber basket, a forest that could be depended on to get out the cut. Its borders encompassed Mount St. Helens, a symmetrical Cascade peak. Interest in protecting Mount St. Helens dated from the 1960s, when a speleologist advocated a national monument to protect unique caves on the mountain's south side. But the likelihood that Mount St. Helens would gain protection diminished as clearcuts climbed higher up its slopes. Between 1949 and 1975, the system of logging roads within the forest nearly quadrupled in length, to 2,300 miles. Roads penetrated most of its large pristine watersheds and obliterated more than half its network of hiking trails.

In 1970, environmentalists in Longview, Washington, wrote to Brock Evans demanding, "What is the Sierra Club going to do to protect Mount St. Helens?" Evans agreed to meet with them. But he told them they would have to save Mount St. Helens themselves. That meeting was the genesis of the Mount St. Helens Protective Association.

Early on, the association and the Sierra Club worked together to fight a proposed road through an old-growth valley along the Green River, to the north of the mountain. Environmentalists walked the proposed right-of-way and wrote a report saying the valley was so narrow the logging road would have to be put in the river. The Forest Service later abandoned the project.

VANISHED REDWOODS

In California, home to the Sierra Club and a heavily urban population, enthusiasm for nature conservation was high. In 1890, with strong public support, Congress passed legislation designating three national parks in the Sierra Nevada Range: Yosemite, Sequoia, and General Grant (later to become part of Kings Canyon). Yet the California conservation ethic was no match for the timber industry in the remote redwood region and Klamath Mountains, in the state's northwest corner.

The modern conservation movement came too late to save significant stands of the coastal California redwoods. These behemoths rose more than 300 feet from the forest floor and grew to diameters of 15 feet or more in a narrow fog belt that extended 450 miles, from just north of the Oregon border to the southern tip of Monterey County.

Large timber companies began acquiring and liquidating virtually all of the giant redwood stands in the mid-19th century, working north from Monterey Bay to the Oregon border. Between 1905 and 1929, even with the primitive logging equipment of the times, timber companies leveled an average of 500 million board feet of virgin redwoods annually.

The extent of destruction did not become widely known until a party of San Francisco civic leaders visited the Redwood Coast in 1917. When they learned that not one of these magnificent trees was protected for future generations, they founded the Save the Redwoods League, which launched a drive for donations to buy redwoods from private owners. Over 75 years, the League raised more than $75 million to purchase and protect more than a quarter-million acres of coast redwoods.

In 1968, 50 years after the idea was first seriously broached, President Lyndon B. Johnson signed the bill that established a 30,000-acre Redwood National Park. By the 1970s, only a few old-growth redwood groves survived on private land. One was the Headwaters Forest, owned by Pacific Lumber Company. Another was a grove owned by Georgia Pacific Corporation adjacent to Sinkyone Wilderness State Park. Both eventually would become the subjects of passionate preservation campaigns.

ROCKS AND ICE

The 1964 Wilderness Act conferred protection on most of the major peaks of the Oregon and Washington Cascades and the botanically unique heart of the Siskiyou Mountains. Little forest of commercial value was included within any of these wilderness areas, however. Across the Northwest, logging roads continued to penetrate unprotected wilderness.

The 1964 act created the enabling legislation for an expanded national wilderness preservation system. Lovers of wild places throughout the West soon inundated Congress with citizen-initiated wilderness proposals. In 1967, to get control over the process and limit the pool of potential wilderness areas, the Forest Service directed regional foresters throughout the nation to review and report by 1969 on areas that qualified for wilderness designation. The deadline for this Roadless Area Review and Evaluation, nicknamed RARE, soon was extended to 1972.

The Forest Service refused to withdraw any of its commercially valuable timberlands from logging during the wilderness survey, because to remove land from this "timber base" would mean that at some future date the pace of cutting on the remaining lands would have to slow. The Northwest delegation concurred in this decision.

The pressure to keep the cut high was political, but it was also institutional and cultural. Under a 1930 law called the Knutson-Vandenberg Act, forest supervisors got to keep a share of timber receipts for reforestation and other projects on their forests. The more timber they sold, the more money they had for projects. Most supervisors and district rangers had been trained as foresters and engineers. They saw their principal job as deciding which tracts would be opened to logging and where the roads would go. Until the Wilderness Act, they had given little thought to qualities the forests under their stewardship possessed beyond timber, alpine scenery, and habitat for big game.

George Leonard, retired Forest Service deputy chief, acknowledges as much. "Historically we looked at the goal of forest management as producing timber and game animals. If you look at those goals, management was a great success. Everything that was viewed as important to humans was being managed."

A GOLDEN ERA

Between 1969 and 1976, Congress passed a series of landmark environmental laws that would prove critical to the forest preservation campaign. The National Environmental Policy Act (NEPA), signed by President Richard Nixon in January of 1970, required federal agencies to disclose to the public the environmental impacts of all major projects and to involve the public in the decision-making process. The 1973 Endangered Species Act established strict protective measures for plants and animals threatened with extinction and for habitat critical to their survival. The 1976 National Forest Management Act required the Forest Service to adopt forest management plans balancing timber, grazing, and recreation and to protect the diversity of plants and animals found within national forests.

The modern environmental movement, which began to coalesce in the late 1960s, was a manifestation of this golden era of ecological awareness. It made its national debut on the first Earth Day, April 22, 1970, an event that began as a kind of national teach-in and became a spontaneous outpouring of commitment to the ecological health of the planet. The movement popularized recycling, won a law banning the pesticide DDT, and scored significant gains in reducing air and water pollution. In the Northwest, many high-school and college students were inspired by Earth Day to become involved in saving forests.

A number of grassroots forest protection groups sprouted in the years following Earth Day. One of the first was the Northcoast Environmental Center, established in 1971 in Arcata, California, to work for protection of roadless forests in the remote Six Rivers, Klamath, and Shasta–Trinity National Forests. The Oregon Wilderness Coalition, based in Eugene, followed soon after.

In the early 1970s, wilderness politics dominated debate about the future of the national forests, and the Sierra Club and the Wilderness Society dominated the national wilderness campaign. After Earth Day, the Sierra Club and the Wilderness Society helped to mobilize grassroots groups in the Northwest for the coming wilderness wars.

RARE I

As the Forest Service undertook its first roadless area review of national forests, initially the agency expected to set aside a few scenic areas unsuitable for commercial timber production in the Pacific Northwest as wilderness, then proceed with the task of converting the nation's most productive forests to second-growth tree plantations.

Between the fall of 1971 and the summer of 1972, the Forest Service inventoried 1,449 roadless areas greater than 5,000 acres in size, 56 million acres in all. It applied a rigid and rigorous definition of wilderness to its lands. At the end, it announced that it had selected 274 areas totaling 12.3 million acres nationwide for further study. The remainder would remain open to logging.

The Sierra Club and the Wilderness Society tore into the proposal. They accused the Forest Service of conducting a hasty review to justify liquidating most of the West's remaining forests and of arbitrarily splitting large wilderness tracts into smaller units to lower their wilderness value. The Sierra Club promptly sued in federal court under NEPA to stop the agency from offering timber sales in roadless areas it had found unsuitable for further wilderness study. In August of 1972, the club won a preliminary injunction preventing logging in these unprotected wild areas.

Bowing to the inevitable, the Forest Service put on the brakes. Each national forest supervisor was ordered to prepare an environmental impact statement that assessed the consequences of logging and road-building in roadless areas. NEPA required the agency to solicit public involvement at every step of the way. Suddenly environmental groups had standing to go head-to-head with the feds over logging.

"For the very first time in years, we are on an equal footing with the timber industry and the Forest Service with regard to our wilderness resource," Brock Evans exulted. "The de facto wilderness areas no longer belong to them first as they have thought for so long."

Chapter Three

Paper Warriors

In 1972, Joe Walicki left his native Pennsylvania and moved west to Oregon to save wilderness. But during his first few weeks in Eugene, he wasn't sure he could take living in the belly of the timber beast. His response to logging was visceral. The sight of a log truck loaded with massive firs barreling down the highway gave him a stomach ache. The way logging was done in the Northwest—taking every tree, leaving a tangled, churned-up landscape of mud and slash—made his blood boil.

Walicki joined the Sierra Club and threw himself into the fight to save French Pete. Students at the University of Oregon were signing up for the environmental crusade in the euphoric aftermath of Earth Day. With a tiny stipend from the Wilderness Society, which was just beginning to pay attention to the Pacific Northwest, he began recruiting students and holding wilderness workshops around the state.

A more fertile base for organizing than Eugene would have been hard to find. The Vietnam War protests of the 1960s had consolidated the town's reputation as Berkeley North. Eugene in the early 1970s was a magnet for liberal arts majors and a favorite gig for the acid-rock Grateful Dead. It was a center for vegetarianism and alternative schooling; a city where the counterculture put itself on display at an annual Renaissance Faire and hippies sold hand-thrown pots at a weekly Saturday market redolent with incense and hashish. Eugene was the world's foremost track town, birthplace of the national jogging craze, and a magnet for hikers, rafters, and backpackers. Eugeneans young and old, from every walk of life, trekked regularly to the nearby mountains to feast at nature's banquet.

Eugene and Springfield, its blue-collar neighbor, were timber towns as well, where rusted metal wigwam burners glowed in the night sky, log trucks rolled down the main streets, and the sweet smell of fresh sawdust wafted on the breeze.

One day in 1974, over a few beers, Walicki and two friends from the Sierra Club, Bob Wazeka and Holly Jones, thought up the Oregon Wilderness Coalition. A front group for their respective national organizations, it would bind Oregon's fledgling cells of wilderness advocates together. "We put out a letterhead and off we went," Walicki said. "That was when it was simple and clean and pure. The early to mid-1970s was the golden era of the wilderness movement in this state." He turns nostalgic when he recalls those days before lawsuits, high-stakes lobbying, and divisive arguments split conservationists into bitter camps.

Fred Swanson, a Sierra Club activist who taught a wilderness course at the University of Oregon, agreed to become the coalition's first coordinator. In the fall of 1974, James Monteith, an intense graduate school drop-out, succeeded him.

THE VISIONARY
Monteith grew up in the ranching and logging community of Klamath Falls, surrounded by the open ponderosa pine forest that grows on the arid east slope of the Cascades. Most of his classmates went straight from high school to jobs in the local sawmills or hired on at cattle ranches. But he had a different future in mind.

After high school, Monteith traveled and attended college, first abroad, at Oxford University, then at MIT, Stanford University, and the University of Alaska. In his youth, he had taken his place of origin for granted. When he returned to the West Coast after several years, he saw his state afresh. Now, he said, "I was totally stunned at what Oregon was."

As a student at Stanford, he became obsessed with wilderness. In 1970, he submitted a grant proposal to the Sierra Club, offering to conduct a wilderness study covering all the national forests of Oregon, Washington, and Idaho for $500, over summer break. The club turned him down, saying his price was too high.

After graduating from Stanford with a biology degree, Monteith enrolled in a graduate program in wildlife biology at Oregon State University in Corvallis. He studied with Howard Wight, the director of an interagency wildlife research program, who had a strong interest in the ecology of old-growth forests. Across the campus at the School of Forestry, future foresters were being taught the dominant paradigm of the day—that the Northwest's old-growth forests were "biological deserts" of decadent trees, and that their highest and best use was to be clearcut, burned, and replanted with plantations of Douglas-firs.

Monteith loved wilderness for its own sake. But intuition, reinforced by his studies with Wight, told him there were other values locked in the old-growth forests. He dropped out of graduate school and landed in Eugene in June of 1974, where he was recruited to fill in as temporary director of the Oregon Wilderness Coalition. He planned to appeal a few timber sales, try to delay some logging operations, and then move on. But within weeks he was caught up in the campaign. Soon he became consumed by it.

THE STRATEGIST
Andy Kerr came of age in Creswell, a small timber and farming town south of Eugene. During summer vacations, he helped his father build

houses. He paid little heed to the antiwar demonstrations taking place on the University of Oregon campus, but he was impressed when 1,500 people marched through the streets of Eugene to save French Pete. Young Andy had never been to French Pete, but he had seen plenty of clearcuts in the forests near his home. He recalled thinking, "What a novel idea! Part of the national forest system that you don't log!"

Kerr too enrolled at Oregon State, where he majored in American studies. He was a mediocre biology student and not much of an outdoorsman. He thought backpacking was overrated. Even in the 1970s he saw that protecting wilderness was not about recreation, that keeping wild places intact was intrinsically important even if people never visited them. But it was the politics of wilderness, not the science, that intrigued him most.

By late 1975, Kerr was spending most of his time volunteering for the Oregon Wilderness Coalition. In the charged political climate of the period, environmental politics seemed more relevant than school. Kerr's destiny was sealed the day he called Monteith to discuss appealing a timber sale on southern Oregon's Fremont National Forest. They met— and connected. In 1976, as the wilderness campaign moved into high gear, Kerr dropped out of college and Monteith put him on staff as the coalition's western field coordinator, based in Corvallis.

Kerr was to become the movement's political strategist, a role he would take to with relish. His short-cropped curly hair and pugnacious features, and his profile—which vaguely resembled that of a spotted owl—gave him an easy-to-recognize visage that would later appear on "wanted' posters in timber communities throughout the Northwest. As the power and influence of the movement grew, his cool, arrogant rhetoric and his knack for sound bites would make him a media hit.

THE EAST-SIDER

Tim Lillebo spent much of his childhood in Prairie City, a ranching and timber town surrounded by the spectacular rimrock canyon and pine forest country of central Oregon. In 1970, after graduating from Lewis & Clark College in Portland with a biology degree, he returned to Prairie City to work as a timber faller, road-builder and log truck driver.

Lillebo knew this sparsely populated land east of the Cascades from living, working, and playing on it. And he could see it changing before his eyes. "My buddies and I liked to hunt and fish," he said. "Like Aldo Leopold, we wanted to find the blank spots on the map. But we'd go to our favorite place and it would be logged. We'd go over the next ridge, but the next ridge would be logged too."

Lillebo began appealing timber sales to get the Forest Service to save some of the blank spaces on the map. But to his surprise, the agency ignored his appeals. He met Monteith in 1975 in the eastern Oregon town of Baker, where local activists and concerned ranchers were meeting to discuss protecting the nearby Elkhorn Mountains from logging. Monteith was put off by Lillebo's pessimism. But

Lillebo refused to go away, so Monteith gave him a list of names. From that list Lillebo created a group called Friends of the Malheur, to appeal sales on eastern Oregon's Malheur National Forest. In 1976, Monteith hired Lillebo as the coalition's eastern field coordinator and began putting his local knowledge to work.

SCRAPING AND SCAMMING

With Kurt Kutay, a land-use analyst and Sierra Club activist who was Monteith's first hire, the Oregon Wilderness Coalition now had a staff of four—and funding for one. Monteith shared his $400-a-month salary, giving Kerr, Lillebo, and Kutay each $100. All of them were subsidized by parents, girlfriends, and the university community.

As Oregon natives, Monteith, Kerr, and Lillebo knew the forests on a gut level and cared fiercely about their fate. "We all had that same sort of obsession, that this is the most special place in the world," Monteith said. "We grew up seeing how fast it was being cut down, and thinking it was normal, that it was an anomaly that we might save something."

In 1974, the coalition began working out of the Survival Center, a student club on the University of Oregon campus. Monteith and his field organizers hit the road to begin signing up recruits in Oregon's hinterland who would help them wage the coming battle for the forests. Walicki, now working full-time as a field organizer for the Wilderness Society, did the same. The response, as often as not, was hostile. But in every town they found two or three people who were willing to stand up for the forest. As the battle for the forests unfolded over the next 20 years, these groups would make their voices heard far out of proportion to their numbers.

THE VISION

In the fall of 1974, Monteith, exhausted, took a break from wilderness recruiting to go camping in the Rogue–Umpqua Divide, a small roadless area straddling the Rogue and Umpqua River watersheds in southwestern Oregon. He had not slept for two nights and was churning inside over a dispute he was having with his board of directors about the coalition's wilderness strategy. Some board members believed the coalition should focus exclusively on saving the largest unprotected roadless areas. Monteith was convinced the coalition must fight to protect all remaining roadless areas, no matter their size, if it hoped to preserve the biological integrity of the forested landscape.

Politically, Monteith's goal was naive. Oregon's timber industry had the state's political leaders on its side. No industrialized nation had saved a significant remnant of its native forests. There was little reason to believe the United States would be different.

During his wanderings in the Rogue–Umpqua Divide, Monteith hiked to the top of the ridge dividing the two watersheds. From there, the vista opened to buttes, peaks, and other small roadless areas on the Umpqua National Forest. Then he headed down into a river drainage he thought would take him back to his camp. Instead, several hours later, he found himself lost, hungry, and on the verge of hypothermia as darkness approached. Sitting on a knoll, eating his last piece of jerky and gazing downhill at an unfamiliar stream, he saw it: a beautiful, multicolored eagle, flying toward him.

"It veered to the right, up a small tributary," Monteith wrote later. "Its size diminished. It flew up the tiny stream, and it was a tiny bird. An hour later I saw it again, flying down the larger creek. As the stream grew larger, so did the eagle, even though it was flying away from me. I headed downstream, following the stream and the eagle. I saw my camp. And then, from the corner of my eye, the eagle flew by again, just off the water. It was very large now, and the colors were vivid. I watched it grow with the size of the stream, and shrink in size as it darted up the tributaries. It flew over the ridge, glanced back, as if to be sure I understood, and then rolled over on its back and dived out of sight. Two hours later I sat on the bank of the South Umpqua and it flew by, its wings spanning the river. It was huge."

"I understood. It was all connected. Large is small. Small becomes large. I had my answer."

In a letter to the board of directors, Monteith translated his vision into a political objective: The campaign would fight to save 100 percent of the unroaded virgin forests. "Regardless of so-called realities, it is this goal which will enable us to save maximum wilderness acreage," he wrote. "This goal, by rational perspective, is not unrealistic or unattainable."

GLOMMING ONTO THE SCIENCE

As a high-school student in Portland in the late 1960s, Randal O'Toole dabbled in the antiwar movement. But after Earth Day 1970, he decided to devote himself to the environmental cause and to enroll in the Oregon State University School of Forestry, so he could learn more about the "environmental ideas" of forest management. On the first day of classes in the fall of 1970, a forestry professor threw down a challenge: By the end of four years, only 8 of 100 freshmen would remain. The rest would have transferred out, dropped out, or flunked out of the rigorous program. O'Toole vowed he would be one of those eight.

With his shoulder-length brown ponytail, O'Toole stood out like some alien being among his cleancut classmates, who would come up to him in the halls and warn, "You're not going to be able to get along with long hair around here." This did not bother him. He studied forestry techniques and forest economics. He became convinced that if wilderness advocates were to prevail over the economic arguments of the timber industry, the environmental movement would have to transform itself. The more he learned about forestry, the more convinced he became that he was the man to effect this transformation. "I could see all the technical expertise was on the other side," he said. "I felt like I was helping the underdogs. At least if both sides had some expertise it would make things more fair."

At the time, opposition to clearcutting was an article of faith in Oregon environmental circles. But O'Toole refused to toe that particular party line. He had a strong aversion to the emotional faction of the movement.

A few months after he graduated in 1974, O'Toole got a late-evening phone call from James Monteith, who soon showed up on his doorstep and spread maps all over his living room floor. Monteith asked O'Toole to help the Oregon Wilderness Coalition save the Wild Rogue, a stretch of wild country along one of Oregon's premier whitewater rivers.

O'Toole was skeptical at first. "I don't feel comfortable with maps," he said. "I'm a quantitative person. I want to know how much timber there is, how much it's worth, how much it's going to cost to get it, how much fish are going to conflict with that, how much deer are going to conflict with that." But he agreed. He went to the Siskiyou National Forest and collected reams of quantitative data on timber, fish, and water quality that ultimately helped the coalition get the Wild Rogue protected as wilderness.

His opportunity to influence the environmental movement came at the coalition's 1975 meeting in the mountain hamlet of McKenzie Bridge. For the occasion, he was attired in his favorite costume: a floor-length, flowing blue cape with a fake-fur hood and a cowboy hat. On his belt he wore a big holstered Hewlett-Packard pocket calculator.

"The discussion turned to clearcutting," he says, "and there were all these people there who just had this emotional response: 'Clearcutting is bad. We can't have any clearcutting in our forests.' And I remember someone got up and said, 'I don't want a single tree cut. It's immoral to cut a single tree!'"

Finally, O'Toole couldn't take it anymore. "I stood up, I put my leg up on the bench, swung my cape back, and you could see this holster, and I remember somebody told me later she thought, 'My god, he's got a gun.' And I said, 'I'm a forester and I know about clearcutting. Clearcutting is good sometimes and it's not good other times, and what we should do is figure out when it's not good and fight that.'"

Monteith and Kerr were listening. They were already coming to believe that wild land was intrinsically valuable, even if no one ever laid eyes on it. They also knew they needed to make science their friend.

O'Toole went on to become the conservation movement's secret weapon. He challenged 70 national forest management plans. His ability to penetrate the bureaucratic obfuscation of Forest Service planning documents and his mastery of FORPLAN, a computer program that employed a mechanistic formula to determine how much timber each national forest could produce, helped save 2 million acres from the chainsaw.

Over the years, he also grew to believe that the only way to change the Forest Service was to change the system of incentives that encouraged the agency to cut trees at the expense of all other resources.

"The wilderness movement in Oregon was changing from one based on emotion to one based on reason," O'Toole said. "It was people like me, saying, 'We have to come up with sound reasons for saving wilderness, sound reasons for saving old growth, sound reasons for stopping timber sales.' We can't just say, 'Woodsman, spare that tree, because in youth it sheltered me.' And this was the turning point, this meeting."

PENCIL DREAMS

Andy Kerr was fond of analogies drawn from military history. Holding down the fort in the Oregon wilderness campaign, waiting for the national conservation groups to enter the fray, was like being a member of the French Resistance in World War II, waiting for the Allies to storm the beaches at Normandy.

The task at hand in the mid-1970s required an approach closer to guerrilla warfare. It was a critical time in the history of the national forests. To slow the logging, wilderness activists had to become paper warriors, challenging each plan the Forest Service wrote to justify building new roads and carving new clearcuts into the mountainsides. It was quite literally a race, and wild forests were the prize.

In 1976, armed only with Forest Service fire maps, field reports, and adrenaline, the Oregon Wilderness Coalition appealed 200 timber sales and more than 70 roadless area plans. James Monteith felt the destiny of the forests rested on his shoulders. "We inventoried every one of them," he said. "We went in on the ground, we worked with local people, we sent students, we burned ourselves out."

In those frenetic months, Monteith had a recurring dream. It became known around the office as his "giant pencil" dream. "I was looking down the landscape and here was this monster pencil, this big red pencil coming my way, and the guy drawing the boundaries of the roadless area coughs, and the pencil whips out, and about 14,000 acres of land just gets lost."

Much of the roadless country in Oregon was in mountainous areas accessible only by an arduous hike. Monteith and Kerr knew they would have to learn the country they hoped to save if they were to mount credible challenges. They needed bodies to deploy, and they needed them fast.

Energy was high, money was nonexistent, and scamming and scrambling were part of the game. Using the Survival Center as their base, Kerr and Monteith tapped into the Oregon State System of Higher Education long-distance line so they could communicate with other activists. A mole helped them keep their overhead down by feeding them the numbers of recently closed telephone accounts.

Monteith's resourcefulness knew few limits. He persuaded the university to offer an experimental course on wilderness and got himself appointed an instructor. Each student was assigned a roadless area and instructed to collect as much information as possible about it. Monteith used the students' field reports to appeal timber sales and environmental impact statements all over Oregon. Later, he used the same reports to make the case for wilderness preservation.

The debate over roadless areas was *the* debate over the future of the forests—the essential debate over how much would be opened to logging, how much left intact. The conservationists' campaign to hold the line on further penetration of roadless areas would continue into the 1990s under other banners. Over the years its tactics, rhetoric, and politics would change dramatically. What would not change was Monteith's ultimate objective: to go for maximum acreage, and to hell with political realities.

In the 1970s, scientists began studying the ecology of old-growth Douglas-fir forests like this classic stand in the Breitenbush area of the Oregon Cascades. They concluded that centuries-old conifers, a canopy of many layers and an abundance of fallen, decaying logs were essential structural features of the old-growth forest ecosystem.

PART TWO

CONVERGING PATHS

1968–87

"Land, then, is not merely soil; it is a fountain of energy flowing through a circuit of soils, plants and animals. Food chains are the living channels which conduct energy upward; death and decay return it to the soil."

— ALDO LEOPOLD, *A Sand County Almanac, 1949*

"With present knowledge, it is not possible to create old-growth stands or markedly hasten the process by which nature creates them."

— SOCIETY OF AMERICAN FORESTERS, *"Scheduling the Harvest of Old Growth," 1984*

"The best of science doesn't consist of mathematical models and experiments, as textbooks make it seem. Those come later. It springs fresh from a more primitive mode of thought, wherein the hunter's mind weaves ideas from old facts and fresh metaphors and the scrambled images of things recently seen."

— EDWARD O. WILSON, *The Diversity of Life, 1992*

> "Clear-cutting the watershed which is the vital artery that supports the environment in which one lives stirs the emotions and the intellect together in a powerful expression. To be an environmentalist takes on a deep, personal meaning. "
>
> —JUDITH PLANT, *"Revaluing Home: Feminism and Bioregionalism,"* 1986

UNTIL THE 1970S, THE FOREST Service didn't bother to study how the native forests of the Pacific Northwest functioned. Why study forests that would be gone in another half-century? When a few scientists did begin conducting research in old-growth forests, they discovered a remarkably stable ecosystem, teeming with seen and unseen creatures, among them the little-known northern spotted owl. They concluded that clearcut logging was robbing the soil of nutrients, replacing diverse forests with biologically sterile plantations, and fragmenting the forest canopy into isolated islands.

Even as scientists began to report their findings, the old-growth remnants were becoming smaller, the clearcuts larger, the roads carving the landscape more ubiquitous. The end of the old growth was in view at the same time people were beginning to understand for the first time the true value of the region's squandered forest resource.

Grassroots forest activists began using the new forest research to press for protection of old-growth forests as wilderness areas. In 1984, Congress passed wilderness bills that conferred protection on some old growth in Oregon, Washington, and California. Meanwhile, an emerging bioregional movement was building support for forest protection in rural enclaves across the Northwest.

The wilderness campaigns and the new bioregional movement did not succeed in slowing the rate of logging, however. Ronald Reagan's election as president in 1980 ushered in 12 years of conservative control of natural resource agencies. Throughout the 1980s Congress set unsustainable timber sale levels, which the Reagan administration endeavored to meet. By mid-decade, even voices from within the Forest Service and Bureau of Land Management were warning that the forests were being cut too fast.

Chapter Four

A Rather Uncommon Bird

By now, Eric Forsman's first encounter with a spotted owl has become a Northwest legend. In 1968, while working as a summer fire lookout on the Willamette National Forest, he heard an odd barking from deep in the forest. He imitated the call. Two owls flew down from the forest canopy and looked him over with their large, round, black eyes.

Forsman, an undergraduate student in wildlife biology at Oregon State University, was driven by simple scientific curiosity to learn more about this brown-and-white–mottled bird. He was intrigued by the owl's unwariness, its willingness to fly in close when lured with prey. He began calling for owls in other forests. He was fascinated to learn that the owl seemed to live only in the deep shade of old forests. At the time, virtually nothing was known about the ecology of these forests or the wildlife species associated with them.

On a spring day in 1969, while Forsman was looking for owls in the woods near Corvallis, he met Richard Reynolds, a graduate student in biology. Reynolds was searching for hawks. They exchanged information. The next spring they teamed up to track their respective raptors: goshawks, Cooper's hawks, and sharp-shinned hawks by day, owls by night.

Because logging in the Oregon Coast Range was accelerating in the late 1960s, often, when Forsman returned to a site where he had located owls, the stand it had lived in was gone.

INTIMATIONS OF THE COMING CONFLICT

Forsman was drafted into the Army in 1970. In his absence, Reynolds carried on with both surveys. He drew maps of areas occupied by owls and goshawks that were scheduled for logging and prepared to distribute them to politicians and environmentalists. But his advisor, Howard Wight, knew the information Forsman and Reynolds had gathered was politically volatile. He advised Reynolds to prepare state and federal forest managers for the fallout by holding a seminar to present them with the information. Reynolds did so, in the spring of 1971. For the first time, forest managers became aware that the old-growth forests they were managing for timber production had value to species other than *Homo sapiens.*

In 1972, after Forsman's Army discharge, he returned to Oregon

State University and began work on his master's thesis on the owl. He worked closely with Wight, who was convinced by now that there had to be wildlife species closely associated with the unique environment of old forests.

One day soon after his return from military service, Forsman discovered three nesting owl pairs in an old-growth forest within the Corvallis city watershed, on land owned partly by the city. One of the nests, containing a baby owl, was close to a tract the city planned to sell to produce revenue for municipal coffers. Forsman suspected that the owl pair used the drainage around the nest for breeding, roosting and preying on flying squirrels. He explained that and more to Floyd Collins, the city's water and waste plant supervisor, in a series of letters in 1972 and 1973 that presaged the titanic forest management battle to come.

"The Spotted Owl is a rather uncommon species which is found only in large stands of old-growth timber. . . . Very little is known about the ecology of this owl, and sightings are infrequent," he wrote in September 1972. "Prior to my study, there was only one nesting record for the state, and that was in 1926."

Clearcutting or thinning of the stand would destroy the owl's nest tree and surrounding habitat, Forsman warned. "At the present time, the Rock Creek watershed is one of the few remaining areas around Corvallis which still has enough old-growth left to support Spotted Owls. Because of this, I feel that every effort should be made to preserve the habitats of the remaining nesting pairs. If this is not done, the Spotted Owl will soon be gone from Rock Creek, just as it is gone from the cutover lands that surround the watershed."

Collins wrote back offering perfunctory appreciation for Forsman's concerns. The following April a study committee recommended stepping up timber harvests on the watershed to remove old trees that had decayed due to "disuse."

By now, Forsman had a basic grasp of old-growth ecology. He wrote back, retorting, "'Disuse' by whom, certainly not spotted owls? I recognize that most old-growth stands contain a high incidence of decayed and often diseased trees, but this is exactly the factor which attracts the spotted owl. . . . Old-growth trees provide an abundance of nest cavities for owls, squirrels, bats, woodpeckers, tree mice, woodrats and vaux's swifts. Old, decaying deadfalls which litter the forest floor in old-growth stands provide habitat for innumerable rodents, insects and reptiles."

Collins brushed aside Forsman's objections and went ahead with the sale, which cut a large area on the slope facing the nest grove. The owl pair disappeared.

SEEKING SUPPORT

In the early 1970s, when Forsman began his research, the northern subspecies of the spotted owl was virtually unknown in the scientific literature. Forsman was the first biologist to conclude that the owl's survival hinged on the continued existence of large tracts of old forest.

He immediately understood the political implications of his research. Forsman had grown up in Eugene, in the heart of timber country. His father was a carpenter, and all five of his brothers ended up making their living from the timber industry, one way or another. Because he chose to study the owl rather than the bald eagle or the California condor, neither professional recognition nor funding came easily in the early years. He scraped to make ends meet, doing tree-trimming, carpentry, and other odd jobs in the winter and depending on his wife's school-teacher salary to support their family, which eventually grew to include three kids.

An early challenge was finding financial sponsorship for Forsman's owl research. The Forest Service's Pacific Northwest Research Station in Corvallis had no interest in supporting studies on an obscure raptor. Charles Meslow, who became Forsman's advisor after the death of Howard Wight, turned to Jack Ward Thomas, a colleague at the Forest Service's Pacific Northwest Research Station in La Grande, Oregon, for help. Thomas, an elk biologist, never had seen a northern spotted owl. Nevertheless, he agreed to subsidize Forsman's owl studies from his own research budget. Thus, the groundwork was laid for Thomas's future involvement in deciding the fate of the spotted owl.

James Monteith, soon to become the executive director of the Oregon Wilderness Coalition, was a fellow graduate student in wildlife biology at Oregon State University during Forsman's early battles on the owl's behalf. He recalls being impressed by his classmate's outspoken criticism of the federal agency that was funding his research. "He was writing letters to the Forest Service saying, 'Stop liquidating old growth before there's nothing left.'"

Early in his forest wanderings, Forsman found an injured young spotted owl in a nest. He took her home to live in a cage and eventually named her "Fat Broad" because of her propensity to overeat. She survived for more than 25 years in captivity, amid a menagerie of other captive owls that came and went at the Forsman house. Over that time she served as an emissary for her species, making appearances with Forsman before schoolchildren, environmentalists, biologists, and timber industry groups. Eventually, Fat Broad even graced the centerfold of *Life* magazine, where she perched on the shoulder of logger Wilbur Heath.

A CANDIDATE SPECIES

In 1973, soon after Congress passed the Endangered Species Act, the U.S. Fish and Wildlife Service prepared a list of animal and plant species that might be candidates for listing as threatened or endangered under the new law. Biologists who were aware of Forsman's research included the northern spotted owl on the list.

That same year, the state of Oregon appointed a task force to recommend a plan for protecting the owl and other species under the

state's own Endangered Species Act. It was the first of many owl committees that Forsman would serve on or advise. Its modest proposal:
State and federal agencies should set aside 300 acres of old-growth
habitat around each of the 100 known spotted owl sites in Oregon.

It took four years—until 1977—for state and federal forest managers to agree to even these minimal buffers. By that time Forsman had
far more data. Two years of radio tracking had revealed that individual
owls ranged over at least 1,000 acres and in some cases as much as
3,200 acres. It was the beginning of a pattern that would prevail
throughout the 1970s and most of the 1980s, as protection for the owl
on federal lands lagged at least four years behind the growing body of
owl research.

As he searched for owls in forests of all types and age classes, Forsman
found the blue spray paint that marked trees for cutting everywhere
he went. Nevertheless, he managed to locate and track enough birds
to complete a master's thesis on the number, distribution, diet, and
habitat needs of the owl. He concluded that the owl's favorite prey were
probably most abundant in old stands.

So much about the owl remained unknown that Forsman went on
to doctoral research. He began documenting the owls' range on the
west side of the Oregon Cascades through radio telemetry. Living in
an old trailer on the H. J. Andrews Experimental Forest east of Eugene,
he spent 12 months tracking eight adult owls fitted with tiny radio
transmitters. Tuned in to a receiver that picked up their eight distinct
frequencies, he followed them virtually around the clock. He discovered that his owls flew long distances for prey but avoided large
clearcuts. "When they were foraging, they worked around a clearcut,
but when they captured prey they would fly straight across clearcuts
to get back to the nest," he said. In a burned-over area near Eugene,
where all the trees had been salvaged, he observed that owls went to
the edge of the burn and then turned back.

It appeared that spotted owls were becoming prisoners within islands
of old growth surrounded by logged lands. For Forsman, the implica-
tion was obvious: The patchwork quilt of 40-acre clearcuts on national
forest land, and the much larger clearcuts on private land, were fragmenting the owl's habitat throughout its range. If the trend continued, he concluded, prospects for the owl's long-term survival looked
bleak.

Forsman completed his doctoral dissertation in 1980. His eight years
of graduate study had cost $35,000. And the Forest Service had footed
the bill.

Chapter Five

"Biological Deserts"

As late as 1970, neither the Forest Service nor university-based schools of forestry showed much interest in studying the virgin forests that were rapidly disappearing from the mountains and foothills of the Pacific Northwest. It took the international scientific community to focus attention and research dollars on this vanishing ecosystem.

In 1970, President Richard Nixon authorized U.S. participation in a United Nations project intended to increase understanding of Earth's major ecosystems. Oregon State University received a grant from the National Science Foundation to take part in the worldwide study. Jerry Forest Franklin, then a young forestry professor at OSU, was tapped to head a study of old-growth Douglas-fir forests. He assembled a team of scientists and selected the H. J. Andrews Experimental Forest, part of the Willamette National Forest east of Eugene, as his laboratory.

Suddenly there was money for old-growth research on bats and raptors, small mammals and insects, birds and reptiles. There was money to study the structure and function of the forest itself: how old-growth trees received, stored, and used water and nutrients; how the dead snags and the fallen logs that covered the forest floor contributed to the life of the forest; and what role the soil played in sustaining the living ecosystem. Jim Trappe, a Forest Service mycologist on Franklin's team, began studying the fungi beneath the forest floor.

The early results of the new forest research and Eric Forsman's owl studies filtered into the environmental community. In 1978, at a conference at Lewis & Clark College in Portland, Glenn Juday, an OSU graduate student in forestry, read a paper extolling the ecological characteristics of old forests and criticizing the prevailing system of clearcut logging. Juday, a classmate of Forsman's, had done his doctoral research on spotted owls in the old-growth forests of the Oregon Coast Range. He was continuing his research with Franklin's team on the Andrews Experimental Forest.

A Reed College student named Cameron La Follette wrote a paper for the Oregon Student Public Interest Research Group, a Ralph Nader–inspired statewide organization, describing the Franklin team's work. Activists circulated her report. The pieces of a scientifically based old-growth forest campaign began to fall into place.

AN ECOLOGICAL SYMPHONY

Chris Maser's no-nonsense supervisors in the Bureau of Land Management in the late 1970s couldn't understand the biologist's obsession with the insects and fungi that live in rotting logs. For Maser, a man of withering intensity, the internal workings of the old-growth forest ecosystem held an almost mystical fascination.

As Franklin's old-growth team pursued its research, Maser was engaged in a separate three-year ecological survey of the Oregon Coast. Maser had concluded that many of the creatures he was studying survived by eating the fungi beneath the forest floor. He induced Jim Trappe to join him in a study of small-mammal food habits. In this work, Maser began to glimpse an unseen and intricately balanced world.

On tours of an old-growth forest near Mary's Peak, where he conducted most of his research, Maser would point out the secret lairs of ambrosia beetles, carpenter ants, and clouded salamanders within the logs strewn in moss-covered humps over steep hillsides. He would show off the burrow of a red-backed vole, admire the tiny star-shaped hemlocks sprung from a decomposing log, and point out how fallen logs anchored the soil on an uphill slope.

Maser and Trappe discovered that northern flying squirrels, fungi, live coniferous trees, and northern spotted owls, together with many other species, lived in a carefully balanced symbiotic relationship. Small mammals ate the fruiting bodies of the fungi and spread their spores through defecation. Flying squirrels and other small mammals were eaten in turn by northern spotted owls nesting high in the broken tops of the old trees. They first described this symbiosis in 1978, in an article in the journal *Ecology*.

They concluded that when the natural cycle was interrupted by logging, tractor-piling, and slash-burning, what grew in place of the original forest was not really a forest at all. Removal of woody debris from logging sites robbed the soil of nutrients and speeded soil erosion. Removal of live trees from streambanks destabilized the banks and deprived fish of shade. Removal of fallen logs from streams destroyed pools where migrating fish rested on their journey.

In a report on their research studies completed in 1981, entitled "The Seen and Unseen World of the Fallen Tree," they documented the importance of decaying trees and asked difficult questions that challenged prevailing assumptions about forest management practices of the times. Maser and Trappe boldly urged their agencies to begin looking at forests as ecosystems, not as commodities.

"What will happen to the Douglas-fir ecosystem when fallen trees are no longer added, as will be the case under intensive forest management with increased utilization of wood fiber?" they asked. "And what will happen under short rotation management, when large trees are no longer produced?. . . . We must not sacrifice the options of future generations on the altar of cost-effectiveness through decisions based on insufficient data."

The implications were stark: Clearcut logging as practiced in the Northwest was biologically unsound and indefensible. It left no organic legacy for the next generation of trees: no snags for woodpeckers; no big logs to decay slowly on the forest floor, providing hiding places for voles; no woody debris to fall into streams and create riffles and resting pools for salmon.

Their report caused consternation among industrial foresters and federal agency heads. In western Oregon, in the early 1980s, the BLM was a timber-cutting agency. How, Maser's bosses wondered, could they deal with these new concerns and still meet timber sale mandates?

A fierce three-year struggle over publication of the Maser-Trappe study ensued within the BLM, reaching the agency's highest levels.

AN ECOLOGICAL DEFINITION

In 1981, after many delays, the Forest Service published a landmark report by Jerry Franklin, Chris Maser, Glenn Juday, and five others entitled "Ecological Characteristics of Old-Growth Douglas-Fir Forests." The report described for the first time the ecological features and functions of the Northwest's original conifer forests. Old-growth forests could be identified by four key features, the scientists said: large live trees, ranging in age from 200 to 1,000 years; large dead snags; large fallen logs; and large logs in streams. Each played an important role in the life of the ecosystem.

But the scientists did more than define and describe the old-growth forest. They also sounded a warning. "At current harvest rates, old-growth stands will not be completely cut over for at least four decades," they wrote. They acknowledged that some of the primeval old-growth forest enjoyed permanent protection. "Nevertheless," they said, "these reserves occupy less than 5 percent of the original landscape, and the end of the unreserved old-growth forests is in sight. The public, scientists, and land managers are increasingly concerned about whether species, communities, and functions are in danger of being eliminated."

In 1982, the Forest Service and BLM at last initiated their own old-growth wildlife research and development program and began to fund studies on spotted owls and other denizens of the ecosystem their agency was fast liquidating. That same year, Maser, wildlife biologist Larry Harris, and ecologist Arthur McKee published a research paper describing the implications of old-growth logging in the Cascades for native wildlife and laid out the concepts around which a system of old-growth reserves might be designed. Though it was not a spotted owl strategy, the report foreshadowed the owl plan that would rock the Northwest eight years later.

"How much old growth should be perpetuated is only part of the question," they wrote. "Size and spacing are of equal importance." Reserves must be large enough to include core areas free of outside influences such as wind and temperature extremes. Reserves of 300 to 500 acres might be needed to provide for natural populations of small rodents, and reserves of 1,000 acres might be necessary to sustain a pair of predatory birds.

SAVING SOME

The forestry profession began paying attention. In 1984 the Society of American Foresters, the nation's largest professional foresters' association, published a slim report entitled "Scheduling the Harvest of Old Growth." Though it was little noticed outside the profession, its significance was profound. The foresters called for federal forest management agencies to develop an updated inventory of the extent of old growth so they could make informed decisions about the future of this rapidly shrinking ecosystem.

"Old-growth forests are valuable for biological, scientific, and aesthetic reasons in addition to their value for timber production," the foresters wrote. "Some should be maintained in their natural state to realize all of these benefits."

In words unusually vivid for a scientific manifesto, they stressed that the old-growth forests were irreplaceable. "With present knowledge, it is not possible to create old-growth stands or markedly hasten the process by which nature creates them. Certain attributes, such as species composition and structural elements, could perhaps be developed or enhanced through silviculture, but we are not aware of any successful attempts. Old growth is a complex ecosystem, and lack of information makes the risk of failure high. In view of the time required, errors could be very costly. At least until substantial research can be completed, the best way to manage for old growth is to conserve an adequate supply of present stands and leave them alone."

As important for the future of forest management as the message were the messengers. They included Franklin; John Gordon, dean of the School of Forestry and Environmental Studies at Yale; and wildlife biologist Jack Ward Thomas, Eric Forsman's benefactor, who was at the time researching the habitat requirements of Rocky Mountain elk. The report was written by Jim Lyons, a young Yale forestry graduate and the society's director of resource policy. This would not be the last time the four came together to discuss the future of old-growth forests.

OWLS 101

In the early 1980s, other wildlife biologists began visiting Eric Forsman to learn his spotted owl survey techniques and to share information. Harriet Allen, a Forest Service biologist in Olympia, Washington, and others began tracking owls on the Olympic Peninsula and discovered that they ranged over much larger areas there than in western Oregon. Rocky Gutiérrez, a professor of wildlife biology at Humboldt State University in Arcata, California, and Alan Franklin, one of his graduate students, began a detailed long-term study of spotted owl habitat associations in California coastal forests. They concluded that in every area where they tracked owls, the birds showed a clear preference for older forests.

In April of 1984, the Wildlife Society, a professional association, published Forsman's wildlife monograph on the owl. The following year, after many delays, Forsman and Meslow at last got permission from federal officials to publish an article on the owl's plight in the *Audubon Wildlife Report*. Meslow said even his own supervisors in the U.S. Fish and Wildlife Service opposed its publication. "We were pretty darned honest," he said. "We criticized management as practiced by the Forest Service and BLM, and that's a no-no. You don't criticize a sister agency."

By that time, scores of biologists from Olympia to Fresno were studying the northern spotted owl and the California spotted owl, a close relative. Owl research proposals proliferated. Federal research money followed. *Strix occidentalis caurina* was well on its way to becoming the most studied bird in the history of federal land management.

Meanwhile, researchers produced studies on scores of other denizens of the old-growth forest. Their research revealed that not only the spotted owl but also the fisher and pine marten, the marbled murrelet and pileated woodpecker, the tailed frog and clouded salamander lived in old-growth forests and depended on them to a greater or lesser extent for survival.

In 1985, the magazine *American Forests*, published by the American Forestry Association, printed a piece saying it might be prudent to delay a decision to log the remaining old growth while scientists studied the implications—and to begin helping timber communities adjust to the end of boom years in the Northwest timber industry.

It was clear by now that the science of forestry and the politics of wilderness preservation were traveling convergent paths.

Chapter Six

Going for the Maximum

In the late 1970s, members of Congress from the Pacific Northwest signaled their intent to win passage of statewide bills that would resolve the fractious wilderness preservation issue once and for all. Wilderness advocates knew this might be their last best chance to save roadless areas. Grassroots forest activists hoped to bring the new scientific awareness of old-growth forest ecology to the political debate.

Within the environmental community, however, a difference of opinion was developing over the purpose of wilderness. The debate focused on whether intact forested watersheds warranted wilderness designation even if they offered no grand scenic vistas or outstanding recreational opportunities. The Sierra Club was not persuaded that its members would want to hike in these gloomy forests, or that they were important enough to risk alienating the powerful Northwest congressional delegation in order to win their protection.

The increasingly influential Oregon Wilderness Coalition, and grassroots forest activists across the Northwest, dissented. They saw how quickly the old growth was going. They determined to engage the political power structure directly, to make the ecological arguments, and to claim as much of this commercially valuable forest as possible for posterity.

EARLY VICTORIES

Oregon's first big wilderness victory came in 1978, with passage of the Endangered American Wilderness Act. In this first major national wilderness campaign, the Sierra Club and the Wilderness Society worked closely with grassroots groups, mounting a lobbying effort in Washington, D.C., while local activists promoted protection on the home front.

The act created 17 new wilderness areas scattered across the West. One-third of the acreage protected was in Oregon. The act established the Wenaha–Tucannon Wilderness, encompassing two remote canyons east of the Cascades that provided critical habitat for elk herds of the Blue Mountains. It established the Wild Rogue Wilderness in the Siskiyous, protecting a popular whitewater rafting river and its premier runs of chinook salmon, steelhead, and rainbow trout. And it added the entire French Pete watershed to the Three Sisters Wilderness.

The French Pete victory proved for the first time that environmentalists could mobilize broad support for wilderness preservation, even over the opposition of influential Northwest congressmen. Though Oregon's junior senator, Republican Bob Packwood, supported protection for French Pete, Republican Mark Hatfield, the state's senior senator, was opposed.

The Many Rivers Group of the Sierra Club and the Save French Pete Committee had taken the lead on French Pete, however, they shared credit with the Oregon Wilderness Coalition, which had thought up the successful strategy of fighting to extend protection to 55,000 acres of intact forest, more than triple the original 16,000 acres proposed. The strategy worked. The victors toasted their victory with French champagne.

By bringing unprecedented publicity to a beautiful old-growth forest, the French Pete victory helped to redefine wilderness. The valley had no alpine meadows, no glaciers, no craggy peaks. What it had were huge old conifers that hugged the riverbanks, fallen logs that created pools and riffles for fish, delicate wildflowers in spring, fiery vine maples in autumn. French Pete was the quintessential low-elevation old-growth forest.

Timber industry leaders, sensing a shift in the political winds, hunkered down to plot strategy. Until then, the wilderness movement had made no serious incursion into the national forest lands the industry regarded as part of its commercial timber base. These were the lands that were supposed to carry wood products companies through the gap between the last of their old growth and the maturing of their second-growth plantations. Now, suddenly, environmentalists were after the same thing the industry coveted: big trees.

In 1979, as the Oregon Wilderness Coalition continued to build its case for saving old forests, scattered grassroots activists in Washington formed the Washington Wilderness Coalition to coordinate their own separate wilderness campaign. The main event in the wilderness wars—the big wilderness bills of 1984—lay ahead.

A NATURAL LABORATORY
In the spring of 1980 Mount St. Helens, dormant for 123 years, rumbled to life. A 300-foot bulge formed on the mountain's north side. On May 18 an earthquake measuring 5.1 on the Richter scale triggered a massive eruption. The mountain's swollen north flank slid into the green basin of Spirit Lake and raced down the North Fork Toutle River, forming the largest landslide in recorded history. A lateral blast produced a 650 degree Fahrenheit current of ash and hot gas that traveled at speeds up to 330 miles an hour. The ash cloud, driven east by prevailing winds, circled the Earth in two weeks.

The blast leveled 150 square miles of forest, including national forest land to the north and a large swath of the Weyerhaeuser Company's 473,000-acre Longview Tree Farm, which extended around the mountain's western flank. Sixty percent of the timber destroyed was privately owned.

A great debate ensued about how to manage the public lands leveled by the blast. Overnight, these lands had become not only a world-class tourist destination but also a priceless laboratory for studying how life reestablishes itself after a natural cataclysmic event. The Mount St. Helens Protective Association, an environmental group based in Longview, Washington, wanted Congress to designate a 216,000-acre national monument, where recovery could proceed at nature's pace.

But in 1981, the Gifford Pinchot National Forest proposed to establish only a 71,000-acre interpretive area around the immediate blast zone and to manage the forests that eventually grew back for timber production and recreation. The Reagan administration opposed legislation to protect the area, maintaining that the Forest Service was quite capable of managing Mount St. Helens on its own. The Washington congressional delegation was split on management.

On a wintry November day in 1982, Susan Saul, the association's president, organized a bus tour of the blast zone for the news media, activists, and members of Congress. Democratic U.S. Representative Don Bonker, whose district included the west slopes of the mountain, asked the Gifford Pinchot National Forest supervisor to send a representative on the tour. But when the bus pulled up at headquarters, no Forest Service representative was there. Bonker was incensed at the snub and decided the Forest Service could not be trusted to manage Mount St. Helens responsibly.

"That was the turning point in the campaign," Saul recalls. "Bonker went back to D.C. and asked his staff to develop the Mount St. Helens Preservation Bill." At hearings, scientists emphasized the mountain's matchless opportunities for long-term research. In 1982, after a number of land trades with private timberland owners, including Weyerhaeuser and Burlington-Northern Railroad, which owned the now-vanished summit, Congress passed a bill setting aside 110,000 acres for public enjoyment and scientific research. It was a stunning victory. Even a portion of the lush Green River valley north of the mountain, untouched by the blast, was included in the monument's boundaries.

One of the first scientists to undertake research in the new monument was forest ecologist Jerry Franklin. He was stunned to discover how quickly life returned to the devastation zone in areas where a biological legacy—seeds, insects, burrowing gophers—survived beneath the ash. It was on the gray slopes of Mount St. Helens that Franklin refined his thoughts about the value of leaving a biological legacy on forest land after logging.

RARE A SECOND TIME

As the wilderness campaign moved into high gear, the Forest Service embarked on a second roadless area inventory. RARE II was intended to settle the issue of wilderness preservation on the national forests and provide certainty to timber companies about future federal timber supplies.

Rupert Cutler, assistant agriculture secretary in the Carter administration, and a former vice president of the Wilderness Society, directed the Forest Service to do a better job with its second inventory and to make specific recommendations this time about which areas should be set aside permanently as wilderness and which should be released for logging and other nonwilderness uses. He told Congress in early 1978 that he believed the job could be done in less than a year.

True to his word, in January 1979, Cutler announced the Forest Service's recommendation: 15 million acres of wilderness nationwide, of which 5 million acres would be in Southeast Alaska's Tongass National Forest. In Oregon and Washington, the Forest Service proposed protecting a total of 637,000 acres, out of nearly 5.5 million acres eligible. In California, it proposed protecting 983,900 acres, out of 6.5 million acres eligible. Most of the rest would be released from consideration as wilderness for at least 10 years.

The Forest Service remained openly hostile to all wilderness proposals except its own. Shortly before his retirement in 1981, Northwest Regional Forester Dick Worthington revealed his bias and his failure to grasp the ecological argument for wilderness preservation when he lashed out at the tactics of wilderness "cultists." "Many wilderness demands are entirely unethical," he said. "They conflict with any sound, esthetic, or biological value; yet they are trumpeted as being in the public interest. In reality classification of lands as wilderness means locking up large acreages for the use of very few people."

The agency began a crash program to build new roads into the roadless areas it had eliminated from consideration. But continuing to destroy the old-growth inventory before the issue of permanent protection was resolved by Congress was a practice of questionable legality. Soon after RARE II was released, Huey Johnson, director of the California Resources Agency, sued and won an injunction blocking development of 47 roadless areas on California national forests until the agency prepared an environmental impact statement for each one.

James Monteith and Andy Kerr were itching to stop development of roadless areas in Oregon. But they had no money to file a lawsuit. In Oregon, the Sierra Club was the only group that did.

By then, a schism had opened in the movement. In 1982, the Oregon Wilderness Coalition became the Oregon Natural Resources Council (ONRC) to reflect the board's expanding interest in issues besides wilderness preservation. ONRC believed the Sierra Club was too quick to compromise, too recreation-minded, too slow to understand the scientific significance of old growth. The Sierra Club, which dominated wilderness politics in California and Washington, was uncomfortable with what it regarded as the Oregon group's increasingly confrontational tactics.

As mainstream groups debated, a band of radical environmentalists from another dimension moved in.

NO COMPROMISE

The Siskiyou Mountains rise at the intersection of the Oregon Coast, Oregon Cascade, and Klamath Ranges. They hold the largest block of wild forest remaining in Oregon and the most botanically diverse conifer forest ecosystem in North America. In 1936, wilderness advocate Bob Marshall recommended establishment of a million-acre wilderness park in the Siskiyous. But in 1964, Congress protected just 77,000 acres at the heart of the range, and in 1978 Senator Mark Hatfield blocked attempts by Representative Jim Weaver, a maverick Oregon Democrat, to expand the Kalmiopsis Wilderness. Most of the roadless Siskiyou forest remained open to logging.

In 1983, the Siskiyou National Forest began laying out a high logging road that would snake along the ridgeline forming the northern boundary of the Kalmiopsis Wilderness, effectively severing it from the roadless area to the north and cutting this last big chunk of wild Oregon in two. Bald Mountain Road was one of Hatfield's pet projects; he had included an appropriation in the Forest Service budget specifically to build it. Once it was completed, any proposal to annex the North Kalmiopsis to the existing wilderness would become moot.

As the bulldozers moved in, Mike Amaranthus, a young soil scientist working on the forest, contacted some local environmentalists. One of the most beautiful old-growth forests in the world was about to be destroyed, he said. Wasn't there something they could do?

On April 27, 1983, Earth First! made its Northwest debut on Bald Mountain Road. Four men, Mike Roselle and Kevin Everhart of Wyoming and local activists Steve Marsden and Pedro Tama, walked out of the woods and blocked the bulldozer as it punched a road into the mountainside. Before they were arrested, they hung an Earth First! banner on the dozer's side.

Dave Foreman, former chief lobbyist for the Wilderness Society, and four friends—Roselle, Ron Kezar, Bart Koehler, and Howie Wolke—had conjured Earth First! in 1980, during a legendary week-long hike in the Arizona desert. Foreman had quit his job out of frustration with the ineffectiveness of the national conservation groups and out of disgust with the Forest Service over its RARE II recommendations. All of the others except Roselle, a veteran of the radical left, also had worked for mainstream conservation groups. From their desert experience came the decision to start a movement that would counter the destruction of nature directly.

The Earth First! mantra, No Compromise in the Defense of Mother Earth, struck a chord with many grassroots activists in the Northwest. They saw the results of accelerated logging firsthand, and they perceived that nothing the national conservation groups were doing seemed to be stopping the destruction.

The arrival of Earth First! ushered in an era of direct action and civil disobedience in the Pacific Northwest. Earth First! engaged the political and industrial juggernaut that was leveling forests directly—disabling equipment, blocking logging roads, sitting in trees as chainsaws whined below. Earth First! tactics drew national attention to the wars being waged on frontiers of wilderness across the West and brought drama and increased tension to the forest protection movement.

The action on Bald Mountain continued sporadically for months, drawing national news coverage. Money poured in to save the North Kalmiopsis and halt Bald Mountain Road. Monteith and Kerr at last had the resources they needed to hire a lawyer and raise the stakes.

DRAWING A LINE

On December 13, 1983, Monteith called a press conference in Portland to announce that the Oregon Natural Resources Council had filed suit against the Forest Service to halt all logging in roadless areas. Monteith was visibly nervous. His voice shook, and he perspired heavily under the television lights, but his message was firm:

> *Today we have filed suit in federal district court to stop illegal development of de facto national forest wilderness lands. Conservationists have asked the court to halt road-building and timber sales on slightly less than 3 million acres of roadless areas until an adequate wilderness review is completed, or preferably until Congress passes legislation to resolve this issue.*

Between 1979 and 1983, about 90,000 acres of roadless national forest land had been sold and logged in the Northwest. Over the next two years, the Forest Service planned to open up nearly 200,000 acres more. With the filing of the Bald Mountain Road lawsuit, environmentalists drew a line in the forest. The ONRC/Earth First! suit was the first citizen-initiated, statewide lawsuit in the nation over the future of these roadless areas. U.S. District Judge James Redden, new to the federal bench after a career in state politics, granted an injunction halting Bald Mountain Road—and logging in all Oregon roadless areas—until the wilderness issue was settled.

Suddenly, the timber industry was pushing harder than anyone for a wilderness bill that would resolve the issue and let business as usual resume in the national forests.

WILDERNESS POLITICS

The Oregon, Washington, and California wilderness bills passed by Congress in 1984 were overtly political documents, and the political dynamic was different in each state.

Oregon

Senator Mark Hatfield personally brokered the Oregon Wilderness Bill. Oregon's senior senator was a master at the art of the deal. Because

Hatfield wielded his power on the Senate Appropriations Committee to keep Oregon's timber industry well supplied with federal timber, Kerr and Monteith referred to him privately as "the Godfather." They had few illusions about where his heart lay, but they knew the fate of the forests rested in his hands. Hatfield's natural resources aide, Tom Imeson, personally visited nearly every roadless area in Oregon that was under consideration for wilderness protection.

Representative Jim Weaver had clout too, as chairman of the House Agriculture Forestry Subcommittee. Weaver had been among the first Oregon politicians to attack the timber industry for sending its own unprocessed logs, and lumber mill jobs, overseas. In 1977, when loggers in his timber-dependent congressional district complained that his support for adding French Pete to the Three Sisters Wilderness would cost their jobs, Weaver retorted that log exports to Japan could produce as many jobs as "860 French Petes every year."

The shaping of the Oregon wilderness bill became a contest between Hatfield, the titan of the Senate, and Weaver, the maverick of the House.

By now, Oregon grassroots forest activists knew the wilderness real estate intimately. They fought to get the maximum amount of roadless forest included in Hatfield's bill. The fiercest battles were fought over proposals to protect large blocks of commercially valuable old-growth timber: the Middle Santiam in the central Oregon Cascades; Drift Creek in the Coast Range; the North Fork John Day in northeastern Oregon; and Grassy Knob, on the South Coast.

The Sierra Club's Seattle office, which was directing the Northwest wilderness campaign, was particularly opposed to including Drift Creek, the largest remaining intact watershed in the Oregon Coast Range. Drift Creek, on the Siuslaw National Forest, lay entirely within Representative Les AuCoin's district. AuCoin, a liberal Democrat, represented Oregon timber interests on the House Appropriations Committee. He vehemently opposed withdrawing Drift Creek from logging, though even local Forest Service officials favored its protection. Hatfield ultimately added a 5,800-acre Drift Creek Wilderness to his bill after noticing that AuCoin was enthusiastically supporting a bill that included no wilderness at all in his district.

The organizing the Oregon Wilderness Coalition had done in the 1970s now paid dividends. Virtually every area under consideration had its local advocates. Some local activists resorted to desperate tactics to keep roads out of unprotected areas. Twice in the early 1980s, road survey stakes were removed from the Grassy Knob Roadless Area, a rare old-growth Port Orford cedar forest just seven miles from the Oregon Coast. The delay helped keep the 17,200-acre unprotected wilderness intact until Congress stepped in.

Because local support for these areas was so passionate, Kerr and Monteith had a hard time dealing away any of the 4 million acres eligible for protection during last-minute negotiations over the final shape of the bill. Hatfield, however, insisted that his bill had to come in at under 1 million acres. In the end, the Oregon bill created 23 new wilderness areas totaling 853,000 acres. When Grassy Knob was added at the last minute, the Forest Service was ordered to stop work on the road it had finally begun pushing into the lush coastal forest. The forest is now gradually reclaiming this monument to the agency's defiant stance against wilderness preservation.

Washington

The Washington delegation was more systematic in its approach to crafting a wilderness bill. Each member developed recommendations for his district. Senator Henry "Scoop" Jackson, a Democrat and a powerful figure in Washington politics, assumed responsibility for shepherding the bill through. When Jackson died suddenly in 1983, Dan Evans, a progressive Republican, was appointed to fill out his term.

"The switch when Jackson died and Evans succeeded him made a huge difference," said Charlie Raines, a longtime Sierra Club activist in Seattle. "Evans was a hiker. He knew the land on the ground, knew the value of wilderness."

The Gifford Pinchot Alliance, a successor to the Mount St. Helens Protective Association, pressed for protection of three large roadless areas in the heavily roaded forest: Indian Heaven, Trapper Creek, and Dark Divide. But Republican Senator Slade Gorton, looking after the interests of Washington's timber industry, balked at setting aside that much valuable timber.

Representative Mike Lowry, a liberal Democrat who represented a pro-wilderness Seattle constituency, introduced a wilderness bill designed to protect intact watersheds. Environmentalists credit Lowry with making the case that resulted in designation of the 6,000-acre Trapper Creek Wilderness, which contained rare low-elevation old growth. But the much larger Dark Divide Roadless Area, which encompassed 57,000 acres of the Cispus and Lewis River Valleys, and which was renowned among hikers in southwest Washington for its old-growth valleys, craggy rock formations, and incomparable views of four Cascade mountain peaks, was left out of the bill.

Representative Tom Foley, a Democrat who represented the Spokane area of eastern Washington, fought designating any wilderness in the Kettle Range, which lay within his district. This was a great disappointment to wilderness advocates. "Kettle Range was the model for grassroots activism in the state," recalled Tim McNulty, a forest activist on the Olympic Peninsula. "They had the support of county administrators, they had local businesses, they did everything right."

Representative Sid Morrison, a moderate Republican, supported several high-elevation wilderness areas in his district on the eastern slope of the Cascades.

On the west side of the Olympic Peninsula, where the fantastic Olympic rainforest grew, the Forest Service had moved quickly in the

1970s to preempt wilderness designation. Unit plans prepared by the Soleduck and Quinault Ranger Districts called for opening virtually all roadless areas to logging. Environmentalists proposed wilderness designation for large roadless watersheds adjacent to Olympic National Park in both districts, but to no avail.

The outlook was more hopeful on the peninsula's east side, across Puget Sound from the state's heavily populated Seattle-Tacoma metropolitan area. McNulty credits botanist Ed Tisch for persuading the Forest Service that the upper watersheds of the Quilcene and Dungeness watersheds should be protected because they harbored rare endemic plants.

Grassroots activists like McNulty and Tom Jay of the group Wild Olympic Salmon worked closely with an established group, Olympic Park Associates, which had built a national constituency for forest protection on the peninsula. The park, McNulty said, was an important selling point for wilderness. "We could talk about the ecological value of Forest Service lands surrounding the park and their importance to wintering elk and salmon."

When the first round of hearings on a Washington wilderness bill was scheduled, McNulty wanted to testify in Washington, D.C., but he had a major tree-planting contract to fulfill. His crew encouraged him to go and kept him on the payroll during his absence.

One of McNulty's top priorities was saving the watershed of the Gray Wolf River, on the north side of the park. In January of 1984, in deep snow, he drove Joe Mentor, a member of Senator Dan Evans' staff, to see the area in his beat-up Volvo. "Somehow we made it and had a magnificent view," he said. "Joe went back and briefed Evans, and the Gray Wolf, virtually the whole valley, ended up in the Washington wilderness bill."

On March 9, 1984, the entire Washington delegation met in Tom Foley's office to hammer out the final bill. Even staff members were excluded from the meeting. "At 9:00 P.M., after five intense hours, the delegation emerged from Foley's office, arm-in-arm and smiling," Karen Fant of the Washington Wilderness Coalition wrote in the coalition's newsletter. "The deals had been cut and, for better or worse, the major decisions on the Washington Wilderness Act of 1984 had been made." Environmentalists had proposed protection for 2 million acres. The final Washington bill established 19 new wilderness areas and expanded four others, protecting 1.03 million acres in all.

Forest activists declared victory. To celebrate, Tim McNulty married his sweetheart, Mary Morgan, on the Gray Wolf River that fall.

Northern California

The California Wilderness Act was even more generous. The Forest Service's RARE II inventory had identified 6.5 million acres of roadless national forest in the state. The final bill, spearheaded by Democratic

U.S. Senator Phil Burton, designated 1.8 million acres as wilderness and set aside an additional 1.7 million acres for further study.

Though most of the newly designated California wilderness was high-elevation rocks and ice, the Northcoast Environmental Center in Arcata managed to win protection for some ecologically significant old growth in the state's northwest corner. A significant victory, said Tim McKay, the center's director, was the designation of the 153,000-acre Siskiyou Wilderness, on the Siskiyou, Klamath, and Six Rivers National Forests, which conferred permanent protection on 10,000 acres of rare low-elevation old growth. The act also added land to the Marble Mountain Wilderness in the rugged Klamath Mountains and gave permanent protection to 500,000 acres of the spectacular Trinity Alps Primitive Area.

NOT ANOTHER ACRE

A key issue for wilderness advocates after 1984 was the fate of the millions of acres left out of the wilderness bills. Senator Hatfield vowed that not another acre of national forest land in Oregon would become wilderness as long as he served in the Senate. His position, and the timber industry's, was that roadless areas left out of the bill should be released forever from consideration as wilderness and opened to logging. Environmentalists opposed this blanket giveaway to the timber industry, known as "hard release" language. The Forest Service also opposed hard release, for a different reason: It took away the agency's discretion to manage the land.

Congress ultimately decided that the roadless areas would be returned to multiple-use management—but not necessarily to timber production. The door to protection of these areas remained open, if only a crack. Dispirited, Andy Kerr and James Monteith plotted their next move.

At 5 o'clock one bleary morning in late 1985, Kerr approached Hatfield at Chicago's O'Hare Airport, where they were both between planes. The home-building industry was in its worst slump since the Great Depression, and Hatfield had introduced a bill to aid the industry by allowing federal timber purchasers to get out of their high-priced contracts. If it passed, it meant less timber would be logged over the next several years. Kerr told Hatfield he was headed for D.C. to support the bill because it would slow the development of roadless areas.

As Kerr recalled the early morning exchange, Hatfield said, "There are no more roadless areas. We released them."

"And I said, 'Oh, well, Senator, but you know, they are still out there in fact, and they still don't have any roads.'

"He said, 'There are no more roadless areas.'"

For Kerr, the conversation was a turning point. The Godfather was unmovable. Environmentalists had won all the wilderness they were going to get.

The Big Creek watershed in the Shelton Unit of the Olympic National Forest was logged clean, leaving no buffers to protect downstream fish runs (photo taken in 1992).

Logs on the docks at Coos Bay, Oregon, await export to Japan. Because Japanese mill-owners paid a premium for fine old-growth timber, companies continued to export unprocessed logs from state and private land even as some Northwest mills faced log shortages in the early 1990s.

Flooding in February of 1996 inundated farmlands at the confluence of the Santiam and Willamette Rivers in western Oregon. Followup studies showed flooding was most severe in areas of the Oregon Coast Range and the Oregon Cascades, where heavy logging and road-building had occurred on steep slopes.

Logging of old growth ordered by the 1995 timber salvage rider was under-way in Oregon's Umpqua National Forest by December of 1995.

A northern spotted owl, totemic symbol of the ancient forests, perches in a stand of Douglas-fir and cedar.

Opposite: *Fallen logs and boulders create pools and riffles for salmon in an undisturbed tributary of the Breitenbush River in the Oregon Cascades.*

Beth Howell, a southern Oregon environmentalist, surveys the aftermath of logging at the Sugarloaf timber sale in October of 1995. Sugarloaf, in the Siskiyou National Forest, became a rallying point for protests over the effects of the timber salvage rider.

Disaster Creek, in the Elk River watershed on the southern Oregon Coast, was logged to its banks in 1993 as it flowed through private land. Throughout the 1990s local activists and fisheries biologists fought to stop logging that threatened the Elk, one of the top coho salmon-producing rivers on the Pacific Coast.

Francis Eatherington of the environmental group Umpqua Watersheds poses with a fallen fir at the Yellow Creek timber sale on Bureau of Land Management land near Roseburg, Oregon. To publicize the forest destruction, Eatherington established a Web site on the Internet, "In Memory of Yellow Creek," featuring color photos of the stand before and after logging.

A scorched tree falls in the North Kalmiopsis roadless area in 1988. The North Kalmiopsis, part of the largest unroaded wilderness in western Oregon, was left unprotected by the 1984 Oregon Wilderness Act.

By the 1970s, unsustainable rates of logging on private lands in the Northwest had created an imminent timber supply gap, prompting the timber industry to press for increased access to timber on national forest lands. This enormous clearcut on Weyerhaeuser Company land in the Oregon Cascades borders the Middle Santiam Wilderness in the Willamette National Forest.

Opposite: *A truck hauls its bounty of old-growth logs out of Oregon's Umpqua National Forest in June of 1996. The salvage logging rider opened many areas of the Umpqua to clearcutting and triggered civil disobedience actions in the woods.*

A visitor gazes upward from the base of a 600-year-old Douglas-fir in the Mount Hood National Forest.

Chapter Seven

Loving a Place

While lobbyists and politicians were cutting final deals on the 1984 wilderness bills, a quieter and more profound movement was taking shape in rural enclaves across the Northwest. By 1983, it had a name: bioregionalism.

Rooted in environmental and utopian ideals, and nurtured by the back-to-the-land movement of the 1970s, bioregionalism was a politics of place. It flourished in remote, sparsely populated areas. Among other things, it was a reaction to nightmare visions of a technological society like the one portrayed in George Orwell's *1984*, where Big Brother and the Thought Police quashed autonomy and independent thought.

One of the places where bioregionalism flowered early was in the Siskiyou-Klamath country of southwestern Oregon and northwestern California.

SISKIYOU COUNTRY

In late 1983, a few people living in Oregon's Illinois Valley, in the heart of the Siskiyous, began publishing a bioregional magazine about their corner of the world, *Siskiyou Country*. Many of those involved had taken part in the 1983 Bald Mountain Road blockade and had stayed on to put down roots and build an alternative community.

In an early issue, *Siskiyou Country* published an essay by Mark Roseland, a writer and teacher living in the small community of Applegate, describing how bioregionalism could defeat Orwell's vision. Roseland wrote:

> *The way to decrease the threat of centralized power is by ex-*
> *panding the realm of decentralized power—that is, by making*
> *decisions at the level of maximum participation, where those*
> *who are most affected by a decision have the most say about it;*
> *and by concentrating on relations that stem from reciprocity*
> *and voluntarism rather than on law or judicial obligation.*
> *The goal is not to capture power but to break it down to a point*
> *where it is human-scale, a level at which people can have a say*
> *or a vote about how to manage the energy, food, products and*
> *resources of the area where they live.*

Siskiyou Country became a communications medium for people who shared this vision of society.

In the Pacific Northwest, living bioregionally meant getting to know the flora and fauna of your particular forest ecosystem, the geology of your watershed, and the policies and practices of your local Forest Service or BLM district. It wasn't a new concept, but it was an important one in the context of the times. Knowledge was power in the campaign to protect the public lands.

Bioregionalism also meant learning the history and culture of your corner of the planet, including the history of its indigenous people. It meant going deeper than wilderness politics, deeper than science, in an effort to understand the spiritual essence and natural wisdom of a place.

In the same 1984 issue of *Siskiyou Country*, Felice Pace, an environmental activist living in Scott Valley, California, in the heart of the Klamath Mountains, contributed an eyewitness report describing a rare performance of the Brush Dance by the Karuk Indians of the Klamaths. "Mainstream ignorance of the lives and traditions of our bioregion's native tribes is deep," he wrote. Most whites, he said, "are either unaware of these events or would never dream of attending them."

Pace went on to found the Klamath Forest Alliance, a bioregional group that worked for responsible forestry and preservation of roadless areas on the Klamath National Forest.

SAGE OF THE SISKIYOUS

Lou Gold, a former political science professor at Oberlin College and the University of Illinois, was one of many newcomers drawn to the Siskiyous by the 1983 Bald Mountain actions. Gold left that life behind in 1983 to devote himself to saving the Siskiyous.

After the blockade, Gold held a solitary 56-day vigil on Bald Mountain, camping just inside the boundary of the Kalmiopsis Wilderness, where he watched as workers bulldozed the road into the heart of the wild country. In July, he learned that a federal judge had halted road construction in response to the Earth First!/Oregon Natural Resources Council lawsuit.

Gold returned to Bald Mountain each summer for a dozen years. His camp became a destination for forest activists and hikers. He developed his own rituals for honoring the sanctity of wilderness, and shared them with visitors. In 1987, wildfire swept across Bald Mountain, burning through old-growth stands both within and outside the protected wilderness, and Gold fled for his life. Later he kept watch as loggers salvaged burned trees from the North Kalmiopsis Roadless Area.

With his long beard and gray ponytail, Gold became the gentle sage of the Siskiyous. When he was not on Bald Mountain, he lived with friends in the Oregon counterculture community of Takelma, near the California border. He spent much of each winter traveling around the country with a compelling slide show and lecture that described the beauty of the Siskiyous and the Forest Service's plan to destroy it.

Single-handedly, Lou Gold built a national constituency for protection of the wild Siskiyous. By 1990, he had made more than 500 presentations across the nation. Siskiyou National Forest managers could track his travels by the letters they received from people in distant states, commenting on their draft forest plan.

Lou Gold never enjoyed the political combat involved in saving wilderness. His connection to the Siskiyous was deeply personal. In a 1990 interview on Bald Mountain, he confided that he was weary of "the politicking, the horse-trading, the chess-playing, the back-room deals." His message, he said, was more basic.

"What I really want to say is, I love a place. It's important to love a place. We have to be part of a total community, human and nonhuman. It's about having a relationship with the Earth that we live and die on."

COMMITTING TO THE CAUSE

Julie Norman acquired her passion for wild places as a Girl Scout. She was a computer specialist for IBM in Houston when she first went rafting on the Colorado River. With scarcely a backward glance, she traded her business cards for a raft and paddle and moved to the West Coast to become a wilderness river guide. Fate brought her to the Rogue River, renowned by whitewater rafters. As she learned this rugged country, she fell in love with the dazzling Siskiyou forests of tanoak and madrone, rare Brewer's spruce and sugar pine.

In the victorious aftermath of the Bald Mountain action, Earth First! held its first Round River Rendezvous at Galice on the Rogue. Norman was living in the river outpost of Galice that summer. She had never heard of Earth First!. Out of curiosity, she attended the rendezvous. There she met Steve Marsden, Chant Thomas, Dave Foreman, Mike Roselle, and Robert Brothers. Brothers, who had adopted the name Bobcat, was crippled by polio. He had collected several Ph.D.s before dropping out of academia to fight for wilderness in the Siskiyou backwoods.

Norman and Bobcat moved to the hippie community of Williams and became part of the Earth First! culture. Norman also joined a new group called the Siskiyou Citizens' Task Force and began to study computer models of timber sales on the Siskiyou National Forest. Another group in Williams, Headwaters, was monitoring logging on the Medford BLM district, which until 1979 had sold timber without any management plan at all.

In 1985 Norman joined the Headwaters board of directors. She remained active in Siskiyou Earth First! as well, until 1987. But in the aftermath of the 1987 Silver Fire, when the future of the North Kalmiopsis became a high-stakes political issue, she decided that wearing both hats was no longer politically tenable.

Together, Norman and Bobcat put their computer skills to work analyzing 30 years' worth of timber sales in the Siskiyous. In the trunk of her 1966 Dodge Coronet, Norman carried color-coded maps and computer printouts containing the details of those sales. They revealed a history of inappropriate forest management: logged areas at high elevations where the soil and climate were so harsh that trees could not regenerate, and clearcuts in unique transition zones where flora and fauna of the Coast, Cascade, and Sierra Nevada mountain ranges converged. She became a mainstream activist, lobbying Congress, appealing timber sales, and cajoling foundations to give Headwaters money.

Siskiyou Country eventually folded, but out of it grew the Siskiyou Regional Education Project. Based in Takelma, the project drew a number of Siskiyou Earth First! activists and others from the Bald Mountain Road protests, including Steve Marsden and Lou Gold. The Siskiyou Project also gradually became more mainstream, applying for grants to conduct ecological mapping and challenging destructive hardrock mining projects.

KNOWING YOUR WATERSHED

Out of the bioregional movement came the concept of local organizing along watershed boundaries. The formation of local watershed councils held the possibility of bringing together people with conflicting values around a mutual commitment to protecting or restoring the watersheds they shared.

In the Mattole Valley, along a remote stretch of northern California's Humboldt County coast, loggers, ranchers, and back-to-the-land refugees from the San Francisco Bay area set aside their differences and came together in the late 1980s to restore salmon runs in the damaged Mattole River watershed. The onetime adversaries celebrated the success of their project in a ribald touring musical comedy called *Queen Salmon*.

Bonnie Phillips moved to Washington state from Wisconsin after college to climb mountains. In the mid-1980s she developed a progressive form of rheumatism that ended her days as a mountain-climber. In 1987, looking for a new way to use her energy, she joined the Pilchuck Audubon chapter in Everett, Washington, and threw herself into a series of environmental campaigns focused on Puget Sound and the sprawling Mount Baker–Snoqualmie National Forest to the east.

Phillips educated herself about the old-growth issue and about how logging practices on the Darrington Ranger District in the mountains east of Everett affected the Stillaguamish watershed she called home. With her fierce commitment and her impressive organizational skills, Phillips would become a force in the regional and national ancient forest campaigns of the 1990s. "A lot of my effectiveness is because I remained here," she said. "You gain credibility with the Forest Service first, if you file lawsuits, and second, if you stay around a long time. Then you have standing."

BREITENBUSH

In the central Oregon Cascades, a group of counterculture entrepreneurs came together in 1981 to form the Breitenbush Community, a cooperative centered on a dilapidated hot springs resort in a beautiful setting near the Breitenbush River. Members of the co-op didn't plan to become forest activists; their activism was thrust on them as logging roads and clearcuts in the Detroit Ranger District of the Willamette National Forest rapidly encroached on their new age sanctuary.

"We were a bunch of idealistic young hippies who were trying to hide out from the world," said Michael Donnelly, one of the original members of the Breitenbush Community, who went on to found Friends of the Breitenbush Cascades. "The movement came to us, in the form of chainsaws at dawn and scars climbing up the hillsides."

Beginning in the mid-1980s, Breitenbush became a base of operations for forest activists who blocked logging roads and sat in trees to slow the rate of logging in the North Santiam Canyon, a timber stronghold long accustomed to getting its way with the Forest Service.

HOSTILE TERRITORY

Living bioregionally didn't come as easily east of the Cascades, where the culture was hostile to environmentalists. Some bioregional experiments failed to flourish as communities dependent on natural resources shattered along predictable fault lines.

Geraldine Payton, New England–born, moved from Berkeley to a remote corner of northeastern Washington's Okanogan County in the mid-1970s to become part of an organic wheat farming cooperative. In 1983 she moved to the tiny hamlet of Chesaw, reached by a twisting 20-mile mountain road that connects it with Oroville, the closest town of any size. On a clear day, from Buckhorn Mountain near her home, the view to the north takes in a forested wilderness across the British Columbia border.

Payton and her partner Rick Gillespie got involved in a local anti-herbicide campaign, drawing the ire of the county's apple orchardists. They monitored forest practices on the Okanogan National Forest. In 1987, they began producing a bioregional journal, *Columbiana*, which carried stories about the ecology and culture of the Interior Columbia Plateau—the vast area drained by the Columbia River east of the Cascades, which encompasses parts of seven states and British Columbia. *Columbiana* published essays about natural history, agriculture, appropriate technology, indigenous people, and early pioneers in the region, as well as environmental issues. But to many of their rural neighbors, their political views made Payton and Gillespie outsiders who would never fit in.

THINKING BIG

The new discipline of conservation biology, just emerging in the 1980s, supplied a scientific context for bioregional consciousness. Conservation biologists stressed the need to manage large landscapes for the preservation of biological diversity. Where large chunks of wild land remained—the Siskiyou-Klamath province, the North Cascades, and the

Northern Rockies—environmental activists adapted the concepts of conservation biology to argue for saving these last, best wild places.

In 1989, a former Earth First! activist named Mitch Friedman founded the Greater Ecosystem Alliance, based in Bellingham, Washington, to bring together U.S. and Canadian environmentalists in a campaign to protect wildlands on both sides of the international boundary. This knot of mountainous wilderness, centered on the North Cascades, is one of the last places in North America large enough and wild enough to harbor gray wolves and grizzlies.

The high-profile ancient forest protection campaign to come was built on the work of these and other environmental activists who chose to live bioregionally, think globally, and act locally.

Chapter Eight

Early Warnings

On May 19, 1983, nine national forest supervisors who held the fate of the Northwest's big-timber forests in their hands gathered at Portland's elegant Benson Hotel. They were by definition "timber beasts"—politically astute managers committed to their agency's mission of getting out the cut. Yet they had asked their boss, Forest Service Chief Max Peterson, to fly out and meet with them face-to-face so they could warn him that the forests were being cut too fast.

After years of politically inspired delay, the supervisors were writing new 10-year forest plans to comply with the 1976 National Forest Management Act. These plans were supposed to balance timber production with recreation use, scenery, and protection of streams, soil, fish, and wildlife. The field reports were in, and the news was not good: all of those nontimber amenities were at risk unless the pace of logging slowed immediately. If it continued, a crash in Northwest timber supplies was inevitable when the new forest plans were completed. And if that happened, there would be hell to pay in the hardball world of Northwest timber politics.

No one said anything about preserving a vanishing ecosystem. The concern was more pragmatic. "The message was that there had to be a day of reckoning," said Dick Pfilf, at the time supervisor of Oregon's Mount Hood National Forest. "We said we ought to prepare the political climate so it wouldn't be a big surprise when the plans came out."

Peterson listened, but he was a political realist. It was he who had to face the powerful Northwest congressional delegation at budget time. Then he doled out a dose of political reality. The timber industry wouldn't stand for a premature reduction in timber sale levels, and neither would the delegation.

The overcutting was to continue for six more years, until a federal judge ordered the Forest Service to put on the brakes.

THE REAGAN FACTOR

In the political climate of the early 1980s, any attempt to reduce logging on the national forests was met with great resistance in Washington, D.C. The Reagan administration had turned over the nation's

natural resources to a band of conservative westerners, led by Interior

Secretary James Watt, who were bent on exploiting them for quick profit. Max Peterson's boss was Assistant Agriculture Secretary John B. Crowell, a former Louisiana Pacific Corporation timber executive. Crowell was dissatisfied with the way the new national forest plans were shaping up.

To his mind, forest managers out in the Northwest weren't building a convincing case for increasing protection of wildlife and scenery at the expense of timber production.

Crowell had set off a firestorm within the Forest Service when he announced that the national forests of the Northwest ought to be able to double timber production to 10 billion board feet annually by the 1990s without harmful environmental consequences.

Three months before Max Peterson's meeting with forest supervisors in Portland, Crowell had warned in an internal memo that "appropriate changes" would be made in Forest Service personnel unless the plans began to "improve significantly soon." In response, Northwest Regional Forester Jeff Sirmon had ordered a "pause" in preparation of management plans for the 19 national forests in Oregon and Washington so supervisors could figure out how to implement Crowell's directive.

A WARNING UNHEEDED

Sirmon was a voice for restraint. He had reviewed early projections of timber yields in the forest plans, and he could foresee the political donnybrook to come. "I decided that I needed to begin taking slings and arrows for the region as a whole," he said.

In 1984, he went public with warnings that the cut would be coming down. He met with the timber industry-dominated Oregon Board of Forestry and with the governors of both Oregon and Washington. He explained why the Forest Service soon would be selling less timber in the Northwest. "My message to them was, 'There's going to be a falldown in timber output. We need your cooperation.' But everyone was in denial; no one wanted to grapple with the issue."

Sirmon met with environmental groups, too, and asked for their help in discussing and debating the planning process, but with Crowell pushing for a doubling of timber sale levels, they were distrustful. "Environmentalists said, 'Don't expect any help from us as long as your generals are rattling their sabers,'" Sirmon recalled.

He went to all the major timber associations with his warning, but they weren't ready to concede that the cut would be coming down. They were too heavily invested in trying to influence the timber yield estimates in the new forest plans. "They had their own economists and forest planners," Sirmon said. "Their computers were as good as ours."

HARDBALL

In 1986, three years after the meeting at the Benson Hotel, Forest Service Chief Max Peterson appeared before the House Interior

Appropriations Subcommittee, the panel that decided how much timber his agency would sell each year. He was grilled by Democratic Representative Les AuCoin of Oregon, who touted his conservation credentials while taking money from the timber industry to do its bidding. At AuCoin's insistence, the 1986 timber target for the Pacific Northwest had been hiked by 700 million board feet beyond the amount the Forest Service had requested. In April, halfway through the fiscal year, national forests in Oregon and Washington were having a hard time finding timber to sell. AuCoin had been hearing from his timber industry constituents. Why, he asked Peterson, was the Pacific Northwest dragging its feet in meeting its 1986 timber targets?

In 1985, during a depression in the home-building industry, Congress had passed special legislation allowing federal timber purchasers to get out of contracts for timber they couldn't afford to log. Now, with the market still in a slump, the industry was pushing for the Forest Service to rush large volumes of timber back to market at bargain-basement prices for harvest later, when the price of lumber had rebounded. Peterson was trying to cut his budget to comply with a new congressional deficit reduction law. And he had not forgotten the warnings delivered at that long-ago meeting in Portland.

AuCoin was not sympathetic. He warned Peterson that if timber sale levels in the Northwest didn't start climbing soon, the chief might not remain chief for long. His grilling paid off—in the short run. The Forest Service scrambled to meet its quota. The following February, Peterson left the Forest Service for a job in the nonprofit sector.

The confrontation was unusual only because it occurred in the open. The pressure from the Northwest delegation to get out the cut in those years was unrelenting. The regional forester and forest supervisors in the Northwest routinely received orders from members of the delegation to expedite timber sales on behalf of timber industry constituents.

"Probably a half dozen times during my tenure someone put out the word that it was time for me to leave," Peterson said years later. "I don't think there's any question that some in the Pacific Northwest were glad to see me go."

NOW OR NEVER
Meanwhile, a few employees in the federal Bureau of Land Management were sounding their own warning about the pace of cutting on the 2.5 million acres the agency managed in western Oregon, where BLM land was interspersed with logged-over private land in a giant checkerboard of mile-square blocks. They tried to take steps to avert a showdown by proposing a system of forest reserves to protect the tattered old-growth forests under their jurisdiction before it was too late.

In 1937, when Congress gave these former Oregon & California Railroad lands to the BLM to manage, it also gave the agency a simple mandate: Sell timber, and pump half of all receipts into the 18 counties where the former railroad lands were located. This revenue-sharing arrangement created a strong political constituency for the BLM among the counties that depended on timber revenue as their lifeblood.

By the mid-1980s the BLM had been liquidating the mature and old-growth timber on the O & C lands for nearly a half-century. As the agency prepared required timber management plans for the 1990s, some officials saw a day of reckoning on the horizon. "It became clear that the end of the old growth was now predictable with relative certainty, and that it was basically now or never if a representative sampling of functioning old-growth ecosystems was to be preserved," wrote Ronald Sadler, chief of forest planning in the BLM's Oregon office from 1973 to 1984, after his retirement in 1991.

In the late 1970s the BLM set aside 90 small owl reserves under a voluntary agreement with the state of Oregon. But it did not reduce logging to reflect the land withdrawn. To meet its timber goals it was forced to log more heavily on land outside the owl reserves. The stepped-up logging dumped more sediment into streams, eliminated more wildlife habitat, and created more ugly clearcuts.

QUASHING REFORM
The 1983 plan, drawn up by employees of the BLM's Coos Bay District, proposed setting aside a number of large old-growth forest blocks where logging would be prohibited and connecting them with smaller blocks that would be logged no more frequently than every 350 years. The proposal contrasted sharply with the agency's existing plan to log most of its western Oregon lands every 60 years. Sixty years is far too little time for young forests to acquire the ecological characteristics of old growth that make them ideal habitat for spotted owls.

Sadler took the plan to Washington, D.C., for review by Interior Department officials. Because of its impact on timber production, it received in-depth scrutiny from BLM Director Robert Burford and Assistant Interior Secretary Garrey Carrothers, both of whom worked for Interior Secretary James Watt. They gave it tentative approval, but a week later that approval was rescinded. Burford later issued a directive boosting the annual timber sale level on the BLM's Coos Bay District and told the state BLM office not to reduce timber production to benefit any wildlife species unless it was already federally listed as threatened or endangered.

In 1986, a BLM wildlife biologist named Mike Wisdom made another attempt to head off disaster when he developed a system for ranking the shrinking old-growth stands in the Coos Bay District based on their size, distance from each other, and suitability as spotted owl habitat. Sadler and most of the agency's field managers endorsed the system as a way to protect some old growth. This time, it was state BLM officials who vetoed the plan.

In the meantime, logging on BLM and private lands continued to carve the Coast Range with roads and clearcuts. In 1990, when the U.S. Fish and Wildlife Service listed the owl as a threatened species, federal biologists singled out the severely fragmented BLM lands of the Oregon Coast Range as an area of critical concern.

STANDING UP TO CENSORSHIP

In the mid-1980s, BLM biologist Chris Maser continued to wage an uphill struggle to get his research on old-growth forest ecology published. At last, in 1988, the BLM and Forest Service jointly published "From the Forest to the Sea: A Story of Fallen Trees." The report, co-authored by Robert Tarrant, Jim Trappe, and Jerry Franklin, warned that current logging practices would profoundly affect forest, stream, and ocean ecology.

By then, Maser had resigned from his job. The BLM's forestry and science staff in Washington, D.C., had tried for three years to squash the old-growth report. Maser had been directed to place himself under censorship for what he said and wrote, but he had refused to fudge data or to lie to the public. By 1987, when he quit, federal agencies no longer could keep a lid on the proliferating old-growth research studies.

In 1988, Maser published *The Redesigned Forest,* a small, profound book in which he wove together his own evolving philosophy with descriptions of forest ecology and raised fundamental questions about the wholesale conversion of complex forest ecosystems to simplified monocultures. He punctuated the text with pithy contrasts between the natural forest and the fully regulated forest that was rapidly replacing it:

> *"Nature designed Pacific Northwest forests to live 500–1200 years. We are designing a forest that may seldom live 100 years."*

> *"Nature designed Pacific Northwest forests to be unique in the world—25 species of conifers, 7 major ones, the longest lived and largest of their genera. We are designing a forest based largely on a single-species' short rotation."*

Maser began to write and speak in whatever forums he could find. To many forest activists, he was a hero, a scientist who had spoken truth to power and who was unafraid to express his contrition. "We have the right to redesign the world," he said in a 1989 speech to a Corvallis, Oregon, standing-room crowd. "What we don't have is the intellect, the knowledge."

In his speeches, Maser expressed empathy for timber workers who had lost their livelihood. "The small loggers, the independent loggers, are part of our heritage," he said. "They're part of what makes us us. They're fighting for their dignity. I know what it's like when the paychecks stop. You can't take something away from people and not replace it with something else."

However, he did not attempt to disguise his frustration with his former employer. "The BLM was lying behind closed doors to retain its homeostasis," he said in a 1989 interview. "One BLM district manager told me that as far as he was concerned, he was going to run an industrial forest and what happened afterward was not his concern."

A FINITE FOREST

By the mid-1980s, forest supervisors were hearing reports from their field employees about slopes too prone to stream-burying landslides to risk logging them and about hikers who objected to clearcuts along their favorite trails. An environmentally awakened public was putting new pressures on national forests to provide wilderness and back-country recreation, trails and campgrounds, and scenery and wildlife viewing opportunities.

Forest managers faced hard professional choices. Meeting timber targets, especially on the big-timber forests, was a sure route to career advancement. But the toll exacted by excessive logging was now impossible to ignore. Some watersheds had been logged so heavily that the Forest Service had no choice but to put them to bed for decades.

As vast and productive as the old-growth forests of the Northwest had once seemed, they were not infinite. The end game for these forests was now in sight.

A logger attacks a giant scorched in the 1987 Silver Fire, which burned 96,000 acres of protected and unprotected wilderness in the Siskiyou Mountains of southwestern Oregon. Environmentalists sued to stop salvage logging in the North Kalmiopsis roadless area, but in 1988 members of Congress from the Northwest passed a measure ordering the project to proceed.

PART THREE

DAY OF RECKONING

1987–92

66 Like the other forms of land preservation, wilderness areas are doomed to be islands surrounded by what constantly threatens to invade and damage them, but that is what we get for learning slowly. 99

—WALLACE STEGNER,
"A Capsule History of Conservation," 1990

---

66 Recreational development is a job not of building roads into lovely country, but of building receptivity into the still unlovely human mind. 99

—ALDO LEOPOLD, *A Sand County Almanac, 1949*

---

66 We had a bunch of cheap timber, a cheap labor pool, and cheap mills. If you'd take any one of those three things away, a lot of the pain would have been gotten over with by now. 99

—TOM HIRONS, *Oregon logger, 1992*

IN THE 1980S, AS LOADED log trucks rolled out of 500-year-old forests and clearcuts climbed higher into the mountains, the timber industry stayed competitive by automating its mills, downsizing its work force, stockpiling cheap federal timber, and exporting unprocessed logs from state and private land overseas, where a premium price was to be had for fine vertical-grain Douglas-fir. By 1990, private companies in the Northwest were exporting 3.6 billion board feet of raw logs annually from state and private lands—more than the Forest Service expected to sell annually from all the national forests of western Oregon and western Washington under its new forest plans. Mountains of logs piled up at ports in Aberdeen, Longview, and Astoria.

After passage of the 1984 wilderness bills, some forest activists began laying the groundwork for a litigation campaign that would use the northern spotted owl as a legal stand-in for wild forests. In late 1987, environmentalists took the government to court in the first of a series of lawsuits to force compliance with environmental laws.

The region erupted in early 1989, when a federal judge blocked logging in national forests inhabited by the owl until the Forest Service adopted a credible plan for preserving its habitat. The timber industry responded by organizing timber towns and encouraging workers to blame the owl, blame environmentalists, blame anything but its own rapacious and short-sighted practices. However, some federal employees who had warned privately for years that the pace of logging in the Northwest was unsustainable now found the courage to speak the truth.

In 1989, in an exercise of raw power, Northwest lawmakers pushed a bill through Congress that released 1.1 billion board feet of timber from the federal injunction and exempted 8 billion board feet more from environmentalists' lawsuits.

Confronted with a crisis in the Pacific Northwest, the Bush administration appointed a committee of scientists to devise a strategy for protecting the owl's old-growth forest habitat across 24 million acres of federal land. The plan's release triggered protests in logging communities throughout the region. Polarization accelerated in 1990 after the U.S. Fish and Wildlife Service listed the owl as a threatened species and undertook steps required by the Endangered Species Act to save the subspecies from extinction.

The Forest Service seized on "new forestry," a less brutal alternative to clearcutting, to defuse opposition to the continued logging of old-growth forests. But President George Bush refused to grapple with the fundamental cause of forest gridlock—decades of overcutting on federal lands. Instead, he pursued a cynical "train-wreck" policy designed to weaken support for the Endangered Species Act and build political support in disaffected timber towns.

Chapter Nine

The Perfect Surrogate

As logging on national forests in the Northwest climbed toward record levels in the mid-1980s, the fight to save old growth moved into the courts.

In a remote hilltop house in the Sierra Nevada foothills, two bright, home-schooled California teenagers, Eric and Willow Beckwitt, decided to conduct a research project on the national forests. They studied the Endangered Species Act. They learned that any citizen could petition to list a species for protection under the 1973 law. On their own, they discovered the spotted owl studies published by Eric Forsman and other biologists. In 1985, they mailed off a petition to the Portland office of the U.S. Fish and Wildlife Service, asking the agency to list the owl as an endangered species.

THE BIODIVERSITY HOOK
As a student at the Oregon State University School of Forestry, Andy Stahl had heard about Forsman's research on the owl too. He knew that in the early 1980s, the Forest Service had declared the owl a "management indicator species"—a barometer for the health of old-growth forests.

In 1985, Stahl was working for the National Wildlife Federation in Portland. When he learned of the Beckwitt brothers' owl petition, Stahl made a trip to North San Juan, California. He explained to the Beckwitts that Northwest environmentalists had not yet laid the scientific groundwork for a campaign to protect the owl. Reluctantly, the Beckwitts agreed to withdraw their petition. Soon after, Stahl took it upon himself to begin laying that groundwork.

The emerging field of conservation biology drew on biology, geography, and many other disciplines to solve real-world problems related to the loss of genetic diversity. Because a growing number of studies showed that the loss of species due to habitat destruction was accelerating worldwide, many conservation biologists considered their field a crisis discipline.

Stahl could see the implications of conservation biology for the owl and for all other species affected by the loss of old-growth forests. He asked his father, Frank Stahl, a professor of molecular biology at the

University of Oregon, to suggest a conservation biologist he could talk to. His father recommended Russell Lande, a University of Chicago population geneticist who specialized in the esoteric science of modeling wildlife populations and habitat conditions.

Stahl tracked Lande down in Maine. Over a meal at a lobster shack, he explained what was known about the owl's relationship to the old-growth forests. He showed Lande the Forest Service's latest plan for protecting the owl. The 1984 plan, known as a regional guide, called for setting aside small reserves across the bird's range, each large enough to support a single breeding owl pair. He asked Lande to assess whether the plan was adequate and to develop a mathematical model predicting how habitat loss might affect the owl's viability. Lande was intrigued by the subject and had time on his hands. He agreed.

As Lande checked the scientific literature cited in the regional guide, he discovered that it relied heavily on work he himself had done on mathematical modeling of genetic variability for his doctoral dissertation. He realized that the Forest Service assumed it could guarantee the owl's survival across 24 million acres by maintaining a population of just 500 mating pairs—a number more appropriate for animals in zoos than species in the wild.

Stahl sent Lande a sheaf of published and unpublished reports by owl biologists. Lande studied the reports and maps of forest habitat, talked to the biologists, and critiqued the regional guide. He concluded that the habitat reserves set aside for the owl were severely deficient. "It was clear they were shaving it down to a minimum and spacing the reserves too far apart," he said.

Lande spent three months in the spring of 1985 writing a paper detailing his findings, submitted it for peer review, and later published it in the professional journal *Oecologia*. In the paper, he concluded that the Forest Service's long-term plan for the owl was likely to lead to its extinction.

AMMUNITION

Lande's findings were all that Stahl had hoped for. With Terry Thatcher, a lawyer for the National Wildlife Federation, he paid a visit to Northwest Regional Forester Jeff Sirmon. Thatcher and Stahl told Sirmon they now had ammunition to shut down logging on national forests west of the Cascades. But they said they would hold off on filing a lawsuit challenging the existing owl protection plan until the Forest Service completed a new one—if Sirmon would agree to withdraw six old-growth timber sales in Oregon and Washington. Sirmon did agree. They sealed the deal with a handshake.

Lande said he was only vaguely aware in 1985 of the legal weight his paper might carry. "I knew that the owl was important not only for itself but for other species and for its habitat," he said. "We were talking about owls, but I knew they had other purposes."

Not every owl biologist agreed with Lande's conclusions. In 1985 the National Audubon Society formed its own blue-ribbon advisory panel of biologists to review the bird's status in Washington, Oregon, and California. Its May 1986 report concluded that, although the owl's habitat was disappearing rapidly, the bird was not in imminent danger.

In 1986 the timber industry, which had been watching the developing owl issue with mounting concern, established the National Council on Air and Stream Improvement in Corvallis, Oregon. The industry hired wildlife biologist Larry Irwin to conduct his own research on the owl, focusing on lands with younger forests in the hope that his research would show that owls could flourish outside old-growth forests.

In 1986, grassroots conservation groups from throughout the Northwest met in Portland and decided that, despite Lande's paper, the time still was not ripe to petition for listing of the owl. The issue, however, would soon be taken out of their hands.

THE LITIGATION CREW

On New Year's Day 1987, lawyers Vic Sher and Todd True moved into a high-ceilinged suite of offices near Seattle's historic Pioneer Square with their newly hired staff forester, Andy Stahl. For embattled Northwest environmentalists, the arrival of the San Francisco–based Sierra Club Legal Defense Fund (SCLDF) was akin to the cavalry coming over the hill. Forests and spotted owls quickly worked their way to the top of the litigation list.

SCLDF, a nonprofit public interest law firm, was founded in 1971 by a group of lawyers who did work for the Sierra Club, but had long since severed its formal ties with the club. Northwest environmentalists had approached SCLDF about opening an office in the region. The SCLDF board also had concluded on its own that the Northwest's rivers, forests, fish, wildlife, and other matchless natural resources needed strong legal advocates. "The Northwest was underrepresented in court on public lands issues although the problems were huge and the threats to the environment immense," Sher said.

A graduate of Stanford Law, Sher left a solo practice in San Francisco, where he specialized in land-use, pesticides, and toxics litigation, to head the SCLDF Seattle office. True, who had graduated first in his 1981 University of Oregon Law School class, was practicing law with a large Seattle firm and doing pro bono work for environmental groups in his spare time. He jumped at the chance to work full-time on environmental litigation.

In the beginning, persuading some Northwest groups that the time was ripe to pursue an aggressive owl-based legal strategy was a tough sell, Sher said. "The environmental community had developed a way of doing business because they weren't used to having access to the courts. They pursued their agenda by trying to maintain access to the congressional delegation. A number of environmental groups tried hard to talk us out of filing the early owl suits. Their fear was that they would lose their seat at the table."

Instead, the opposite happened. The litigation campaign launched in 1987 quickly leveled the playing field and assured that the Northwest delegation would have to deal with environmentalists one way or another.

ENFORCING THE LAW

The strategy Sher, True, and Stahl and their clients decided on was as simple as it was devastating. Federal natural resource laws and the rules implementing them were written broadly, and federal agencies had seldom taken them literally. SCLDF would sue to hold the agencies to the letter as well as the spirit of the law.

Though the Endangered Species Act would later grab all the attention, the law that provided the key to ending the logging of old-growth forests was the less celebrated National Forest Management Act. The 1976 act requires the Forest Service to "provide for diversity of plant and animal communities." However, it was a rule called the "viability standard," written in 1979 by a committee of scientists to provide guidance on the act's implementation, that provided the key the legal team was looking for. The rule requires the Forest Service to protect "viable populations" of vertebrate species, well distributed throughout their range. What constitutes a "viable population" is a matter for biologists, not politicians or timber sale managers, to decide.

The National Environmental Policy Act also was critical to the success of the litigation campaign. NEPA is a process law. It does not dictate to government agencies what actions they may take, but it does require them to lay out various options for conducting major projects and to assess their environmental impacts.

Taken together, the two laws were to ensnare the Forest Service in a legal Catch-22 of its own making. By suing under NEPA, environmentalists could force the agency to state clearly the environmental consequences of a timber sale project. By also suing under NFMA, they could require the Forest Service to choose an action that met the strict "viable populations" standard.

The third major law available was the Endangered Species Act. Unlike other natural resource laws, which attempt to balance protection and exploitation, the ESA clearly and unequivocally puts threatened and endangered plants and animals first. It was a loaded gun. Northwest activists feared wielding it prematurely.

FORCING THE ISSUE

Debate over whether to petition the U.S. Fish and Wildlife Service to list the owl as a threatened species was at a high pitch as Sher and True set up shop in Seattle. The national groups in particular worried that if they were successful, the political impact of shutting down the forests could threaten the very survival of the act, which would be up for reauthorization by Congress in 1992.

That debate became moot overnight when a maverick group in

distant Boston rudely inserted itself into the process. Max Strahan of GreenWorld saw no reason to wait. In January 1987, GreenWorld filed a one-paragraph petition asking the service to list the northern spotted owl as an endangered species.

Strahan described GreenWorld's strategy as "saturation bombing." "We attack in the most ruthless and uncompromising manner," he boasted. "We won't cut deals, we won't compromise, because the species are our clients. We have a policy of no extinction. We feel if that line is crossed with any species, you lose the ability to protect life."

He criticized environmental groups in the Northwest for delaying efforts to protect the owl. "There was a refined conspiracy not to let the owl be listed," he said. "They blatantly sold themselves out."

Northwest activists who had encountered Strahan considered him a blustering jerk. Nevertheless, the die had been cast. In March of 1987, 35 groups jumped into the deep waters of the Endangered Species Act when they signed a separate petition to list the owl. The national groups remained on the sidelines. The Sierra Club and National Wildlife Federation in particular opposed the owl strategy.

Lynn Greenwalt, a National Wildlife Federation vice president and former director of the U.S. Fish and Wildlife Service, said he saw a tactical error in using the owl early on. "I felt pretty sure that what we would end up with would be a schism that had the owls on one side and the local communities on the other, because the focus was on the owl, not the forest. The issue we should have been addressing was, What are we going to do when we run out of trees?"

THE OWL SUITS

SCLDF began laying the groundwork for lawsuits against the Forest Service and Bureau of Land Management over the inadequacy of their owl protection plans. But in early 1987, those suits were not yet ripe. Both agencies were reviewing their owl plans in response to administrative appeals. Until the appeals process was exhausted, environmentalists couldn't take the government to court.

In late 1987, when the BLM announced that it would not immediately write a new plan for protecting owls in western Oregon, SCLDF filed its first owl suit. Lawyers argued that the existing BLM owl plan was inadequate to ensure the owl's survival and that the BLM was required under NEPA to write a new plan, using the best scientific data available.

In 1988, U.S. District Judge Helen Frye in Portland granted a preliminary injunction blocking BLM timber sales in stands of trees more than 200 years old. But Republican Senator Mark Hatfield and Democratic Representative Les AuCoin promptly fought back. They attached language to a spending bill for the BLM that said its management plans could not be challenged solely on the basis of new scientific information. Judge Frye, bowing to this direction from Congress, lifted the injunction.

It was Hatfield 1, environmentalists 0.

The development sent a clear message that litigation alone would not save the forests. From the beginning, Sher and True had warned their clients that court victories were not permanent, that they must build public support for saving old-growth forests at the same time they sued the government to protect them. The task was made more difficult because at that point the disparate forest protection groups in the Northwest had no formal coalition to speak for them.

ARBITRARY AND CAPRICIOUS

Meanwhile, biologists in the Fish and Wildlife Service began reviewing more than 10 years of owl research in response to the petitions. Their review found overwhelming evidence of the owl's precarious status. It concluded that logging was destroying 62,000 acres of spotted owl habitat each year. But the review was abruptly cut short when Frank Dunkle, the Reagan administration's director of the Fish and Wildlife Service, summoned the biologists to Washington, D.C., and told them to bring all their notes. The report was rewritten under directions from Reagan political appointees in the Interior and Agriculture Departments. In December 1987 Rolf Wallenstrom, the service's regional director, announced under orders from his bosses that the owl's situation did not warrant protection under the Endangered Species Act.

In May of 1988, SCLDF sued the Fish and Wildlife Service, arguing that the agency's decision not to conduct a full-scale study of the owl's situation was "arbitrary and capricious"—without scientific basis. In November of 1988, U.S. District Judge Thomas Zilly agreed, saying the decision "disregarded all of the expert testimony on population viability, including that of its own expert, that the owl is facing extinction." He ordered the service to go back and try again.

It was now Hatfield 1, environmentalists 1.

TERMS OF ART

In December, in a speech to the Association of O & C Counties, a coalition of counties dependent on timber receipts from BLM land, Hatfield recounted the events of the previous 12 months and their likely effect on federal timber sales. He lashed out at environmentalists, warning that "there are many who do not share the values we hold important."

"These people have little or no stake in the outcome of the conflicts they cause," Hatfield said. "In fact, many times I'm not sure these people have any understanding of the effect these actions have on Oregon and Oregonians—our human resources, our most important resource."

Hatfield warned that environmentalists were now employing such "terms of art" as "long-term productivity" and "biological diversity." "It is clear these phrases reflect a new, sophisticated, legalistic approach by those who make 'preservation at all costs' their exclusive emphasis," he said. "These challenges do not prevail on substantive grounds—they prevail on procedural grounds. They win, in short, because some district ranger or district manager somewhere forgot to dot an I or cross a T."

In late 1988, Forest Service Chief F. Dale Robertson finally responded to the appeal of his agency's spotted owl plan. He said the Forest Service would establish new, larger owl reserves on the 13 national forests inhabited by the owl. The reserves would range in size from 1,000 acres in southern Oregon to 3,000 acres on the Olympic Peninsula.

Once again, the agency was behind the research curve. The same year, a federal interagency spotted owl committee proposed sweeping new management guidelines for the owl throughout its range, including protection of all remaining habitat in heavily fragmented areas such as the Oregon Coast Range. No agency acted on the recommendations.

Environmental groups appealed again. When their appeal was denied, they finally had standing to file the big one against the Forest Service— the most far-reaching lawsuit ever brought under the National Forest Management Act.

SWEET VICTORY

Andy Stahl didn't know the timber industry had spies in the hall when he addressed the environmental law conference at the University of Oregon Law School in March 1988. What he said that day was captured on videotape and soon circulated on Capitol Hill. Stahl confided to the assembled law students the legal strategy that was now driving the forest preservation movement. Because Russell Lande's research tied the owl's survival so closely to the disappearing old forests, he said, the bird could stand in for the forests themselves—a perfect surrogate in court. "If the northern spotted owl hadn't evolved in the old-growth forests of the Pacific Northwest, we would have had to genetically engineer it," he bragged.

Assuming that Stahl had revealed a closely held secret, timber industry lobbyists brandished the videotape in the halls of Congress, to prove, as they said, that environmentalists didn't really care about the owl at all—it was the old-growth forests they were after.

In fact, the obscure owl was not a perfect surrogate. Most people, including loggers who had spent their lives in the woods, had never heard of it. For those looking to polarize the issue, it was easy to cast the debate as owls versus jobs. The job of educating the public to the fact that the owl was a stand-in for the forest ecosystem had hardly begun.

Yet events quickly outstripped environmentalists' ability to control them. In March of 1989, U.S. District Judge William Dwyer issued a preliminary injunction blocking national forest timber sales in western Oregon and western Washington until the Forest Service produced a legally adequate plan for the owl. His order produced screaming headlines across the Northwest and detonated a political bombshell that reverberated all the way to Capitol Hill.

It was Hatfield 1, environmentalists 2.

In the Oregon Legislature, the Dwyer ruling overshadowed a hearing rural legislators had scheduled to hold the Forest Service's feet to the fire over reduced timber sale levels in the new national forest plans. At the Arlene Schnitzer Concert Hall in downtown Portland, where biologists from all over the West convened March 29–31 for a symposium to share their research on spotted owls and other wildlife associated with old-growth forests, the Forest Service hired security guards to keep an eye out for trouble.

At the 1989 University of Oregon Environmental Law Conference in March, the mood was jubilant. John Bonine of the Law School faculty, one of the conference's founders, asked 700 pumped-up activists to join hands in a big lecture hall at the closing session. To the tune of the civil rights anthem, they sang *We Shall Save the Earth*.

In the rapidly evolving history of the forest preservation campaign, it was a transcendent moment.

Chapter Ten

Yellow Ribbons

Gleaming log trucks snaked down the main street of Sweet Home, Oregon, on a warm May evening in 1989. The drivers, in Stihl chainsaw caps, laid on their horns. Their wives and kids rode high in the cabs beside them. People had turned out by the hundreds to wave and cheer. The convoy turned left onto a side street and into the parking lot at Sweet Home High School.

The celebration had the feel of Fourth of July, with yellow, symbolizing solidarity, replacing the red, white, and blue. Someone released hundreds of yellow balloons. Truck antennas flew yellow ribbons. Women wore yellow ribbons braided into their hair. Young men wore yellow ribbons wrapped around the legs of their blue jeans, tied in delicate bows.

But an ugly mood lay just beneath the surface at this first large demonstration staged by the Yellow Ribbon Coalition, a timber industry–funded campaign to organize timber towns for the fight of their lives. Two months earlier, Judge William Dwyer had ordered a freeze on all timber sales in national forests occupied by the northern spotted owl. Sidewalk signs warned, "Your jobs next," beneath a caricature of the owl.

The bleachers in the high-school gym were filled and people stood against the wall. Someone estimated the crowd at 1,300. *Stars and Stripes Forever* blared from the speakers. Tom Hirons, a logging contractor from the next valley north, got up and grabbed the microphone. "How many choker setters here tonight? How many timbercutters? Millworkers? Truck drivers?"

The place erupted in shouts and cheers.

"I'm probably not much different from the rest of you," Hirons said. "I chose to ignore this issue for four years. I imitated an ostrich. Then I pulled my head out and realized, 'I'm an American. God chose to put me in a timber town.'"

"Ladies and gentlemen, you *are* an industry," Hirons said, his voice rising. "This industry has a face. We have accepted this industry as our heritage and we choose to pass that heritage on. Give yourselves a roof-raising shout that can be heard to the congressional halls in Washington, D.C.!"

The Sweet Home rally came on the heels of two mill closures in the community. The town of Sweet Home, far up the Santiam Valley and isolated at the edge of the Willamette National Forest, had languished since the recession of the early 1980s, never entirely recovering. Empty storefronts lined Main Street. But a new energy pulsed through the town this night.

A BROADER AGENDA

That same week a less raucous event, sponsored by Willamette Industries, a company that owned several mills in the Santiam, took place down the valley in Lebanon. Instead of loggers, this meeting featured civic leaders, state legislators, Forest Service officials, and Larry Irwin, the biologist hired by the timber industry to study the northern spotted owl. Though yellow ribbons were everywhere, the intent of this community meeting was to inform rather than inflame.

Irwin carefully explained what was known about the owl's habitat needs and what federal law required. Mike Kerrick, the supervisor of the Willamette National Forest, predicted how the Dwyer injunction might affect timber sales. The only inciting done that night was by Mark Rutzick, a former U.S. Department of Justice attorney with a Harvard Law degree, who had been hired by the timber industry to fight environmentalists head-to-head in court. It was an extraordinary performance.

"You have a problem which could hurt your ability to make a living," Rutzick said. "We're not exactly dealing with the spotted owl problem. The groups involved have a much broader agenda than the spotted owl." In Texas, he said, these same groups had shut down one-third of a national forest to protect the red-cockaded woodpecker. "It's an agenda to try to shut down not just logging but mining, grazing, and productive use of water. They want to turn all public land into parks."

Ultimately, Rutzick said, it was the responsibility of Congress to manage the public land. "You're voters. You can make your voices heard. It's citizens like you who have a stake in whether there's a forest industry in Oregon."

If people hadn't been afraid before, they were now—and they knew who to blame.

"My husband took a $12,000 drop in wages," one woman said tearfully. "How am I going to feed my unborn child? I deserve food on my plate, not an owl."

"How many acres do you need for the things you do in your ancient forest?" a young boy asked. "I just don't see how you can put the spotted owl over your own people. It don't make sense to me."

One young man in the rear of the auditorium found the courage to speak out for the forests. "I'm not a preservationist. I'm a woodworker," he said. "I'm willing to talk to anyone who's willing to talk to me. Ancient forest is what we're trying to preserve a little of. There are old trees out there. There's no need to take all of them. Some should be left to be seen and cherished forever."

In response, someone stood up and waved a book about monkey-wrenching—the sabotage of logging equipment and other machinery, a tactic advocated by some factions of Earth First!. "This is their handbook," he shouted. "Kill the bastards."

By the end, the audience was so agitated that Rutzick felt it necessary to offer a warning: "There are so many comments going on about killing owls and eating owls. First of all, it's a federal crime to kill a spotted owl. Second, it's wrong. It's not their fault. We need more of them, not less."

His warning fell on deaf ears. In May, 1,500 loggers, millworkers, and their families staged a 90-minute parade through Hood River, Oregon, featuring an imposing convoy of 178 log trucks and 33 wood chip and lumber trucks. About 200 people cheered loudly at a passing log truck bearing a sign that said, "Eat an owl, save the economy!" A dozen mills in the area closed for the day so workers could take part in the demonstration.

DIVERSIONARY TACTICS

As colorful as these pro-timber demonstrations were, they were not entirely spontaneous. From the beginning, the timber industry helped to organize and fund them. It was, in a way, a diversionary tactic.

While timber companies encouraged their workers to blame environmental restrictions for lost jobs, giant wood products companies with vast timberland holdings, like Weyerhaeuser Company and Plum Creek Timber Company, were taking advantage of record-high log prices in the late 1980s to export billions of board feet of raw logs from their own lands to Japan and other Pacific Rim countries.

Moreover, Northwest timber industry leaders were well aware that owls were not to blame for the job losses their industry had sustained in the 1980s. Automation of sawmills and plywood mills had reduced the size of the wood products workforce substantially even during the logging frenzy of the mid-1980s. Unions representing timber workers had been forced to agree to major wage concessions to save jobs during the downsizing. A 1988 Portland State University study revealed that in Oregon the timber industry processed more timber in 1986 than it had in 1979, but with 15 percent fewer workers. And despite the doom-and-gloom rhetoric, in the spring of 1989 no immediate widespread federal timber shortage loomed. Federal timber purchasers had a two-year supply under contract—sales that could be logged at any time.

WISE USE

Nevertheless, the environmentalists' court victories had revitalized the Sagebrush Rebellion, a movement dormant since the departure of its patron saint, Reagan administration Interior Secretary James Watt. The Sagebrush Rebellion, which got most of its money from the mining industry, fought to get the government to sell off the federal domain to the states, with the ultimate goal of delivering timber, range, and mineral resources into the hands of private developers.

The new western lands insurgency, christened the Wise Use movement at a Reno conference in 1988, had a broader pro-property rights, pro-resource extraction agenda. The name "Wise Use" came from Gifford Pinchot, the first chief of the Forest Service, who advocated a utilitarian role for the national forest system.

Ron Arnold, founder of the Center for the Defense of Free Enterprise, a conservative think tank in Bellevue, Washington, organized the Reno conference to bring together disaffected loggers, ranchers, miners, and developers. He invoked Pinchot's phrase to describe the political philosophy he believed would be necessary to counter the environmental movement's victories.

Bill Grannell, a former Oregon state representative, and his wife, Barbara, a former legislative aide, also helped launch this incipient movement. In 1988, after moving to Colorado, the Grannells founded the Western States Public Lands Coalition with backing from oil, timber, mining, and uranium companies and the National Association of Counties. When the forest conflict hit the headlines in late 1988, they thought up the Oregon Project, and Barbara Grannell returned to Oregon to mobilize loggers, millworkers, and local business workers against this threat to their way of life. She found no shortage of willing recruits.

Associated Oregon Loggers launched its own organizing effort, forming "yellow ribbon coalitions" in timber towns like Roseburg and Springfield. In Washington state, the Washington Contract Loggers Association mounted a similar effort, based in the Olympic Peninsula timber town of Forks.

Meanwhile Valerie Johnson, a sales representative for Portland-based Stimson Lumber Company and the daughter of a prominent mill owner in Oregon's Douglas County, had grown alarmed about restrictions on federal timber sales. She asked Stimson's staff forester to make a presentation to the sales staff. "His message," she said, "was, 'This is serious. We have to take it seriously.'"

THE OREGON LANDS COALITION

On August 31, 1989, the various pro-timber groups met in Eugene and agreed to form a statewide coalition to increase their visibility and political clout. "We chose the name Oregon Lands Coalition because right then we knew that our job was bigger than just timber," Johnson said.

Tom Hirons, the coalition's first president, and Valerie Johnson, its first salaried coordinator, became rural Oregon's fiercest advocates.

The coalition, financed primarily with timber industry money, worked closely with the Yellow Ribbon groups and, at first, with the Oregon Project. But the Grannells' top-down style did not sit well with locals.

"There wasn't any horizontal communication," Johnson said. "It was all vertical. They felt money needed to come from them, expenditures needed to be approved by them. No money ever went to local groups." The Oregon Lands Coalition finally walked away from the Oregon Project, and the Grannells pulled out of Oregon in 1991.

The Oregon Lands Coalition quickly became a potent force by mobilizing millworkers' and loggers' wives to tell their stories—to Congress, to federal agencies, to the news media. Its work made it impossible for elected officials to ignore the economic implications of locking up vast tracts of federal forests.

Though the timber industry supported the coalition, Johnson insists the industry did not control it. "Did the industry encourage us? Yes. Was there a point in time when they called us together? No. In Washington, the industry tried to convene the grassroots groups, but it didn't work. I remember very specifically feeling that was not the way to go. I said, 'You cannot create the emotion and passion it takes to make this happen. The people will either feel the need to do it or not.'"

The new pro-timber campaign took the rural Northwest by storm. Borrowing tactics from the environmental movement, timber town activists began staging news conferences and rallies, firing off press releases and mounting letter-writing campaigns.

Results came quickly: In September of 1989, a timber industry lobbyist previewed a National Audubon special, *Rage Over Trees,* narrated by Paul Newman and scheduled for broadcast on the Turner Television Network, and the industry went on the attack.

The Yellow Ribbon Coalition immediately activated a telephone network to put pressure on sponsors. Hundreds of people called their local Ford dealerships and soft drink distributors. Within a day, every national sponsor had withdrawn, and Ted Turner was forced to air the program without sponsorship.

A MISSED OPPORTUNITY

Environmentalists were unprepared for the vehemence of the backlash. Confronted with timber industry rhetoric, they talked about log exports, automation, and cut-and-run practices on private land. But most of the national news media weren't interested in those subtleties. They loved the loggers. They were colorful, angry, and rough around the edges— the perfect Northwest denizens to symbolize the other side of the old-growth debate. The issue quickly got framed as loggers versus owls.

Forest activists also failed to summon the appropriate response to the fear that had been unleashed in the timbered Northwest: a dose of compassion for working-class people caught in an economic transition beyond their control. They missed the obvious argument: That corporate greed had exploited timber workers every bit as much as it had exploited the old-growth forests that gave them their livelihood.

Years later, some environmentalists conceded their mistake. "How could we have failed to make alliances with the other people who were getting the shaft?" asked Melanie Rowland, a Seattle attorney who worked for the Wilderness Society during those years.

Others insist the effort would have been futile in any case. Unions representing timber workers had lost members throughout the 1980s because of mill automation. Faced with the threat of mill shutdowns, they had agreed to deep wage cuts. By 1989, they had lost most of their power as well. "Timber workers identified with their captors," said Andy Kerr of the Oregon Natural Resources Council. "Was there a missed opportunity? Sure. We could have spent years trying to make inroads into labor. We didn't have time."

Instead, the timber industry succeeded in turning workers against environmentalists. The Timber Labor Coalition, an alliance of five unions that enjoyed active support from management, made its public debut September 8, 1989, in Salem, Oregon, when it held a rally and march that drew 1,500 workers. Several timber companies chartered buses to carry workers to the rally. Some gave their employees an unpaid day off to attend.

Labor officials insisted they had not become pawns of the timber industry. But whether by tacit or formal agreement, over the next several years organized labor remained silent on the export of billions of board feet of raw logs—and timber processing jobs—from the Pacific Northwest to Japan.

THE BOTTOM LINE

Years later, Tom Hirons recalled the moment he knew he would have to take a stand. It had come in a flash, the culmination of three events that struck close to home in his North Santiam Canyon community: Judge Dwyer had shut down the forests. Earth First! demonstrators had buried themselves up to their necks on a snowy logging road to block a timber sale, attracting national news media to their cause. But the final straw had been the defection of a friend and former business partner, George Atiyeh, who had launched a campaign to preserve an intact old-growth valley called Opal Creek in Hirons' back yard.

"Atiyeh called me up and said, 'You'd better wake up and smell the roses. The environmental movement, and I'm one of 'em, is going to put you out of business.' My reaction was, 'This is war. You have just declared war.'"

Hirons may be quick to anger and slow to give up a grudge, but he's a reasonable man and not blind to his industry's mistakes. Pressed for his opinion about whether the breakneck pace of logging on the national forests in the 1980s could have continued, he said in 1992, "I concede a lot more than most people do. The cut was coming down anyway."

Some mills were bound to go out of business even if the owl hadn't come along, Hirons admitted, once the glory days of the mid-1980s passed and companies had to compete for scarce federal timber. "We had a bunch of cheap timber, a cheap labor pool, and cheap mills. If you'd taken any one of those three things away, a lot of the pain would have been gotten over with by now."

But that admission had not softened Hirons' anger toward environmentalists for threatening his livelihood. He had taken a crash course in owl biology. It had made him deeply cynical. "I don't believe 80 percent of what I hear about the owl," he said in 1992. "It's still nothing more than a theory. I think you have a bunch of biologists who were never listened to before and now all of a sudden they've got the biggest hammer out there. It's gone to their head."

"My sense of morality got offended in this whole thing," Hirons said. "I don't see too much gray. Basically, things are pretty black and white to me. Somebody crossed over a line out there and I felt I had to defend a set of values my old man tried to teach me." He paused.

"You know that flag with the snake that says 'Don't Tread on Me'? That."

Chapter Eleven

Mutiny in the Ranks

When Jeff DeBonis began working as a timber sale planner on the Willamette National Forest in 1989, he experienced what was known in the Forest Service as "westside future shock." The Willamette, the premier timber-producing forest in the national forest system, was a good place to experience clearcut logging on a scale unequaled anywhere else on the nation's public lands. To DeBonis, the extent of forest fragmentation and the cumulative impacts of logging on soils and streams were a revelation.

As a Peace Corps volunteer in El Salvador, DeBonis had seen the destruction of tropical rainforests. As a Forest Service timber planner, he had seen logging practices on Montana's Kootenai National Forest, where clearcutting and slash-burning on steep slopes regularly triggered debris slides and dumped thousands of cubic yards of sediment into streams. He told his co-workers there, "You guys are doing the same thing they're doing in Third World countries."

DeBonis made the remark partly in jest. It took a transfer to western Oregon's realm of big timber for him to realize that his initial apprehension had been correct.

FREE SPEECH

DeBonis first spoke out in early 1989, testing the limits of free speech within the Forest Service. His epiphany came after he attended a conference of forest activists in Eugene. There, he finally understood that conservationists, of whom he considered himself one, widely regarded the agency he worked for as the enemy.

Fired by indignation, he sat at his computer terminal in the Blue River Ranger District and composed an internal memo to Forest Service Chief F. Dale Robertson. "We, as an agency, are perceived by the conservation community as being an advocate of the timber industry's agenda," he wrote. "Based on my 10 years with the Forest Service, I believe this charge is true. I also believe, along with many others, that this agency needs to retake the moral "high ground.""

The memo became public and drew the ire of a timber industry hired gun, Troy Reinhart, who demanded in a letter to the supervisor of the Willamette National Forest that DeBonis be formally reprimanded for expressing such convictions. DeBonis was in fact reprimanded for putting out his message via Forest Service electronic mail. But the incident prompted the Forest Service to consult with its lawyers and draft liberal free-speech guidelines for all employees. Ultimately DeBonis was told that as long as he didn't reap financial gain, misrepresent himself as speaking for the agency, or knowingly publish false information, he was free to speak out on his own time.

Soon after, DeBonis founded the Association of Forest Service Employees for Environmental Ethics and produced the first issue of a newsletter, *Inner Voice,* on a computer in his tiny West Eugene apartment. In it, he printed a lengthy open letter to Robertson, arguing that the agency's timber sale program was responsible for wide-scale deforestation, massive soil erosion, and the probable extinction of many wildlife species. "This stubborn, get-the-cut-out mindset we tend to embrace as an agency blinds us to the actual destructive results of our actions," he wrote. "We see only what we want to see. As the negative impacts of our actions become more and more obvious, we try to pretend its not happening. And yet at some subconscious level we *know* that we are overcutting."

His message struck a chord with federal employees who had seen their warnings about logging, road-building, and livestock grazing practices ignored for too long. The words of people inside the agencies carried more weight in the national debate over the forests than those of any professional environmentalist. The truth was out of the bottle. The Forest Service could find no way to put it back.

SPEAKING OUT

Hundreds of public employees, environmentalists, and interested citizens wrote to offer their horror stories. In subsequent issues, *Inner Voice* published reports on the destruction of Indian ruins by logging in the national forests of the Southwest, the degradation of important salmon-spawning streams in Southeast Alaska's Tongass National Forest, and the abuse of public land grazing leases throughout the West.

The tabloid began showing up on the desks and counters of Forest Service and BLM offices throughout the West. In January of 1990, the environmental group Headwaters sent a copy to each of the 270 employees in the Medford BLM office. When state BLM Director Dean Bibles wrote to Headwaters complaining bitterly about the tactic and saying BLM employees needed no "outside instruction on the topic of ethical conduct in our daily business," Headwaters distributed Bibles' letter as well.

DeBonis's new group swiftly nationalized the internal criticism raging within the Forest Service. It attracted attention from *High Country News, Outside* magazine, and the Fairbanks, Alaska, *Daily News-Miner.* The truth proved to be the most powerful of all weapons.

In testimony before a U.S. House Government Operations Subcommittee in San Francisco on February 14, 1990, DeBonis stressed the importance of free speech rights for government scientists and resource specialists. "If government can muzzle its scientists—if it can assert that it 'owns' the scientist simply because it employs him or her—then the government will control the debate on difficult policy choices. This danger is particularly acute in cases where federal employees discover that scientific objectivity precludes political neutrality."

In late February of 1990, DeBonis announced that he would leave the Forest Service and his job as a timber sale planner and devote all his time to the seven-month-old insurgency movement he had founded. He had the look of a man whose warring sides at last were at peace. "The cognitive dissonance was just getting to be too much," he said. "It was hard for me to go to work every day on liquidating the temperate rainforest."

DeBonis had tapped a deep well of anger, frustration, and professional indignation. People sent him stories of solid biological evidence agencies had ignored, of critical reports they had deep-sixed, of retaliatory disciplinary actions they had experienced for speaking out.

Some federal employees wrote anonymously. Others found courage to speak out openly. Charlie Thomas, a wildlife biologist nearing retirement with the Bureau of Land Management, went public in 1990 with his opposition to his agency's plan to allow logging of old-growth bald eagle habitat in the heavily cutover Coburg Hills, east of Eugene. He took television crews into the hills to show them how little habitat was left. He gave reporters the letters he had sent to his superiors, and the responses he had received.

"Everybody knows about DeBonis," Thomas said. " His paper is out in all of the western United States. Because of him, I know there are people out there who support what I do."

OUT OF TOUCH

DeBonis's effort was only one sign of growing dissension within the ranks. In May of 1989, seven BLM managers in western Oregon wrote an internal report naming specific areas where it was now "very difficult or impossible" to find places to sell timber because the BLM had never adjusted its cutting quotas to reflect the withdrawal of forests for spotted owl reserves. "We are trying to carry out timber management on greatly reduced intensive timber bases without reductions in the annual allowable cuts," they wrote. They urged their bosses to reduce logging levels until the final BLM plans for the 1990s were completed.

However, the report surfaced only in February of 1990, after Congress had passed a measure mandating continued unsustainable levels of logging on BLM land for at least one more year.

In the fall of 1989, national forest supervisors from several western states went public with memos to Forest Service Chief Robertson declaring that the agency was "out of control" and out of touch with the land stewardship values on which it had been founded.

Supervisors from 63 national forests signed a letter to Robertson saying they were weary of agency and congressional priorities that had allocated 35 percent of the agency's operating budget to timber sales over the previous 20 years while recreation, fish and wildlife, and water and soil protection programs each received only 2 to 3 percent of the budget pie. In a separate memo, supervisors from throughout the West urged agency leaders to order a reevaluation of all forest plans to determine whether their timber sale goals were realistic.

A DEBATE OVER ADVOCACY

As science moved front and center in the old-growth debate, the propriety of advocacy by scientists in natural resource fields became a hot issue within many professional scientific bodies.

It was a matter of intense debate within the American Fisheries Society, where some fisheries biologists argued that scientists could not become active in public policy debates and still maintain their professional impartiality. Cindy Deacon-Williams, a Forest Service research fisheries biologist and an active member of AFS, strongly dissented. "I've always been on the other side, which says if you have solid fisheries or aquatic ecology science that has implications in a public policy debate, you are not a professional unless you bring that scientific information to the debate in a useful form," she said.

The Wildlife Society, an international association of professional wildlife biologists, was grappling with the same issue. At a February 1992 meeting of the society's Oregon chapter, the issue of advocacy was at the top of the agenda. The association had recently adopted a policy supporting the preservation of some old-growth forests nationwide. Wildlife biologists were up in arms over attempts by the Bush administration to bar federal employees from serving as officers in professional organizations.

Tom Franklin, the society's assistant director, told the assembled biologists that the new prominence of scientists in decisions regarding public land issues was a welcome and long overdue development. By turning to biologists to help resolve the forest management crisis, he said, policy makers had unleashed a powerful force for wildlife conservation.

Some scientists were paying a high price for speaking out, however. John Mumma, the featured speaker at the conference, had recently become a martyr to the profession. Until November of 1991, Mumma had served as the Forest Service's regional forester for the Northern Rockies—the only wildlife biologist ever to attain that rank in the agency. He had quit rather than accept a transfer after he told his bosses he could not meet timber sale targets he opposed as environmentally harmful.

"I expected my staff members to be advocates for the resources they had responsibility for," Mumma told his colleagues. His own experience, he said, had taught him a different lesson: "You can be classified as an adversary if you do your job responsibly."

Chapter Twelve

The Rider from Hell

In June of 1989, with timber industry rhetoric rising feverishly across the Northwest, Oregon Governor Neil Goldschmidt and the entire Oregon congressional delegation staged a timber summit at Oregon's Capitol in Salem to deal with Judge Dwyer's owl injunction. There, after a half-day of testimony, Republican U.S. Senator Mark Hatfield and Democratic Representative Les AuCoin presented forest preservationists with a take-it-or-leave-it proposition written in advance: agree within 48 hours to a courtroom deal that would release most of the timber sales from the injunction that had locked up the forests, or Congress would do it for them.

A FRAGILE ALLIANCE

For forest activists, the Salem summit was a wake-up call. The various forest preservation groups in the Northwest had been working together for only a few months. Under the umbrella of the newly formed Ancient Forest Alliance, five national groups—the Wilderness Society, the Sierra Club, the National Audubon Society, the National Wildlife Federation, and the Sierra Club Legal Defense Fund—had agreed to join grassroots groups in Oregon, Washington, and California in a campaign to save ancient forests. But the alliance remained a loose coalition of independent-minded activists. It had no national political strategy, no formal agenda, no process for collective decision-making.

For Bonnie Phillips of Pilchuck Audubon in Everett, Washington, the summit was the beginning of a warp-speed introduction to environmental politics. She had recently agreed to spearhead formation of a Washington Ancient Forest Alliance that would pull together grassroots forest activists in her state and communicate with similar statewide coalitions in Oregon and California.

In May, the fragile new alliance began preparing for the Salem summit. At a meeting in Portland, where Phillips met leaders of the national groups and Oregon forest activists for the first time, she was struck by the fact that no one seemed to grasp what was at stake in the upcoming summit. "I don't think anyone understood that this would be more than a flash in the pan."

Her intuition proved prescient. The alliance was ill-prepared to counter the so-called "timber compromise" laid on the table in Salem. The Oregon delegation's proposal called for releasing more than 1 billion board feet of timber from Judge Dwyer's injunction and requiring federal agencies to sell an additional 8 billion board feet by October of 1990—about 90 percent of the volume sold over a recent two-year period, squeezed into a single year. No legal challenges of the released sales would be permitted.

It was obvious nothing was to be gained by accepting this deal, so the alliance rejected it. The next week, in an endless round of conference calls, activists debated what kind of counteroffer would be taken seriously by the delegation. On July 14, they offered a modest proposal for slightly lower timber sale levels and an alternative way of releasing the sales that would not affect future rights to challenge them in court. The timber industry and the Forest Service rejected it out of hand.

OVERRIDING THE COURT

Ten days later Hatfield and U.S. Senator Brock Adams, a Washington Democrat, introduced a bill to implement their "compromise" by attaching it to the 1990 appropriations bill funding the Forest Service and Bureau of Land Management.

Environmentalists knew a "rider"—a measure attached to an unrelated bill—was a distinct possibility. Hatfield and AuCoin were by now practiced at undoing what the federal courts had done to bring restraint to the Northwest federal timber sale program. They had pushed through their first court-stripping rider in 1985, partially overturning a 1984 federal court order that blocked timber sales in part of the Siuslaw National Forest in the Oregon Coast Range because of the threat of severe soil erosion. Since then, there had been a series of riders, most recently one overturning the injunction against the Bureau of Land Management over its owl protection plan.

These measures, typically crafted behind closed doors and seldom debated on the House and Senate floors, were proof of the Oregon delegation's raw political clout. Under Hatfield and AuCoin, riders had become business as usual in Oregon. In 1988, even environmentalists had signed off on a rider that prohibited legal challenges of fire salvage logging in the Siskiyou National Forest.

Sierra Club Legal Defense Fund lawyers Vic Sher and Todd True now understood that their legal strategy could not succeed as long as Northwest lawmakers were able to reverse their courtroom victories with impunity. They launched a media campaign to educate the public about riders and persuade citizens that it was wrong for Congress to override the federal courts.

CALLING IN THE CHIPS

It was clear, however, that nothing was going to stop a rider in the politically charged autumn of 1989. Aides to Hatfield wrote the Senate version with help from Sierra Club lobbyists. It contained some of the environmentalists' counterproposals, including one that required federal agencies to acknowledge for the first time the ecological value of old-growth forests.

Senator Patrick Leahy, a Vermont Democrat with a progressive record on environmental issues, believed the Northwest should solve its own problems, but he also had a strong aversion to court-stripping bills. Leahy chaired the Senate Agriculture Committee, which had jurisdiction over national forest issues. In the summer of 1989 he hired Tom Tuchmann, a political operative with a degree in forestry, and assigned him to kill the Hatfield-Adams rider. But Hatfield wooed the national conservation groups by asserting that he too now understood the ecological value of old-growth forests. At the last minute Brock Evans, now a lobbyist for the National Audubon Society, withdrew his opposition to the rider, undercutting Leahy's efforts.

Tuchmann did persuade Hatfield to take part in a colloquy with Leahy on the Senate floor. In the carefully scripted exchange, Hatfield stated that the rider was a onetime emergency measure, "an action of last resort," and promised to work through Leahy's committee for a permanent fix. Though he may have been sincere at the time, no permanent solution ever emerged from Congress. And six years later, Hatfield would resort to this court-stripping strategy again.

In September, more than 100 congressmen signed a letter to Representative Sid Yates, the Illinois Democrat who chaired the House Interior Appropriations Subcommittee, warning that the rider "threatens to remove administrative decisions—no matter how illegal— from effective judicial remedies." A coalition of groups, including the American Civil Liberties Union, denounced laws that took away the citizens' right to sue.

Hatfield and AuCoin went to work in their appropriations committees, calling in all the political chips owed them. During the last three days in September, as the fiscal year was running out, a select subgroup of the conference committee, which included all the major Northwest power-brokers, met behind closed doors to work over the final language of the rider. Besides giving lip service to the ecological value of old-growth forests, it provided slightly increased protection for spotted owls in sales released from the injunction and directed the Forest Service and BLM to try to avoid increased fragmentation of intact forests.

But it also contained dreaded "sufficiency" language, stating that sales sold under the rider would automatically be considered to be in compliance with all environmental laws. This provision insulated all sales sold under the terms of the rider from legal challenges forever.

Hatfield summoned timber industry lobbyists. They weren't overjoyed, but they said they could live with it. Brock Evans of National Audubon and Syd Butler, a lobbyist for the Wilderness Society, signed off on it as well. Significantly, neither National Audubon nor the Wilderness Society was a plaintiff in the lawsuit that had won the injunction that Congress was about to overturn.

SOPHIE'S CHOICE

Section 318 of the 1990 Interior and Related Agencies Appropriations Bill became law on October 23, 1989. The gates to the forests had been kept open for one more year. The Oregon chapter of the Sierra Club gave Hatfield an award for the rider and praised him for finally recognizing the value of old-growth forests. But most Northwest forest activists understood that their campaign had been dealt a crippling blow. They promptly named Section 318 the Rider from Hell.

On November 7, Judge Dwyer lifted the preliminary injunction blocking timber sales on national forests and canceled the scheduled trial, which was just a week away. But Dwyer retained jurisdiction over the case. In Portland, Judge Helen Frye dismissed the lawsuit against the BLM.

The Forest Service presented environmentalists with what Andy Kerr, of the Oregon Natural Resources Council, aptly called a "Sophie's Choice": They could pick the timber sales to be released from the court injunction themselves, or they could let the Forest Service do it. Either way, 1.1 billion board feet of timber must be given up. Either way, old-growth stands they had worked for years to protect were as good as gone.

Grassroots groups faced the need to make wrenching choices on an impossible timeline with inadequate information. "We had to depend on groups like Headwaters, who weren't even plaintiffs at that point, to help review the timber sales," Bonnie Phillips recalled. "We had no set of criteria for people to use." The Forest Service was uncooperative. On the Mount Baker–Snoqualmie National Forest in Washington, she said, "They wouldn't let us talk to the wildlife biologists without timber staff present."

Phillips wept as environmentalists and their attorneys held a news conference in November of 1989, immediately after turning over their list to Deputy Regional Forester John Lowe. "We had to give up two-thirds of our volume to save one-third," she said later. "We had no plan in effect because people refused to think this could ever happen to us. It's hard, trying to do the best thing, knowing you're going to be responsible for this piece of land being logged."

"I wouldn't want to defend this decision biologically," said Kerr. "With these sales, owls are going to die. But Congress put a gun to our head, so we chose. What got compromised was the owl."

THE LAST OF THE BAD OLD SALES

The Section 318 sales, designed in the 1980s, called for clearcutting old-growth forests with minimal safeguards for fish and wildlife. Insulated from court challenges, more than 600 of them were auctioned. Most were logged soon after. But some were so objectionable that the agencies themselves withdrew them. These leftover sales would flare into the headlines five years later, when another timber rider ordered the government to release them for logging.

Ninety-five percent of the Section 318 sales were in spotted owl habitat. Despite language in the rider, neither the Forest Service nor the BLM could meet the measure's timber targets without further fragmenting owl habitat.

The Sierra Club Legal Defense Fund challenged the Rider from Hell on constitutional grounds, arguing that it violated the separation of powers between the judicial and legislative branches of government. But in 1992 the U.S. Supreme Court upheld the power of Congress to pass such riders.

Many lawmakers nonetheless were uncomfortable overriding the courts on such a volatile issue. Senator Brock Adams vowed he would not support such a measure again. At least for the time being, Hatfield and AuCoin had used up their political capital doing a final favor for their friends in the timber industry.

PUBLIC SCRUTINY

The Rider from Hell had at least one unanticipated positive consequence for the forest preservation movement: It required each national forest and BLM district to appoint a citizens' timber sale review panel to make recommendations about which sales should go forward in 1990. The experience of serving on these committees opened the eyes of many environmentalists to the cost of logging for the first time. For most federal forest managers, it was a first as well—the first time their timber sale programs had been held up to careful public scrutiny.

Each national forest and BLM district had a timber quota to fill. Citizens often were not even given reports by biologists describing how the 1990 sales would affect spotted owls. When they did get the information, it simply confirmed their worst suspicion—the agencies couldn't keep cutting at the rate the rider allowed without further harming the owl.

In March of 1990, the citizens' advisory board for the Eugene BLM District publicly rejected the timber sale review process when it refused to approve enough sales to allow the agency to meet its quota. "It is increasingly clear that the timber sale advisory board system is a sham," said the panel's chairman, Allan Sorenson.

Jim Britell of the Kalmiopsis Audubon chapter on the southern Oregon Coast was shocked to learn while serving on the Coos Bay BLM District advisory board that one of the sales the agency planned to award had 16 owls living within units scheduled for cutting. "The BLM did not take the owl reports as anything but a ticket to be punched on the way to selling the timber," Britell said.

The Rider from Hell contained another little-noticed provision that would have repercussions long after it expired. It instructed the Forest Service to adopt, within 12 months, a scientifically adequate plan for the conservation of the northern spotted owl.

Chapter Thirteen

Best Available Science

In the winter of 1989–90, while the Northwest's attention was riveted on the Rider from Hell, six wildlife biologists working out of an obscure Portland office building were rushing to meet a pressing deadline. The federal government had given them a blank check and a top-priority assignment: Develop a legally and biologically defensible strategy to head off the extinction of the northern spotted owl.

The Forest Service's top officials knew by the summer of 1989 that the owl was headed for the endangered species list. They knew as well that in order to win the lawsuit challenging their owl protection plan they would have to persuade U.S. District Judge William Dwyer that they were at last serious about protecting the bird. The agency's lawyers realized that if the owl case ever came to trial, their own biologists would be subpoenaed to testify against them about the glaring inadequacy of their existing owl plan.

In Washington, D.C., a top-secret "owlworks" committee advised Forest Service Chief F. Dale Robertson to develop an owl strategy that would pass legal muster. In late summer, Robertson and the heads of the Bureau of Land Management, National Park Service, and Fish and Wildlife Service agreed to appoint a team of scientists to produce the plan. They knew they needed someone of unimpeachable integrity, proven leadership skills, and political savvy to head the effort.

THE RIGHT MAN FOR THE JOB

When he got the call from the chief's office at his home in La Grande, Oregon, Jack Ward Thomas heard destiny knocking at his door. Thomas, a portly, silver-haired, Texas-born, Shakespeare-quoting elk biologist, headed the Forest Service research station in La Grande, where he pursued his own research on the habitat requirements of the Rocky Mountain elk.

Thomas felt some trepidation about taking on the owl study, and he discussed it with his wife, Margaret. As he recalled the conversation later, she read him a quote roughly borrowed from the Old Testament: "Oh, come on. The war horse smelleth the battle from afar and paweth in the valley." There was never any question that his answer would be yes. This was the assignment of his life.

Charles Philpott, the director of the Forest Service's Pacific Northwest Research Station, said Thomas was an obvious choice for the job. "The person had to be credible not just with the scientists but with environmentalists and other interest groups. We've probably got 5 to 10 people in the Forest Service who can do that. Jack has a knack for explaining complex things in good, simple English. And he can get folksy when it's appropriate."

His bosses told Thomas he could select whomever he wished, follow the research wherever it led, and develop a conservation strategy free from the political interference that had dogged owl conservation efforts throughout the 1980s. Thomas took them at their word. However, his bosses turned him down when he suggested that the strategy be expanded to include other old-growth species besides the spotted owl.

Thomas picked five of the best owl biologists he knew for his team: Eric Forsman, whose research Thomas had funded and who now worked for the Forest Service's Pacific Northwest Research Station in Corvallis, Oregon; Barry Noon, an expert on mathematical modeling of bird populations, from the Forest Service's Redwood Lab in Arcata, California; E. Charles Meslow, Forsman's academic adviser and the leader of the Oregon Cooperative Wildlife Research Unit; Jerry Verner of the Forest Service's Fresno, California, research station, who had done extensive owl studies in California; and Joseph Lint, a biologist for the BLM. All but Lint had Ph.D.s. A second tier of 11 biologists included representatives from academia, the timber industry, and the environmental community.

To this day, members of Thomas's team are at a loss to explain the broad mandate they were given. "I don't think the higher-ups in the agencies had any idea what they were doing," said Forsman. "They put six scientists on it who were all very concerned about wildlife issues."

"I don't think they recognized what they had created," Meslow added. "If they had recognized, I think they would have shut it off."

SEARCHING FOR A PARADIGM

The scientists met for the first time in a dim basement room at a Portland hotel in early October. Some of them agreed to take a week off in the fall for elk season. Then they set to work. For the next five months, they worked 12-hour days conducting an exhaustive review of all owl studies. They took field trips to the California redwoods, the Oregon Cascades and Coast Range, and the rainforests of the Olympic Peninsula. They organized seminars and invited presentations from anyone with credible information about the owl.

They realized early in the process that this was their chance to put science in the driver's seat and create a new paradigm for management of federal lands in the 21st century.

One of their first decisions involved setting what Thomas called "sideboards"—the parameters within which they would operate. In December of 1989, in formal comments to the Fish and Wildlife Service regarding its proposal to list the owl as a threatened species, they made it clear that they would operate within the bounds of what was politically possible.

"It is obvious . . . that the best management for the northern spotted owl is to preserve all stands of mature and 'old growth' timber within the range of the species and to grow more such stands as soon as possible," they wrote. Recognizing the "real-world" situation, they said, they would pursue a "less than optimal approach" that provided a high probability the owl would survive throughout its range while still allowing the logging of old-growth forests.

FROM THEORY TO PRACTICE

The puzzle the scientists had been called on to solve was unprecedented: how to manage 24 million acres of public land in western Washington, western Oregon, and northern California that had been utterly transformed by logging so that 50 or 100 years in the future, owls still would be around to disperse, stake out their treetop territory, and reproduce their kind.

In trying to conceptualize what a strategy for the owl's survival might look like, they were forced to deal largely in theory. There were no blocks of owl habitat left that they could visit to observe how owls had behaved before logging began to shrink their world. And no one could predict with certainty how long the birds would maintain their hold on existence as that world grew smaller and more fragmented.

They borrowed a number of theories from professional journals, combined them with 20 years of research on the owl and data on the condition of the forests, and applied them to a swath of forest stretching from the Canadian border to San Francisco Bay. It was a bold, even breathtaking leap from theory to application.

The concepts the scientists drew on—landscape ecology, conservation biology, island biogeography—focused on managing the natural world to protect intact ecological systems and nurture biological diversity. Until the Thomas team latched onto them, they had remained primarily theoretical tools. The principles underlying these theories could be stated simply: Think big. Save the wild pieces. Connect them somehow. Manage for the whole, recognizing that it is greater than the sum of its parts. And don't let habitat become so diminished that a species no longer can disperse or maintain its gene pool; by then, the march to extinction may be irreversible.

The biologists looked at the vast clearcut landscape as a kind of hostile ocean surrounding the remaining "islands" of old-growth forest. They examined maps and aerial photos, looking for critical gaps in habitat. Using mathematical modeling techniques previously applied to bird populations on real islands off California and Great Britain, they calculated how large to make these forest "islands" so that someday they would support enough breeding owl pairs to assure genetic mixing and allow young dispersing owls to find mates. They calculated how close together the islands must be to assure that young owls could traverse the hostile terrain between these habitat islands, where great horned owls might swoop down and kill them, or where they might starve for lack of prey.

Ultimately they rejected the small, museum-like reserves the Forest Service and Bureau of Land Management had previously set aside for individual owl pairs. Saving the owl, they concluded, would require redesigning the entire forest.

A BAND OF BROTHERS

All the scientists except Thomas were put up at the same northeast Portland motel. Thomas had an apartment on the other side of the river. They worked late into the evening and spent their few leisure hours working out together, eating together, drinking beer together, and talking about owls. Over time, they developed a strong esprit de corp and a spirited, consensus-building working style. "You get that many highly charged people in one room and there's every reason in the world to get testy," Thomas recalled later. "Everyone was forceful. But by the time it was over, we were like Henry V and his men in battle: 'We few, we happy few, we band of brothers.'"

Barry Noon saw himself as a bridge between the empiricists like Forsman, who gathered and analyzed field data, and the theoreticians like Verner, who devised conceptual models to predict wildlife behavior. Noon himself had little field experience with spotted owls; he had spent the first 12 years of his career studying neotropical migrant birds for the U.S. Fish and Wildlife Service and had taught ornithology at Humboldt State from 1981 to 1987, with an emphasis on biometrics, statistics, and analysis of ecological data.

"I think there was mixed enthusiasm for what I was doing initially," Noon said. He sensed that Forsman and Thomas in particular were skeptical of the principles of conservation biology, which used mathematical modeling to predict wildlife demographic trends. "Someone who is grounded in field studies is uncomfortable with things that are abstract and intangible."

When biologists attempt to solve problems involving wildlife demographics, Noon explained, they need an integrative tool—a set of assumptions—that allows them to use past behavior to predict the future. This means taking a leap beyond what can be documented in the field.

LARGE VERSUS SMALL

The principles of conservation biology pointed inexorably toward large reserves that could support multiple pairs of owls, allowing them to interbreed. But the scientists had incomplete data on the owl's range requirements and dispersal habits and on which areas had enough old forests to support multiple owl pairs.

At a key meeting on February 3 and 4, 1990, several outside scientists were brought in to review the team's work. During the presentations, two members of the team's second tier, David Wilcove, a conservation biologist with the Wilderness Society, and Dennis Murphy, the director of Stanford University's Center for Conservation Biology, scribbled a diagram on a sheet of paper showing large blocks of forest habitat stair-stepping down the west side of the Cascades. Wilcove keeps a copy of the rough drawing in a file cabinet to this day and claims it was the genesis of the plan that finally emerged. Others on the team credit Noon, Verner, and Sandy Wilbur, a biologist with the Fish and Wildlife Service, as the first proponents of the big-reserve concept.

In any case, the idea stuck. The scientists finally took out their marking pens and drew enormous amoeba-shaped blobs across the map, ranging up to tens of thousands of acres in size. To lessen the impact on logging, they clustered these owl reserves around existing wilderness areas and national parks.

The reserves covered nearly 6 million acres, but they were not pristine reserves of old growth. They also encompassed clearcuts, young plantations, and 30-year-old forests that, left alone for a couple of centuries, might become suitable habitat for owls.

REACHING CONSENSUS

For weeks afterward the committee mulled this radical strategy, weighing it against less drastic alternatives. "We were groping in a sense," Noon recalled. "It was unprecedented. We had no model we could pull off the shelf." For scientists, Noon explained, the method by which conclusions are reached is all-important. "The process has to be dynamic. You have to work in an environment where people can challenge each other's ideas. You have to have an open mind."

Finally, he said, the scientists came up with a workable process. "We decided to couch the plan as a way to test hypotheses. People tried to disprove each other's theories. That's when people started to feel comfortable with the process. It was a tense time, but it was a healthy tension. We were searching."

Thomas recalls that the moment of truth came in late February of 1990. "The more we looked and the more we examined and the more we learned about the mathematical model, we recognized that [small reserves] wouldn't do it," he said. "On this particular night there was tremendous frustration, and pressure was building up. We twisted and we turned every direction we could think of to defeat our own hypothesis, and we finally said, 'No, that's the scientifically credible way to go.'"

Thomas polled his team. The vote was unanimous. "And I said, 'We've crossed the Rubicon. The die is cast.'"

Meslow does not recall the "cross the Rubicon" statement. "Jack gets a bit theatrical," he said. "I'm sure he *thinks* he said it. Of all of us, he was the one who thought most globally about how this was going to be presented."

But Forsman remembers the feeling in the room. "We finally made a decision that this was what we were going to do, that it was the best approach politically and practically. From that point on, there was never any discussion of starting over."

In the end, there was no dissent, not even from team member Larry Irwin, a wildlife biologist employed by the timber industry.

CONNECTING THE DOTS

The issue of how to connect these large blocks of habitat remained unresolved. One option was to designate corridors—in effect, pathways through the logged landscape along which young owls could disperse to establish new nests without starving in the clearcuts or getting eaten by great horned owls. The scientists knew that would require withdrawing even more land from logging.

Wilcove called Thomas from Washington, D.C., one day and demanded to know, "Where are the corridors?" Thomas told him there weren't going to be any, because studies showed young owls leaving the nest took off in all directions. Wilcove protested that he would not sign off on the plan unless it provided a way for owls to fly safely between reserves.

What finally evolved from this discussion was the arcane but critically important 50-11-40 rule. It said that agencies must manage the land between the habitat reserves so that at least half the trees were 11 inches or more in diameter and 40 percent of the forest canopy remained intact. Simply put, that meant logging no more frequently than every 80 years.

For the Bureau of Land Management, this rule would have major implications. Because BLM lands were interspersed with private lands that were logged as often as every 40 years, the landscape in these checkerboard-ownership areas was far outside the 50-11-40 standard. That meant no logging could occur in many areas until young trees grew larger and the forest canopy began to close.

THE BRIEFING

Until the scientists began writing their conservation strategy, their deliberations had been open to anyone who cared to sit in. Then the curtain dropped.

In March of 1990, the heads of the Forest Service, Bureau of Land Management, Fish and Wildlife Service, and National Park Service flew to Portland for a briefing on the progress of the Thomas team. Only then did they begin to comprehend what was coming—but it was too late to shove the genie back into the bottle. Timber industry supporters, sensing that something momentous was about to happen, staged a rally outside the hotel where the briefing was taking place and delivered a petition to the agency heads, asking for a guaranteed supply of federal timber no matter what.

At the closed briefing, Forest Service Chief Robertson reportedly gulped at the scope of the plan and the wholesale reductions in logging it would require. But he recovered enough to say, "Well, if it's the best available science, I guess it's the way we'll have to go."

BLM Director Cy Jamison, a Montana conservative who had his eye on a future run for elective office in his home state, recalls that he had a more indignant response. "Oh, no!" he moaned. "There goes my career —and maybe yours, too."

As late as March, only a few environmentalists were aware of what was happening in the owl team's inner sanctum, or of its significance.

In the final days before the plan was unveiled, the scientists worked 14-hour days to complete their report and then 36 hours straight to assemble it. Security surrounding the report was tight. Thomas wanted the owl strategy to make the biggest splash possible. He arranged to unveil it before a congressional committee in Washington, D.C.

THE UNVEILING

On April 4, 1990, Thomas gave members of the Northwest delegation a closed-door briefing on the strategy before its public release. He told them the plan would reduce timber sales on national forests by 25 percent and on BLM land by 30 to 40 percent. Representative Les AuCoin of Oregon emerged looking pale and shaken. "This is staggering news economically," he said. "I was not prepared for the magnitude of the withdrawals being proposed." AuCoin stressed that politicians, not scientists, would have the final say.

The sentence that made the headlines on April 5 came on the first page of the report's summary, at the top of the fourth paragraph: "We have concluded that the owl is imperiled over significant portions of its range because of continuing losses of habitat from logging and natural disturbances."

Meslow was pleased, when the report emerged from review in Washington, D.C., to see that the sentence had survived intact. The team never had discussed whether the owl was threatened or endangered, he said. "The word 'imperiled' just appeared. We edited the hell out of that report, but no one touched that sentence."

Sweeping as their plan was, the scientists emphasized that it was not risk-free. Even if it were followed to the letter, they said, owl populations, then estimated at between 2,500 and 3,000 breeding pairs and an unknown number of single owls, could plummet by up to 40 percent as a result of habitat loss that had already occurred. No one could say for sure how long it would take before owl numbers began rebounding to a state of equilibrium.

The scientists candidly acknowledged that they had taken "human needs and desires" into account. "To ignore the human condition in conservation strategies is to fail," they wrote. "We have searched for a way to assure the continuing viability of the owl that still allows continuation of some substantial cutting of mature and old-growth timber."

The scientific community recognized the owl strategy as a conservation watershed. Yet Thomas also knew that because it was owl-centered, it would not be the final word. He suggested that it contained a blueprint for protecting important remnants of the entire old-growth ecosystem—if policy-makers chose to broaden their vision.

"A balanced assessment of this strategy's various impacts must consider water quality, fisheries, recreation, soils, stream flows, scenic values, biodiversity, and balance," he wrote in the plan's conclusion. "The issues are not limited to questions of owls and timber supply, as important as those are. The matter is not that simple—it never has been."

Environmentalists were ambivalent. The interagency plan might save the owl, but it left many of their most cherished roadless areas open to logging. As it turned out, the owl had its own agenda—and it did not necessarily match theirs.

But it was too late for second thoughts. In June, the U.S. Fish and Wildlife Service listed the northern spotted owl as a threatened species due to destruction of its habitat by logging, and the Endangered Species Act kicked into high gear.

Chapter Fourteen

Season of Blame

The first log trucks and chartered buses from Oregon's hinterland rolled off the freeways into downtown Portland early on the morning of April 13, 1990, slowing rush-hour traffic to a crawl. State police directed the convoys across the Willamette River to the Memorial Coliseum parking lot. Thousands of small-town loggers and millworkers squeezed onto Portland's commuter trains for the trip to Pioneer Courthouse Square in the heart of the city. When the big rally began at noon they were still arriving, stepping off the train and craning to gaze at the office towers that loomed over the red-brick square.

Office workers on their lunch hours paused, bemused, to take in the scene. For the first time, the war in the woods had spilled over into Portland's living room. The square was a sea of yellow ribbons, yellow T-shirts, and signs proclaiming anger, defiance, and bewilderment over the events of the preceding 10 days, including the release of the scientists' owl plan. Some of the messages professed pride in rural self-sufficiency: "America! We don't want handouts, we want jobs!" "Where there walks a logger, there walks a man!" Some were pointedly sarcastic: "Have you read your newspaper today? What will we print it on tomorrow?"

Suddenly, hoots, applause, and derisive laughter rippled through the crowd. A couple of workers in the Oregon Department of Environmental Quality offices across the way had chosen this moment to lower a huge banner in honor of Earth Day 20. "Imagine Environmental Harmony," it said.

But on this Friday the 13th environmental harmony was not to be found in Portland or anywhere else in the Pacific Northwest. The northern spotted owl had become a symbol of a malevolent force that was conspiring to rob timber workers of their livelihood and way of life. More than 300 mills had shut down for the day so workers could attend the Portland rally.

Wives and children of loggers and millworkers often were recruited to speak at timber rallies. Today Audrey Barnes, a young mother from the Oregon timber town of Roseburg, stepped to the microphone with her seven-year-old daughter Jennifer. "Can you look her in the eye and tell her that her father's job may be taken away?" she pleaded as television cameras whirred.

PLAYING THE DEMAGOGUE

Bob Packwood, Oregon's junior senator, was next to the microphone. Packwood, a Republican, had once courted environmentalists with his support for wilderness. But today, in a speech pundits would call one of the most demagogic of his career, he staked out the position that would carry him through his 1992 reelection campaign. He derided arguments that old-growth forests were disappearing. The people who were battling to save old-growth forests, he said, were the same people who had fought for gun control and against the Vietnam War.

"I've been dealing with these people for 20 years and I know what they're driving at," he shouted. "And it's not what Oregon is driving at! I have been to the limit of my patience on this!"

"Folks, the owl is not the issue," Packwood continued in a calmer voice. "If the natural predator of the owl swept in tonight and ate all of the little devils, this issue wouldn't go away. Their goal is *no* jobs. Whatever is left we'll now negotiate about until we've set it all aside. We'll let Canada supply our timber!"

Packwood's decision to embrace the timber industry was a calculated political strategy urged on him by his formidable chief of staff, Elaine Franklin. According to Lauri Hennessey, Packwood's speechwriter during this period, Franklin had told her boss it was time for him to choose between environmentalists and jobs. "Elaine said she would advise him to come down in favor of jobs and labor, because that was where the money was."

This was timber's day in Portland. A few foolhardy tree huggers taunted the loggers and got roughed up in the process. But environmentalists who had any sense stayed away. Some of them were wondering what sort of victory their strategy had wrought. The owl plan wasn't the panacea they had hoped for. And the backlash was growing. Events had outstripped their ability to control them.

DAMAGE CONTROL

In the wake of the owl plan's unveiling, timber lobbyists didn't confine their efforts to organizing rallies and didn't even bother to talk to the chief of the Forest Service. They went straight to John Sununu, President Bush's chief of staff.

Within weeks, Jack Ward Thomas and his team were summoned to Washington, D.C. Thomas could feel the hostility in the room as he appeared before an inquisitory panel of Bush administration henchmen to defend his team's work. His interrogators included John Shrote and Don Knowles, political appointees in the Interior Department; Agriculture Secretary Clayton Yeutter and his deputy, John Moseley; U.S. Representative Edward Madigan, the ranking Republican on the House Agriculture Committee, who would succeed Yeutter as agriculture secretary later that year; and a number of government economists and policy analysts, but no biologists.

They were looking for a way to undermine the plan. The grilling went on for hours. Special attention was directed at the recommendation that no logging of any kind be allowed in the owl reserves. "Clearly, the committee's job was to poke holes in it," Knowles said.

"Madigan never asked me to sit down," Thomas recalled three years later, still miffed at the memory. "I was at parade rest. He treated us like bugs on a pin."

Thomas also was summoned before the Senate Energy and Natural Resources Committee, where he was asked to respond to 150 questions, many of them fed to the committee by timber industry lobbyist Mark Rey. Thomas dealt with the questions one by one, showing a level of responsiveness that defused the plan's adversaries. "Jack defended the plan vigorously, not only with his scientific touch and personal style but with a fair political deftness," Knowles said.

Soon after, Yeutter announced that the administration would submit the owl plan to a panel of scientists of his own choosing for review. But to Yeutter's chagrin, the peer reviewers gave the plan an A plus for its pathbreaking use of the principles of conservation biology and landscape ecology. This owl strategy would not be easy to attack head-on.

DELAY AND DENIAL

Meanwhile, over at Forest Service headquarters in the shadow of the Washington Monument, the agency faced a congressionally imposed September 30, 1990, deadline for adopting a scientifically credible owl protection plan. Bowing to the inevitable, the agency had started the paper work to adopt the Interagency Scientific Committee (ISC) owl plan as official Forest Service policy and submit it to Judge Dwyer in Seattle. "It was clear that Dwyer was in charge," said George Leonard, who was associate chief of the Forest Service—number two in command at the time. "We had to do something to satisfy Dwyer." But before the team had even been named, he said, word came down from John Sununu through Moseley: "Don't adopt ISC."

As the deadline approached, the Forest Service quietly inserted a notice in the *Federal Register* announcing that, for now, it would manage the owl forests "in a manner not inconsistent with" the ISC owl plan.

Interior Secretary Manuel Lujan had no intention of adopting the owl plan. He gave BLM Director Cy Jamison the go-ahead to hatch his own owl plan for 2.5 million acres of BLM land in western Oregon. Jamison did. The "Jamison Plan," written in three days, had zero scientific credibility. Among other things, it waived the 50-11-40 rule. Jamison said later that he was only looking for some breathing room—time for the agency to adjust to the dramatic drop in timber sale levels. But the move would soon come back to haunt the Bush administration.

By refusing to formally adopt the ISC plan on either national forests or BLM land, the Bush administration gave environmentalists ammunition for new court challenges. The administration had been handed an opportunity to lay the contentious forest issue to rest. And it had blown the chance.

TRUTH-TELLING

On April 5, 1990, the day after the ISC owl plan was unveiled in Washington, D.C., Oregon Secretary of State Barbara Roberts delivered a speech to the Northwest Forestry Association. Roberts had just launched a campaign for governor, following the surprise announcement by Oregon Governor Neil Goldschmidt that he would not seek reelection. In her speech, she attacked the export of raw logs from Northwest lands, expressed her desire for a responsible, balanced solution to the forest impasse, and committed herself to working with the industry to build a second-growth, secondary-wood products economy.

But she also attacked the politics of denial. "I am not here to sell you a bill of goods," she said. "The public need and the public pressure on the timber resource base in Oregon is not about to disappear. It long ago passed the point where it was simply a tug-of-war between the environmentalists and the timber industry. We cannot turn back the clock. You cannot change the landscape by name-calling or demonstrations or bumper strips about fried owls."

She concluded, "Now is the time for playing the cards we've been dealt." And that was the line that made the headlines in the next day's papers.

Roberts' willingness to tell her fellow Oregon citizens what she thought they needed to hear won her no friends in Oregon's most powerful industry after she became Oregon's first woman governor in January 1991. She was still living down her "play the cards that we've been dealt" speech.

"The truth is, it was a fine speech," she said later. "I attempted to lay out the history of the timber industry in Oregon. In 1936, the year I was born, there was a report warning that the rate of logging in Oregon was not sustainable. But the Legislature failed to act on it, and so did the industry. If the Legislature and timber industry had not been in deep denial, we wouldn't have come to the point we had reached. The hand we'd been dealt was, we had a harvest deficit, an owl listed under the Endangered Species Act, an industry in major transition. My message was, 'If we don't deal with this, we will end up in court for the next four years or more.'"

Roberts grew up in the farming and timber town of Sheridan, Oregon, where her father owned a machine shop that repaired machinery for local sawmills. She knew the wave of mill closures Oregon was experiencing was not about spotted owls. "We had been closing mills for 10 years because of mechanization, log exports, and overharvesting," she said. "The owl was used by the timber industry to refocus workers away from those issues. It was a brilliant strategy."

As a blue-collar Democrat, she had political roots with organized labor and working people. But as governor, she soon found her efforts to communicate with workers blocked by harsh wise-use rhetoric. She refused to apologize for being an environmentalist. "My commitment was to abide by the law, to find a sound solution for the forests, both state and federal, and to find ways to help local communities. Those were my goals and I didn't think they were in conflict."

Roberts supported federal legislation that allowed states to make their own decisions about whether to ban the export of raw logs from state lands. After the legislation passed, Oregon voters passed a ban on state log exports by a lopsided ratio. They saw clearly the hypocrisy of a timber industry that continued to export logs while mills were closing.

In 1991, she went head-to-head with the timber industry when she pressured the Oregon Board of Forestry to adopt much stricter stream protection rules for state and private land.

The first of three unsuccessful timber industry–sponsored recall petitions against Roberts was filed in February of 1992. Roberts admitted later that she was surprised—and hurt. "When you knew how hard you were trying, it was very painful to be perceived as the enemy. In 25 years in public office, no one had ever questioned my honesty or integrity. I did exactly what I said I would do, no more, no less."

"A DELIBERATE AND SYSTEMATIC REFUSAL"

In early May of 1991, in Seattle, Judge Dwyer held a two-week hearing in the Sierra Club Legal Defense Fund lawsuit against the Forest Service over owl protection. Though the agency had not yet formally adopted the ISC owl plan, government lawyers now said they would adopt it, and they defended it as the best available science.

The testimony at trial was damning. Owl biologist Eric Forsman, testifying on behalf of the government, told Dwyer that at every step of the way biologists advising the Forest Service on owl protection had encountered "a considerable—I would emphasize considerable— amount of political pressure to create a plan which was an absolute minimum. That is, which had a very low probability of success and which had a minimum impact on timber harvest."

Until the ISC plan, he told Dwyer, owl protection recommendations had been "either gutted, ignored, or subverted. I was concerned that this would be another one of those efforts. But it was not. I'm proud to have my name on it."

George Leonard admitted under oath that the Bush administration had ordered the Forest Service to stop work on adopting the ISC plan.

On May 23, 1991, Dwyer issued a permanent injunction blocking all logging of owl habitat on national forests until the Forest Service formally adopted a scientifically supportable plan for the owl's conservation. For forest activists across the Northwest, it was a scary dream come true.

In his ruling, Dwyer systematically rejected the Bush administration's argument that he should lift the injunction and allow timber sales to go forward while the Forest Service belatedly adopted the ISC owl plan. The risk to the owl was too great, Dwyer said, and the administration had done nothing to earn his trust.

He acknowledged that reductions in federal timber sales might harm

Season of Blame

123

some companies and workers but pointed out that the timber industry had more than two years' volume of federal timber under contract and was continuing to export its own logs to Japan.

"To bypass the environmental laws, either briefly or permanently, would not fend off the changes transforming the timber industry," he wrote. "The argument that the mightiest economy on Earth cannot afford to preserve old-growth forests for a short time, while it reaches an overdue decision on how to manage them, is not convincing today. It would be even less so a year or a century from now."

Dwyer saved his harshest words for politicians who had consistently refused to heed warnings from government scientists. "Had the Forest Service done what Congress directed it to do—adopt a lawful plan by last fall—this case would have ended some time ago," Dwyer scolded. "More is involved here than a simple failure by an agency to comply with its governing statute. The most recent violation of [the National Forest Management Act] exemplifies a deliberate and systematic refusal by the Forest Service and the Fish and Wildlife Service to comply with the laws protecting wildlife. This is not the doing of the scientists, foresters, rangers, and others at the working levels of these agencies. It reflects decisions made by higher authorities in the executive branch of government."

FEELING PAIN

As the political wheels spun in Washington, a tableau of pain, anger, and incomprehension played out in owl hearings across the Northwest. Timber families, recruited by the Oregon Lands Coalition and other pro-logging groups, traveled hundreds of miles to vent their fear at public hearings held by the U.S. Fish and Wildlife Service. The service was required to gather public comment on its proposals to list the owl as a threatened species and, later, to designate critical owl habitat. Doing its job—enforcing the Endangered Species Act—had cast the agency as the ultimate out-of-control federal bureaucracy in the minds of many rural Northwest residents. Fish and Wildlife Service employees had been left to defend themselves with little or no help from the Bush administration. They gritted their teeth and took it.

The emotional testimony often ran late into the night, as workers berated the government and demanded answers to angry questions. To them, arguments about habitat fragmentation and population thresholds seemed abstract and unreal compared with the reality of mill closures, worker layoffs, and forests arbitrarily declared off-limits to logging.

At a Medford, Oregon, hearing in September 1991, one logger spoke with tears streaming down his cheeks, and a logger's wife described in shattering detail how her family had been disrupted by her husband's ever-more-desperate search for work.

Jerry Counsil, a logging contractor from Winston, Oregon, in the heart of timber country, bit off his words in barely controlled rage. Two years ago, he said, his company had employed 61 timber fallers. Now it had work for 16. Crime and alcoholism were up in his town and the county sheriff's office was out of money. "We can't afford to destroy our industry, our communities," he said. "Search relentlessly for balance and truth!"

"Shutting down our mills and our woods will not bring one extra tourist to Oregon," declared Gordon Ross, a commissioner from Coos County on the Oregon coast. "But it will leave vacant homes and idle factories to be viewed by those who do come."

Most environmentalists lacked the stomach to confront their adversaries in such settings. They stayed away in droves.

By 1991, the mood had turned nasty in the hinterland as well. Two owls had been found shot and nailed to signs on the Olympic Peninsula. Near Oakridge, Oregon, that same year, arsonists set fire to 9,000 acres of old growth that lay entirely within a habitat reserve for the northern spotted owl in an area called Warner Creek.

FACING REALITY

University of Washington sociologist Robert Lee had spent a year conducting in-depth interviews in Washington timber communities. He came away convinced that the forest debate had assumed a moral dimension, in which logging was viewed as a transgression against the emerging ecological ethic. The victims, he said, were being saddled with the blame for their own demise.

Yet there were a few tentative signs that the region might one day be able to move beyond denial and blame. Virtually alone among the national conservation groups lobbying to save the ancient forests, the Wilderness Society had chosen to invest in the search for solutions to the existential dilemma facing timber towns. In Washington's Grays Harbor County and Oregon's Linn County, Jeffrey Olson, a Wilderness Society economist, was working behind the scenes with local leaders, trying to help them chart a future based on sustainable forestry and economic diversification.

That did not mean community leaders in those towns liked the environmentalists' agenda. "The Wilderness Society has a very strict policy for environmental change that is detrimental to our economy," said Don Clothier, chairman of the Grays Harbor Economic Development Council. "We still sit down at the table together. We need to deal with reality."

Chapter Fifteen

Shasta Costa

In 1989, as District Ranger Kathy Johnson began planning timber sales for the next decade on the Siskiyou National Forest's Gold Beach District, she turned to the forest for guidance.

Wildfire had swept through the parched Siskiyous in the summer of 1987, leaving a vivid signature: a mosaic of bare, burned-over ridges; stringers of surviving green trees running downslope; and patches of charred tree, both alive and dead. Johnson thought the fire's pattern might offer a model for a gentler kind of forestry. She asked her staff to study the pattern of burns left by the Silver Fire and look for ways to make logging emulate nature.

THE ROADLESS AREA DILEMMA

The Shasta Costa watershed on the Gold Beach District was the perfect embodiment of the dilemma facing the Forest Service as it prepared to implement new forest plans for the 1990s.

Shasta Costa Creek flows west out of the Siskiyous, through a forested valley spread between steep ridges, toward its confluence with the Rogue River. Though the creek's headwaters had been heavily logged decades earlier, and roads had been built atop its ridgelines, the core of the 23,000-acre valley remained roadless in 1990, and the watershed provided a crucial link for wildlife moving between the Wild Rogue Wilderness and the North Kalmiopsis Roadless Area. Ecologically too, the Shasta Costa was pivotal; it formed a bridge, east to west, between the Klamath Mountains and the southern end of the Oregon Coast Range. The creek harbored salmon, and the forests were home to at least two nesting pairs of spotted owls.

The new Siskiyou National Forest plan called for building roads into Shasta Costa and selling timber there. Environmentalists in the Siskiyous had drawn the line against logging in roadless areas. Johnson knew any decision to enter Shasta Costa would be controversial.

She decided Shasta Costa was the perfect laboratory for the "new forestry" that forest ecologist Jerry Franklin had lately been preaching. This kinder and gentler forestry called for logging more lightly on the land, creating smaller openings in the forest canopy, and leaving behind some green trees, dead snags, and fallen logs to shelter wild-life and enrich the soil. Johnson enlisted the help of Siskiyou National Forest Supervisor Ron McCormick and some of the best soil scientists, ecologists, landscape architects, and geologists in the Forest Service. She asked them to lay out a new forestry option for a three-year timber sale program in the Shasta Costa watershed.

EARLY EXPERIMENTS

Johnson wasn't the first forest manager to experiment with new forestry. Steve Eubanks had been trying out its concepts for 15 years. In the mid-1970s, while working for the Wenatchee National Forest on the east slope of the Washington Cascades, Eubanks got to know Chris Maser. Maser was on special assignment for the Bureau of Land Management in La Grande, Oregon, working with Jack Ward Thomas. Together, Maser and Eubanks designed a plan to leave some limbs and branches on the ground for wildlife after logging instead of piling them up and burning them.

After his transfer to the heavily logged Bear Springs Ranger District of the Mount Hood National Forest, on the east slope of the Oregon Cascades, Eubanks worked with Maser and mycologist Jim Trappe on guidelines for leaving logs and wildlife trees, both dead and alive, after logging. Eubanks then proceeded to implement them on his own.

In 1984 Eubanks landed a plum job as Blue River district ranger on the Willamette National Forest and found himself at the center of the forestry renaissance taking place on the H. J. Andrews Experimental Forest. Franklin and other leading researchers began sharing scientific findings with him. Eubanks applied some of the new research findings on the ground. It was, he said, "a continual implementation-feedback loop. We had both science and management working together, so we were able to satisfy skeptics on both sides of the fence."

One project involved leaving live trees on logging sites and periodically girdling and killing some of them to create snags for cavity-nesting birds. These "sloppy clearcuts" became standard operating procedure in the Blue River District. Logging them required retraining loggers, who were used to scouring logged lands of fiber. It also required establishing new safety procedures to reduce the risk that fallers might be injured.

Franklin and others also worked with Eubanks on a plan that concentrated logging in areas already carved by clearcuts to avoid fragmenting intact forest stands elsewhere. Eubanks presented the plan to his supervisors and to Forest Service officials in Washington, D.C. But he didn't wait for official approval. In the Blue River District, he replaced the "staggered clearcuts" that had turned the forest canopy into a patchwork quilt with this new design.

Not everyone approved of Eubanks' experiments. When Jeff

DeBonis came to work in the Blue River District in 1989, he warned that some of these new forestry sales threatened to increase soil erosion and watershed impacts. But he said Eubanks disregarded his analyses, and he finally concluded that his boss "was using new forestry as a hook to get the cut out."

The ferment bubbling under the forest canopy in the Blue River District didn't get much attention outside the small team of scientists and forest managers who were making it happen.

In fact, in the late 1980s, when Eubank transferred to a desk job in Washington, D.C., no one from the chief's office bothered to walk down the hall to his office for a briefing. In the mid-1980s, the Forest Service had no incentive to change its forest management paradigm in the Pacific Northwest.

That changed as the agency careened toward gridlock in 1989.

FORESTRY DUELS

By late 1989, Jerry Franklin's theories were gaining wide circulation. In November of 1989, he wrote in *American Forests:* "Forestry needs to expand its focus beyond wood production to the perpetuation of diverse forest ecosystems. . . . Forestry professionals need to acknowledge that what is good for wood-fiber production is not necessarily best for other forest values."

Franklin's piece also carried a subtle warning for forest preservationists that a paradigm shift away from wilderness preservation was underway. He argued that there simply wasn't enough wilderness to provide all the biological diversity the world needed. "Environmentalists must stop relying on setting aside preserved lands as the only approach to the protection of ecological values," he wrote. "Clearly, the reserving of lands is critical to the protection of many values—such as, for example, aquatic habitats and unstable soils. But many of the reserves need to be a part of the commodity landscape, rather than existing apart from it."

By the summer of 1990, spirited debate over the wisdom of clearcutting raged within the forestry profession. The debate was particularly intense at Oregon State University's College of Forestry, where the superiority of clearcutting as a system for converting decadent Douglas-fir forests to young plantations had been treated as received wisdom for nearly a half-century.

During a July 12, 1990, tour of the Andrews Experimental Forest, as Franklin showed off some of the new logging techniques to foresters and the news media, the professional divide over new forestry flared into the public eye. Bill Atkinson, a member of the OSU forestry old guard who headed the college's forest engineering department, challenged him openly. "New forestry is being sold to the American people like a bar of soap," he stormed. "People are using new forestry to get at clearcutting. We're getting new forestry by decree, by dogma. We don't have Chairman Mao; we've got Jerry."

Atkinson acknowledged that clearcutting had been destructive to wildlife, fish, and streams. "But it grows trees," he added defensively. "Plantations outgrow natural forests by 30 to 40 percent. These second-growth forests are going to save the industry."

Franklin, quick-tempered, shot back, "If you want to, you can argue ecological values aren't important enough to interfere with economic values." But he said that argument wouldn't carry much weight in the political climate of the post-owl world. "Let's not argue," he said, "about the train that's coming down the track."

NEW PERSPECTIVES

On October 11, 1989, obeying marching orders from Congress contained in the Rider from Hell, Forest Service Chief F. Dale Robertson announced that his agency now recognized old-growth forests were "valuable as diverse and productive ecosystems." From this day forward, he said, the Forest Service would reduce the use of traditional clearcutting and move toward retaining more trees, snags, logs, and woody debris on the forest floor. It would reduce fragmentation of old growth and manage some stands on extended rotations. The following March, the Forest Service expanded on its new vision, unveiling a vaguely defined program called "New Perspectives for Managing the National Forest System."

On the Siskiyou National Forest, suddenly, there was an opportunity to make this new national policy manifest. The Forest Service embraced Shasta Costa to its bosom. It published a glossy, full-color brochure written in breathless prose that described the project variously as "holistic forestry," "down-home forestry," and an exciting venture into New Perspectives. In all, the Siskiyou National Forest spent $500,000 in 1989 and 1990 preparing and marketing the Shasta Costa plan.

The entire watershed was studied in minute detail. "We looked at it as a huge jigsaw puzzle," said project director Kurt Wiedenmann. "We mapped and analyzed 1,000 stands."

The project recruited members of the public to take part in the process. Eight timber industry representatives and five environmentalists volunteered. One was Jim Britell of Port Orford, Oregon, who still harbored hope that environmentalists could work cooperatively with the Forest Service. Shasta Costa seemed like the last best chance for that.

The draft plan for Shasta Costa, released in the summer of 1990, called for building just two miles of new roads. More than 40 percent of the logs would be removed by helicopter; the rest would be yarded from existing roads. Trees would be individually marked. Only small patches, an acre or two in size, would be clear-cut. On most sites, 10 to 20 trees per acre, of many ages, would be left. Most old growth would remain untouched, and younger stands would be logged in a way that would preserve wildlife corridors. Damage caused by past logging and road-building would be repaired. And the unroaded core of the watershed would remain untouched, at least for three more years.

Britell praised the plan as a way for the Forest Service to produce timber volume without roads or clearcuts. Not all environmentalists were as sanguine. The Oregon Natural Resources Council, smelling an alarming precedent, announced that it would appeal the Shasta Costa plan. "Roadless areas are the anchors of biological diversity, the intact ecosystems that still exist," said conservation director Andy Kerr. "New Forestry is simply a less violent way to rape them."

THE UNRAVELING

Timber industry groups initially gave guarded approval to the plan. But when they studied it further, they discovered that it would it reduce the timber yield from the Shasta Costa watershed by one-third over the next three years. How, they wanted to know, would the Forest Service make up the difference? And what were the implications if this "New Perspectives" paradigm became the modus operandi on watersheds across the Northwest? In that case, some mill-owners suggested, the agency should consider opening up scenic buffers, river corridors, and other reserves to logging.

The Forest Service should have been prepared to answer these questions, but wasn't.

Soon after, the Shasta Costa experiment began to unravel. Forest Supervisor Ron McCormick retired, and Kathy Johnson, a rising star in the Forest Service, was promoted to a job in the agency's Washington, D.C., office. She died later of brain cancer. In late 1990, Mike Lunn replaced McCormick on the Siskiyou, which was rapidly becoming a crucible for conflict.

In January of 1991, Lunn announced that in response to concerns from the timber industry, changes had been made in the preferred Shasta Costa alternative. There would be more roads, more clearcuts. At a follow-up meeting, fisheries biologists who had helped craft the plan pounced on him for this retreat from watershed protection. By the time Judge Dwyer's injunction came down in May of 1991, blocking all logging of owl habitat, Shasta Costa was a fading memory.

That didn't mean New Perspectives was dead. Far from it. In an interview in November of 1991, Franklin said the past 12 months had seen an explosion in new forestry. "It's very hard to find a national forest timber sale anymore that doesn't have some elements of structural retention," he said. Even private companies like Washington's Plum Creek Timber were getting into the act.

For Franklin, the agency's belated decision to embrace his work was a huge career boost. Offers came in from all over the world. Franklin became the guru of new forestry.

But Kerr and a few other activists saw an important point obscured in the rush to champion this kinder and gentler forestry. New forestry might be all right in new forests, they said. But it made no sense in the pristine roadless areas they were fighting to save. They had a nagging hunch that it might become the loophole through which the Forest Service would introduce logging into the last wild forests.

Shasta Costa

Chapter Sixteen

Train Wreck

When the U.S. Fish and Wildlife Service declared the northern spotted owl a threatened species in June 1990, it set in motion a bewildering series of complex, conflicting, and overlapping processes. The agency concluded that the owl was in trouble because of destruction of its habitat by logging. But because the owl's range was so vast—spanning three states and encompassing 24 million acres of federal land alone—the challenge of deciding how to protect the bird under the Endangered Species Act was unprecedented. The act itself provided no clear path through the maze, and the Bush administration was content to stand by and watch the agency flounder.

The 1973 law required the FWS to write a recovery plan—a blueprint for restoring the owl's population to sustainable levels. It required the FWS to designate critical habitat—areas suitable for owls which would receive protection whether owls actually inhabited them or not. It required the FWS to formally review federal projects that might jeopardize the owl's survival—Forest Service and Bureau of Land Management timber sales, primarily. And it required the FWS to protect owls on private as well as public land, forcing the agency to step into the treacherous minefield of private property rights. At the request of several timber companies, the FWS established voluntary guidelines private timberland owners could follow to avoid civil and even criminal penalties for illegally "taking" owls by destroying their habitat. These guidelines, which called for leaving large circular forested buffers around owl nesting sites, drew powerful new adversaries into the fray.

Marvin Plenert, an honest, plainspoken career FWS employee, inherited this mess when he took over as regional director of the service in 1989. Fortunately, Plenert had a sense of humor. He needed it as the owl saga ground on for the next four years, fueled by court briefs, bureaucratic missteps, and administrative delay tactics.

UNDERCUTTING THE ESA
By 1991, the northern spotted owl was well on its way to becoming the most studied bird in the history of avian biology. The federal government was spending $10 million a year to research its birth and survival rates, dietary preferences, and habitat requirements. A small cottage

industry had grown up as state and private timber managers hired owl callers to go into their own forests and hoot the birds out of the treetops. This frenzy of activity was designed to influence the federal courts and federal agencies as they made decisions about how logging and the owl could coexist.

By 1991, it was also apparent that the Bush administration had decided to pursue what Washington, D.C., insiders called a "train-wreck strategy." It would let various processes unleashed by the Endangered Species Act run their course without taking action to resolve the underlying problem of unsustainable logging on federal lands, a tactic designed to build support for weakening the act.

The 1973 law was due to expire in 1992 and would soon be up for reauthorization by Congress. Increasingly, environmentalists were using the ESA to protect not only imperiled species but degraded habitat—overlogged and overgrazed public lands, overappropriated rivers and aquifers, and natural areas under siege from developers. The economic costs of protecting the nation's shrinking islands of undisturbed nature had become a rallying point for the wise-use movement—and not just in the Pacific Northwest. The act was under fire from timber, grazing, mining, and development interests across the nation.

THE OWL RECOVERY PLAN

In March of 1991, Interior Secretary Manuel Lujan announced that he had appointed a recovery team to write a plan for restoring owl populations to viable numbers. Departing from the customary practice of appointing only scientists to ESA recovery teams, Lujan announced that his team would include economists, representatives from the three affected states, and political appointees as well. Lujan chose Donald Knowles, one of his deputies and a seasoned political operative, to head the effort. He asked Knowles to deliver an owl recovery plan that would take the heat off the Bush administration by putting fewer loggers out of work than the owl strategy written in 1990 by the Interagency Scientific Committee (ISC).

At first the recovery team process was dogged by scientific skepticism. Lujan had ordered that no biologists who had worked on the ISC owl plan be included on his team. In fact, Knowles had a hard time finding an owl biologist who wanted to have anything to do with this new project. Finally Rocky Gutiérrez, a talented, acerbic professor of wildlife biology at Humboldt State University in Arcata, California, agreed to take on the assignment.

"People called me up and said, 'You shouldn't do this, it's going to ruin your career,'" recalled Gutiérrez, who had 12 years of spotted owl research under his belt. "I said, 'That's bullshit. Nothing can ruin a scientist but bad science.'"

Soon after it convened, the recovery team retreated behind closed doors. No one paid much attention.

Surprisingly, the team began to click. Representatives from the governors' offices provided useful information about owl habitat on state and private land. Economists gathered employment data. Biologists were left to work out the details of the recovery plan with little interference. As team leader, Knowles was in a sensitive situation: He had his marching orders from Lujan, but as the months went by he built up a level of trust with the scientists that he was loath to betray.

At Knowles' direction, the recovery team, like the ISC before it, stuck to the owl. A subcommittee gathered detailed information on 364 other species, both plants and animals, that shared old forests with the owl, including 30 species already listed as threatened or endangered. But the administration passed on the opportunity to address the status of these species in its plan. The information was relegated to an appendix.

Knowles held monthly congressional briefings in Washington, D.C., to update the administration on the team's progress. "Everyone wanted the same thing," he said, "a scientifically credible plan with no impacts."

CRITICAL HABITAT

Because the FWS did not immediately designate critical habitat for the owl at the time of its listing, environmentalists sued to require that the agency finish the job as the law required. In February of 1991, U.S. District Court Judge Thomas Zilly ordered the FWS to publish a critical habitat rule by the end of April. The overwhelmed agency had to scramble to meet the deadline, and it showed. Its draft rule called for designating a whopping 11.6 million acres, including 3 million acres of private land, as habitat for the owl.

FWS officials tried to explain that the proposed rule didn't mean these areas would be closed to logging, only that logging within them would be subject to agency review. Nevertheless, timber towns erupted once again, and their anger turned to ridicule when a close examination of the maps accompanying the rule revealed that some of this "critical habitat" had no trees. "It is time for President Bush to intervene and 'reel in' the Fish and Wildlife Service," declared Mike Draper, executive secretary of the Western Council of Industrial Workers. At a raucous hearing on the critical habitat rule in the small Oregon town of Creswell, loggers shouted down environmentalists and blasted air horns to support pro-timber testimony.

Timber company executives who found the owl now had designs on their own land took a more direct approach. In July 1991, George Weyerhaeuser, chairman and chief executive officer of Weyerhaeuser Company, met with Bush administration officials to discuss how the owl's listing would affect private lands. In August, the FWS announced that it was dropping 3 million acres of private land from its critical habitat rule. By the time the agency adopted its final rule, it had whittled critical habitat to 6 million acres, but it was still living down this public relations disaster.

THE GOD SQUAD

In September of 1991, BLM Director Cy Jamison asked Lujan to convene the Endangered Species Committee to consider whether 44 BLM timber sales in western Oregon should be exempted from the Endangered Species Act. The FWS, after reviewing the sales, had concluded that logging them would jeopardize the owl. Biologists said the forests involved provided essential dispersal habitat for owls flying between the Oregon Coast Range and the Southern Oregon Cascades.

The committee, nicknamed the God Squad, was an invention of Congress, a loophole added to the 1973 act in 1978 at the request of Senator Howard Baker of Tennessee. Congress gave the committee the power to exempt a species from the ESA's protections if it judged the cost to society to be too high—in effect, to sentence a species to possible extinction. Baker hoped the God Squad would vote for an exemption that would allow the Tennessee Valley Authority to finish Tellico Dam despite its likely impact on a tiny fish called the snail darter.

The composition of the God Squad made for an unlikely assemblage. Its members were the secretaries of the Interior and Agriculture Departments, the secretary of the army, the chairman of the Council of Economic Advisers, the administrator of the Environmental Protection Agency, the director of the National Oceanic and Atmospheric Administration, and a representative from the affected state or states, to be appointed by the governor.

Lynn Greenwalt, director of the FWS during this period, helped write the God Squad amendment. It was his idea, he said, to require that the actual Cabinet-level officials, not their representatives, meet to vote on the exemption. "It's not a small thing to say to oneself, Dear Diary, Today I decided against the continued existence of a species."

In the case of the snail darter, the strategy failed. The committee convened for the first and only time on a stage at the Interior Department on January 23, 1979, and voted against an exemption for Tellico Dam. "It was a little like a morality play," Greenwalt recalled. "The parties said their piece, and then Charles Schultz, head of the Council of Economic Advisors, stood up and said, 'There's no need for this dam, to hell with it, I'm leaving.'" Baker, miffed, had to resort to a midnight appropriations rider to push the dam project through.

The same day the God Squad considered the snail darter, it approved a negotiated agreement between the state of Nebraska and the Rural Electrification Administration over a proposed dam and reservoir on the Platte River that threatened habitat for the endangered whooping crane. The agreement committed the project's operators to assure adequate water releases for the whooping crane. It would be 13 years before the God Squad convened again.

DEBACLE IN PORTLAND

Republican Senator Bob Packwood of Oregon, a friend of the timber industry, first proposed convening the God Squad in 1990, soon after release of the ISC owl plan. But in 1990, Packwood's idea went nowhere.

In 1991, after the Fish and Wildlife Service found that 44 sales on BLM land posed risks to the owl, the BLM cut short negotiations with the service over changing the sales to make them less harmful. That laid the groundwork for Interior Secretary Lujan to invoke the God Squad.

In order to grant an exemption, the God Squad had to find, among other things, that the project was of regional or national significance. In the case of the 44 BLM sales, that was a hard case to make. The timber involved amounted to less than 1 percent of the nation's annual timber supply.

In that context, the tedious evidentiary hearing that unfolded in Portland in January of 1992 was at once less and more than it seemed.

Invoking the God Squad cast two Interior Department agencies, the FWS and the BLM, as adversaries. There was no question which side the Bush administration was on. Lujan put his top lawyer, Interior Solicitor Tom Sansonetti, on the case. The Fish and Wildlife Service, forced to turn to outside counsel, hired Patrick Parenteau, a politically savvy attorney in private practice who had helped argue the case against the Tellico Dam exemption. A retired administrative law judge from Salt Lake City, Harold Sweitzer, presided.

The cast of characters also included the Sierra Club Legal Defense Fund, which argued against the exemption, and three pro-timber groups—the Oregon Lands Coalition, the Northwest Forest Resources Council, and the Association of O & C Counties—which argued in its favor.

On January 8, 1992, this passel of lawyers met in a Portland federal office building to present evidence and call witnesses. Because the administration had heard that emotions were running high, security was elaborate. But it soon became apparent that the biggest danger was boredom. Ahead were three weeks of arcane testimony and convoluted legal arguments. Even the rallies held concurrently were listless affairs.

Sansonetti, the Interior Department's top lawyer, was the impresario charged with orchestrating this circus. He had received his orders straight from the Bush White House: Find out whether the escape hatch in the ESA created a big enough loophole to drive several hundred log trucks through. "I really don't care who wins," he insisted to the press. "I just want to make sure the process goes right."

To Jamison and Lujan, the owl case seemed the perfect test of whether the act was flexible enough to consider what they called "the human dimension." Either way, they couldn't lose. If it worked, they could take credit for helping out struggling rural communities. If it failed, they could attack the act as a job-stealer when it came up for reauthorization in Congress.

But Sansonetti also had to worry about the BLM's legal exposure in a separate case underway across the river at the federal courthouse. There, U.S. District Judge Helen Frye was hearing a lawsuit brought by the Sierra Club Legal Defense Fund against the BLM's so-called

"Jamison Plan." Sansonetti had to try to block testimony in the God Squad proceeding that might hurt the BLM's legal case. But he failed to squelch damaging testimony that the BLM had failed to consider new biological information about the owl's decline. Lawyers for environmentalists quickly submitted the written testimony as evidence in the case before Judge Frye.

The spectacle that unfolded as the evidentiary hearing began was a transparently political show. Roger Nesbitt, the inept government attorney representing the BLM, received repeated scoldings from Judge Sweitzer, an infinitely patient man, for his delays and his rambling, often incoherent questions. Timber industry attorney Mark Rutzick seized the opportunity to interrogate Jack Ward Thomas, Barry Noon, and other scientists from the ISC owl committee in an attempt to discredit their work.

In one of the low points of the evidentiary hearing, Rutzick railed against the "high priests of the cult of biology." It didn't help that the timber industry's own representative to the owl team, Larry Irwin, testified that he supported the owl strategy.

It was all pretty obscure stuff, not the compelling show Lujan and Jamison had hoped for.

On the last day of the hearing, as if to punctuate the pointlessness of the process, word came from across the river that Judge Frye had just ruled in the Jamison owl plan lawsuit. She had issued an order blocking all BLM old-growth sales—including the 44 at issue in the God Squad hearing.

LUJAN'S OWL EXTINCTION PLAN

Meanwhile, the recovery team had finished a draft owl recovery plan and was awaiting further instructions. The plan, based on the ISC owl strategy, was scientifically solid. But Interior Secretary Lujan's in-house economists told him it would cost 32,000 timber jobs. Republican senators from the Northwest said they wouldn't countenance job losses on that scale.

On February 14, 1992, Lujan announced that although the team had fulfilled its mission, he wanted a different owl plan, one that would cost fewer jobs. In the meantime, he suspended action on the draft recovery plan.

The states of Oregon, Washington, and California objected. They were eager to get a recovery plan in place so they could begin planning for the future. Four days after Lujan's announcement, the state of Oregon sued the Interior Department to halt the God Squad process. Oregon Governor Barbara Roberts, a Democrat, accused the Bush administration of initiating the process illegally, without a good-faith effort by the BLM to modify its timber sales so they would pose less risk to the owl. The God Squad, she said, offered no hope of a long-term resolution to the state's timber woes.

Donald Knowles, the recovery team leader, had to quell a rebellion among biologists on the team, who had vowed to walk and blow the whistle if their science fell victim to election-year politicking.

Lujan himself was growing impatient with all the simultaneous processes his agencies had set in motion. Knowles recalls that Lujan exclaimed to him one day, "Look, I'm the Secretary of Interior. Why can't I just say the owl isn't endangered and take it off the list?" Tom Sansonetti, his solicitor, explained to Lujan that he could indeed do that—if he wanted to find himself embroiled in yet another owl lawsuit.

Lujan asked Knowles to head the development of his new owl plan. This time Knowles knew better than to ask owl biologists to help him. Though he had no scientific background, he handled the job himself, with the help of other Interior policy works.

The plan they came up with proposed eliminating protection for owls in huge sections of Washington, Oregon, and northern California, effectively isolating the birds in pockets of the Oregon and Washington Cascades. Biologists who reviewed it said bluntly that while some owls might still remain in the forests after 100 years under such a strategy, it would create conditions that would almost certainly spell doom for the species over time. They called it "a recipe for extinction." Environmentalists immediately labeled it Lujan's "owl extinction plan."

Lujan agreed that his new plan did not comply with the Endangered Species Act, but he said it could be implemented through a special act of Congress. Senator Slade Gorton, a Washington Republican, later introduced the "owl extinction plan" in the Senate, where it died an unheralded death.

LUJAN'S CIRCUS

As inept as Lujan appeared, he did have a plan. The day of denouement was set for May 14, 1992. On that day the seven Cabinet-level members would meet to vote on the God Squad exemption. Lujan needed five of those votes to win his exemption.

Lujan could count on his own vote and those of Agriculture Secretary Edward Madigan, Secretary of the Army Michael Stone, and Council of Economic Advisers Chairman Michael Boskin. But Tom Walsh, Oregon's representative, was a sure no vote. As the day approached, the Bush White House engaged in personal arm-twisting with the other two God Squad members, Environmental Protection Agency administrator William K. Reilly and National Oceanic and Atmospheric Administration Director John Knauss.

The atmosphere in the wood-paneled Interior Department ceremonial conference room was frantic on the morning of May 14. Interior functionaries stood at their posts and press aides darted in and out with quick glances at their watches. Seating in the small chamber was limited. Ten reporters and 10 invited timber industry constituents were allowed inside. No environmentalists were in attendance. Lujan, the chairman of the God Squad, was the last to arrive.

Last-minute negotiations with Knauss had won Lujan the fifth vote he needed for an exemption on 13 of the 44 timber sales. But it had been a pyrrhic victory. Knauss attached a high price to his vote: The BLM must agree to follow the owl recovery plan—the same plan that Lujan was trying to deep-six—until it developed its own scientifically credible plan for the owl's survival.

Hours before the God Squad was to convene, Lujan's aides threw up their hands and agreed. When the members of the committee filed into the secretary's conference room, most had not even seen a copy of the Knauss amendment. Knauss was caustic in his comments. If the BLM didn't get its act together and adopt a scientifically credible owl plan, he said, the God Squad would be back next year, considering another exemption for next year's BLM timber sale program.

Immediately after the God Squad met and voted, press aides hustled reporters into a news conference, where Lujan unveiled his now thoroughly repudiated 63-page "owl extinction plan." On the other side of the country, in Portland, Fish and Wildlife Service officials quietly released the draft 662-page owl recovery plan, a document that biologists, ecologists, and economists had labored over for 14 months.

Cy Jamison was conveniently out of town that day, traveling in the West. By then, he was disgusted with the whole mess. Lujan's office had called him to brief him on the political intrigue. "I said, 'Life goes on,' and I hung up," he recalled later, with a chuckle. He admitted that convening the God Squad was a mistake.

In all, the debacle had cost taxpayers well over $1.5 million, consumed 11 tons of paper—and destroyed whatever shreds of credibility the Bush administration had left on forests in the Pacific Northwest. And the ancient forests remained under lock and key.

Carl Ross, Mark Winstein (at lectern), and Chris Van Dalen speak at the Save America's Forests kickoff rally in Washington, D.C., on September 16, 1990. Ross and Winstein started Save America's Forests after seeing a touring presentation that featured a 730-year-old Douglas-fir log.

PART FOUR

RAISING THE STAKES

1987–92

“ . . . the historic richness of the salmon and steelhead resource of the West Coast will never be known. However, it is clear that what has survived is a small proportion of what once existed, and what remains is substantially at risk. ”

> —AMERICAN FISHERIES SOCIETY, *"Pacific Salmon at the Crossroads," March 1991*

“We must now pay for the billions of board feet of cheap pine logged earlier in the century. ”

> —BOYD WICKMAN, *"Forest Health in the Blue Mountains: Insects and Disease," March 1991*

“Management that harms native ecosystems, or management out of ignorance or lack of respect for biodiversity, is no longer excusable. ”

> —REED F. NOSS AND ALLEN Y. COOPERRIDER, *Saving Nature's Legacy, 1994*

WHILE THE BUSH ADMINISTRATION pursued its strategy of delay, denial, and polarization, the ancient forest campaign in the Pacific Northwest was attracting belated attention from the national conservation groups, which had long maintained that the disappearance of the old-growth forests was a regional rather than a national issue. The Wilderness Society launched a forest inventory and forest mapping project to help lay the scientific and educational groundwork for a national campaign, and in 1989 opened an Oregon office to increase its visibility. The National Audubon Society launched its own forest mapping project, using volunteers. The National Wildlife Federation contributed the on-the-ground expertise of Rick Brown, a former Forest Service biologist hired to monitor timber sales out of its Portland office.

But though the national groups brought new visibility to the ancient forests, they failed to mount an effective lobbying effort to get Congress to protect them. In 1990, Indiana congressman Jim Jontz introduced a bill to create a system of ancient forest reserves. The following year, several large foundations agreed to fund a new organization that would work in Washington, D.C. to protect the Northwest's ancient forests. Meanwhile, grassroots activists were taking their ancient forest campaign on the road. Two political neophytes, inspired by the message, started a group called Save America's Forests to work for protection of forests in every region of the country.

Awareness of the broader consequences of forest liquidation was growing. In the early 1990s, fisheries biologists went public with a warning about the plight of Pacific salmon and the role of habitat destruction in their demise. At about the same time, forest activists unveiled new information about the extent of old-growth forest loss east of the Cascades. By the end of 1992, it was obvious that the conflict flaring in the forests of the Northwest involved far more than loggers versus owls.

Chapter Seventeen

Going National

It was on a trip to the Pacific Northwest in early 1987 that George Frampton, president of the Wilderness Society, had his eyes opened to the rampant rate of clearcutting in the region's native forests. At the time, the carnage occurring in the nation's upper-left corner was not on the radar screen of any national conservation group in Washington, D.C. The nationals had departed the field of battle in the Northwest after passage of the 1984 wilderness bills. Since then, grassroots groups still fighting to save roadless forests had been pretty much on their own.

"The local groups felt they weren't getting any help from the nationals," Frampton said. "I realized that something had to be done, that this was a national issue."

In the summer of 1986, Sierra Club President Doug Wheeler had organized a six-day trip to Southeast Alaska for an elite cadre of national conservation leaders known as the Group of 10. When he saw the scarred mountains of the Northwest, Frampton decided to bring the Group of 10 to the West Coast again.

In the spring of 1988 these conservation bigwigs flew to Seattle and then got a bird's-eye view of the extent of logging courtesy of Lighthawk, an environmental air force that conducted aerial tours of the forest to show off the worst of the timber industry's handiwork. At a meeting in Seattle, James Monteith, executive director of the Oregon Natural Resources Council, made a pitch for assistance from the Group of 10.

Grassroots activists in the Northwest were now ready to take their forest campaign to the next step, Monteith said. ONRC was widely regarded as one of the most effective statewide environmental groups in the nation. After a three-year fundraising effort, Monteith was in the process of moving its headquarters from a funky wood-frame house in Eugene to a tasteful suite of offices in downtown Portland to gain increased visibility.

By trip's end, the Northwest's old-growth forests were on the nationals' radar screens. For better or worse, the dance between the nation's conservation establishment and the zealous tree huggers of the Pacific Northwest had begun.

DOING THE GOVERNMENT'S WORK

Under Frampton's leadership, the Wilderness Society took on three critical tasks: Inventorying and mapping the forests, describing their ecological significance, and analyzing the region's changing timber economy.

Barry Flamm, the society's staff forester, was the first to identify the need for accurate, up-to-date maps of old-growth forests. Frampton hired Peter Morrison, a forest ecologist with a master's degree from the University of Washington, to do the basic mapping and inventory work the Forest Service had failed to do. Using state-of-the-art geographic information system software, Morrison produced maps documenting how much old growth remained, where it was, and the extent of forest fragmentation. At the peak of his project, he was assisted by a paid staff of seven and a cadre of volunteers from among Seattle's computer hacker elite.

In June of 1988, the Wilderness Society published Morrison's work in "End of the Ancient Forests: A Report on National Forest Management Plans in the Pacific Northwest." The report analyzed draft management plans for 12 national forests in western Washington, western Oregon, and northern California. Using the Forest Service's own ecological definition, Morrison concluded that just 2.4 million acres of roadless old-growth forest—about half as much as the Forest Service claimed—remained in forests west of the Cascades.

The disparity was explained by the fact that individual forests were not required to use the ecological definition of old growth developed by Jerry Franklin's team. The definitions they did use varied widely from forest to forest. Moreover, the accelerated logging of the late 1980s typically was not reflected in national forest inventory data. The numbers derived were thus sloppy and unreliable.

Morrison's report was a wake-up call on how fast the old growth was disappearing. Throughout the 1980s, he found, the 12 forests had been logged at a phenomenal rate. By 1987, the timber industry was logging an estimated 70 acres of old growth—the equivalent of 129 football fields—every day. He warned that under forest plans for the 1990s, most future logging would occur in roadless areas. Over 15 years, if cutting at 1988 rates continued, nearly half the unprotected roadless acreage on the 12 forests would be gone. Over 50 years, two-thirds would disappear.

Morrison's most effective maps contrasted the extent of unlogged Olympic National Forest lands in the 1940s, in the 1960s, and in 1988. They showed an unbroken canopy transformed over four decades into a shredded quilt. The contrast with the adjacent intact forests of Olympic National Park was stark. "I used the slides often," said Melanie Rowland, an attorney for the Wilderness Society. "People literally gasped."

In a series of five other carefully researched studies, published in 1989 and 1990, the Wilderness Society laid out the scientific and economic arguments for protecting old growth. In 1990, the Wilderness Society and Island Press published *Ancient Forests of the Pacific Northwest,* a collection of essays edited by staff ecologist Elliott Norse, which described the ecological values of the forests in more depth and breadth.

In 1989 the Wilderness Society opened an office in Portland, signaling its growing commitment to the ancient forest campaign.

ADOPTING FORESTS

Meanwhile, the National Audubon Society had undertaken its own, more modest mapping project. Audubon's Adopt-a-Forest campaign recruited volunteers to map old-growth tracts in several parts of the national forest system. In the Northwest, volunteers used Forest Service data, aerial photos, and on-the-ground observation to map all groves at least 300 acres in size that had trees at least 100 years old. The project's goal was to show the location of forest stands that still provided intact interior forests for native plants and wildlife.

Adopt-a-Forest mobilized grassroots activists throughout the Northwest. In Washington and Oregon, many local Audubon chapters became far more militant than their parent organization, filing lawsuits and appeals to challenge logging on lands they had come to know through in-the-field research.

In November of 1989, representatives of 100 Audubon chapters met in Eugene with members of the National Audubon staff from Washington, D.C. They hoped to persuade the national staff that it was time to approach forest protection in a new way—to focus on the ecological importance of old forests, not just their recreational and esthetic values. "The challenge was to persuade this venerable conservation group that it might be necessary to save fragmented forests for the owls, and save cutover forests for the fish," recalled Bonnie Phillips of Pilchuck Audubon in Everett, Washington, who organized the meeting. She found Audubon lobbyist Brock Evans, a veteran of the Northwest forest wars, quite resistant. "His concern," she said, "was, 'What can I sell back there?'"

THE TONGASS CAMPAIGN

Meanwhile, another regional forest protection campaign, this one in Alaska, was attracting national attention and the ear of Congress. This was due largely to the efforts of the Southeast Alaska Conservation Council, a coalition of environmentalists, commercial fishing groups, and subsistence groups based in Juneau, Alaska. Formed in the early 1970s, SEACC worked to expose the waste, corruption, and environmental destruction Congress had set in motion with passage of the 1980 Tongass Timber Supply program. Bart Koehler, an intense, politically astute former Earth First! activist, became SEACC's executive director in 1983. He spent much of the next seven years traveling through the Lower 48 with a slide show on the Tongass, generating letters to Congress, and building a national campaign.

SEACC had plenty of ammunition. The Tongass had become virtually an extension of two pulp companies that held 50-year contracts to log its timber. The Forest Service had given the companies veto power over land management decisions and had allowed them to destroy some of the most ecologically sensitive forests on the Tongass while taxpayers across the nation subsidized their operations to the tune of $40 million a year. The 1970s and 1980s had seen blatant abuses of the contracts, including antitrust violations and efforts to defraud the government of timber revenues.

The U.S. House of Representatives passed a strong reform bill in 1989. No reform bill emerged from the Senate that year, but SEACC's on-the-ground documentation of environmental abuses kept the heat on. In October of 1990 Congress passed the Tongass Timber Reform Act, designating 300,000 acres of the Tongass as wilderness and protecting a million acres in all from logging. The bill represented not only a stunning victory for environmentalists but also a body blow to Alaska's three-member Republican congressional delegation, which had fought to protect the interests of Southeast Alaska's timber industry.

The major conservation foundations took notice of the Tongass victory and began discussing whether a similar model might work in the Pacific Northwest. "SEACC had the idea they should actually go to Washington and communicate directly with members of Congress, the administration, and the national media," said Tom Wathen of the Pew Charitable Trusts, a Philadelphia-based foundation that was just getting involved in environmental grantmaking. "We proposed that the same model be used in the Pacific Northwest."

A FRIEND IN CONGRESS

U.S. Representative Jim Jontz, a combative Indiana Democrat, first visited the Pacific Northwest in 1987 at the invitation of Representative Bob Smith, a conservative eastern Oregon Republican with whom he served on the House Agriculture Forestry Subcommittee. Smith took Jontz to a meeting in his district on the timber situation. "I discovered there was a civil war going on, but you wouldn't have known it from the Northwest delegation or from the national environmental groups at that time," Jontz said.

In 1989 Jontz returned to Oregon to attend a forest reform conference organized by forest economist Randal O'Toole, who had become the nation's foremost advocate of incentive-based solutions to the federal timber conflict. O'Toole was convinced that if the Forest Service got more of its money from recreation and hunting and wildlife viewing fees and less from timber receipts, it would shift its priorities and begin managing the forests for those purposes. It was a view not wholeheartedly shared by his compatriots within the environmental community.

At the conference, Jontz described how Northwest lawmakers were using the appropriations process to override court decisions affecting national forests. Afterward he toured the beautiful Metolius River Basin of central Oregon with forest ecologist Jerry Franklin and met with forest activists, who told him they had no hope that the Northwest delegation would support legislation to protect old-growth forests. Jontz said, "I'll help."

In the spring of 1990, Jontz introduced the Ancient Forest Protection Act, written by James Monteith and Brock Evans, among others. The bill called for setting up a process by which a group of independent scientists would choose areas worthy of protection in a system of ancient forest reserves based on their ecological significance. Though it was opposed by the entire Northwest congressional delegation, the Jontz bill eventually attracted 145 sponsors.

Over the next two years many other bills offering solutions to the forest impasse surfaced. Republican Senator Bob Packwood of Oregon introduced a bill written by the timber industry; Oregon's four Democratic House members introduced a middle-of-the-road forest protection bill. Democratic Representative George Miller of California introduced a bill offering relatively high levels of protection. None of them, including the Jontz bill, got as far as a vote on the House or Senate floor.

Environmentalists had enough power by then to stop a bad bill, but not enough power to pass a good one.

FREE-LANCING

By 1990 some activists had gone on the road with their message about what was happening to the forests of the Pacific Northwest.

Lou Gold's winter road show was building a national constituency for protection of old-growth forests in the Siskiyous. Passionate and articulate, Gold touched people everywhere he went with his words and images.

Tim Hermach, a Eugene businessman and member of the Sierra Club Many Rivers Group, became a convert to the forest preservation movement after he reviewed the Willamette National Forest Plan. Hermach, a volatile and uncompromising activist, found the plan full of unwarranted assumptions about how much old-growth timber the Willamette could sell in the 1990s and how fast it could grow new trees to replace the native stands. In 1988, frustrated with the Sierra Club's incremental approach to halting the destruction of ancient forests, he formed the Native Forest Council to promote a devastatingly simple proposition: zero cut on the national forests.

Hermach scraped together $2,500 and published the first issue of *Forest Voice*, a tabloid that featured photos of the ugliest clearcuts in the Northwest, including many on the Olympic National Forest's Shelton Unit. He had 25,000 copies printed initially and sent them to Sierra Club members and other activists around the country. Eventually 1 million copies of that first issue circulated, delivering a payload of shocking images to a national audience.

In the early 1990s Hermach became a favorite environmental source for East Coast reporters who were trying to sort out the tangled Northwest forest conflict for readers far from the scene of battle. His zero cut message had the ring of integrity and the beauty of simplicity. He believed that only a national campaign could save native forests. "I was always of the opinion that the forest issue could not be resolved forest by forest, state by state, or region by region," he said. "It was a national policy issue of concern to all Americans."

In 1989 former Earth First! activists Mitch Friedman and Ric Bailey bought a 730-year-old Douglas-fir log from a Port Angeles, Washington, timber exporter for $3,040, loaded the behemoth onto a flatbed truck, and drove it across the country to introduce the rest of America to the magnificence of the ancient forests that were falling in the Pacific Northwest.

Mark Winstein had recently sold his business in St. Louis and was looking for new challenges. He caught the Ancient Forest Rescue Expedition in a St. Louis parking lot and was moved to instant political commitment. Winstein had visited Washington's Olympic Peninsula and had hiked in the surreal Hoh River rainforest. He had never forgotten it.

When he asked what he could do, Mitch Friedman told him about Randal O'Toole's forest reform conference in Oregon. Winstein went. There he met Brock Evans and Jim Jontz. Jontz invited him to come to Washington, D.C. and work on forests as a volunteer. Winstein agreed. He rented a tiny apartment with a view of the Capitol Dome from his window.

After two months in Washington, Winstein's money was running out. He called Brock Evans at National Audubon to find out what he was doing to save ancient forests. "I was shocked to find there was no national campaign," he said. Evans offered him $1,500 to compile a data base of people who had written to Audubon saying they wanted to protect forests.

Carl Ross, a musician in Long Island, New York, also took in the Ancient Forest Rescue Expedition. Unlike Winstein, he had never set foot in the Pacific Northwest. Nevertheless, he immediately dropped everything and began proselytizing in the Big Apple to save ancient forests.

"I said, 'This is the most important thing,' and I threw myself into it," Ross recalled. "I made up ancient forest postcards and I handed them out at Jones Beach. I got up a petition to Congress. I called the local Audubon Society to get them involved. I was calling around the nation saying, 'We've got to have a national campaign.' I was like a nut."

In the fall of 1989 Ross went to a Washington, D.C., meeting of forest activists who were trying to stop the Rider from Hell. He was handed a list of congressmen and told to call them. Like Winstein, he was shocked. "I thought, 'Here's the most important issue in the world and they don't have a national campaign.'" The following February, he too tried to call Brock Evans to discuss ancient forests. Instead, he got Winstein. Ross came down to Washington. The two of them stayed up all night talking forests.

SAVE AMERICA'S FORESTS

In April of 1990, Ross and Winstein attended a forest reform pow-wow in Asheville, North Carolina, where Winstein spoke about the need for a national campaign. "I said it would cost $10,000 a month to start this. No one had any idea where it would come from." After his speech people came by to discuss the idea. Someone passed the hat and collected $500. Later, someone else sent Winstein and Ross a check for $2,000. And Save America's Forests was born.

Every legislative campaign needs a vehicle. Ross and Winstein wanted a bill that dealt with forests across the nation. They seized on a bill sponsored by Senator John Bryant, a moderate Texas Democrat, which prohibited clearcutting on the national forests. The Bryant bill wasn't going anywhere, and some mainstream groups saw it as a poorly written non-starter. But Ross and Winstein saw it as a rallying point.

From the beginning, it was scrape and hustle for Save America's Forests. Mainstream conservation groups raised money through membership dues, sale of magazines, and hefty foundation grants. At first, Ross and Winstein got no support from those traditional sources, and they got the cold shoulder from the nationals.

They decided to hold a rally in front of the Capitol, and sent out more than 4,000 postcards. Winstein's tiny apartment suddenly became the nerve center for a huge happening. On September 16, 1990, more than 800 people showed up for the Save America's Forests kickoff. The event, complete with people in animal costumes, made page one of *USA Today*.

Chapter Eighteen

A Voice in Washington

In 1990, after putting out a few newsletters, holding a few meetings, and failing to stop the Rider from Hell, the Ancient Forest Alliance faded. This first attempt by national conservation groups and Northwest activists to work together in a campaign to save old-growth forests fell victim to internal politics within the Washington, D.C., conservation establishment.

National conservation groups seldom worked together effectively, in part because they were natural competitors. They competed for members, competed for press coverage, competed for access and influence on Capitol Hill, competed for the same pool of money from environmental grantmaking foundations.

Working with grassroots forest activists 3,000 miles away in the Pacific Northwest was, in some ways, an even bigger challenge for the nationals. The chasm in values and lifestyles that separated conservation professionals inside the Washington, D.C., Beltway from tree huggers in rural communities was in some ways wider than the divide between forest activists and timber workers, who at least shared the same physical turf.

The growing professionalism of the national conservation organizations by 1990 had increased their distance from the grass roots. By then, many of the largest organizations relied on direct-mail consultants to hone their message and boost their membership, on pollsters to test the political winds, and on their own lawyers, scientists, lobbyists, and policy analysts to advance their agenda. Increasingly, they also depended on funding from large foundations. Many of these foundations weren't content to write a check; in exchange, they wanted a piece of the action—a chance to set priorities and help design campaigns.

In the Northwest, the ancient forest campaign was on a roll by 1990. It was winning in federal court and attracting national media attention. The Ancient Forest Protection Act, introduced by Representative Jim Jontz, had given the campaign a legislative tool for winning permanent protection of ancient forests. But there still was no real coordination of the forest campaign at the national level, no strategy for countering the wise-use backlash, no strategy for lobbying Congress to pass a

strong ancient forest protection bill.

CULTURE CLASH

Melanie Rowland, a Seattle attorney, experienced the clash of cultures between the nationals and the grass roots directly after she accepted a job with the Wilderness Society that frequently took her to D.C. for strategy sessions. As conservation chair for Seattle Audubon, she had experience in the grassroots world. "I was used to discussing issues," she said. "Out here in the Northwest, we'd discuss how much old growth, and where's the science, and how are we going to draw lines on the map, and which areas are really critical to protect, and what effect is it going to have on the spotted owl."

The talk around the table in D.C., she discovered, was all about access and influence, not issues. "We're sitting in a meeting and there are all these names of representatives and senators flying around. It was, 'If we do this, you can imagine what Volkmer is going to do about that,' and 'If Sid Yates won't support us on this, we're dead, so has anyone talked to Sid Yates?' And I'd say, 'Wait. Who's Volkmer? Who's Sid Yates?'"

Pragmatism was the currency of access. Lobbyists had to go to Capitol Hill with proposals that were perceived as politically viable. "If they thought you were going to come and waste their time by saying, 'Protect all old growth in the Northwest,' they wouldn't even let you in," Rowland said.

The lot of an environmental lobbyist during the Reagan-Bush years was tough, she said. "You felt assaulted, you felt like an island. And it wasn't just the administration. Congress, although nominally Democratically controlled, was not real friendly environmentally. Trying to protect ancient forests, and having to deal with the Oregon and Washington delegations, you felt anything you could accomplish was a major, major thing."

In the early 1990s, the national groups were working on myriad issues besides ancient forests, from saving the Everglades to keeping oil drilling out of the Arctic National Wildlife Refuge. The job of an environmental lobbyist was to juggle those issues.

The single-mindedness of the forest activists who made the trip to D.C. contrasted starkly with that Beltway reality, Rowland said. "They're looking at one piece of the country, one issue, and it is so important in their lives that they are willing to give up practically everything else in their lives. If they have another job, which most of them do, they're working that job full-time and the rest of their time they're working this issue, and probably next to their family it is the most important thing in their lives. And many of them don't have families. Their environmental group *is* their family, and the forest *is* their family. And the reason they are willing to make a shambles of their personal lives by spending thousands of hours working as volunteers in environmental organizations is that they are passionately, passionately dedicated to keeping the forests alive.

"Put those two world views together and what have you got? It goes beyond a failure to communicate. You grow up with completely different views of what's important, what's essential for your mental well-being, what is doable, what is not doable."

THE WESTERN ANCIENT FOREST CAMPAIGN

By 1990, James Monteith realized that although the national conservation groups had brought national publicity to the destruction of ancient forests, they were not inclined to help finance a regional grassroots political campaign to win permanent protection for those forests. As executive director of the Oregon Natural Resources Council, he had been wooing small foundations since 1988, trying to raise money for a national campaign that grassroots activists could run themselves, with their own lobbyist based in Washington, D.C.

By early 1991 the time was ripe for an infusion of serious foundation money into the campaign. The Seattle-based Bullitt Foundation had received a large bequest from Dorothy S. Bullitt, the recently deceased matriarch of a national media empire, and was about to become a major player in Northwest environmental politics.

The Pew Charitable Trusts, a Philadelphia-based foundation built on the Sun Oil fortune, had recently reorganized. Its board of directors wanted forests to be a focus and had considered a tropical rainforest campaign. But Josh Reichert, who had been hired by Pew to develop an environmental program, argued that the foundation should start closer to home, by investing in saving the ancient forests of the Pacific Northwest.

The major foundations supporting environmental causes had formed Environmental Grantmakers to coordinate their philanthropic programs. It was Donald Ross of the Rockefeller Family Fund, coordinator of Environmental Grantmakers, who suggested that the foundations create a new group to represent the grass roots in D.C.

"There seemed to be agreement that the issue needed to be nationalized," Tom Wathen of Pew said. "You needed a media campaign to get people in other parts of the country to care. What we found was that there was no strategy, no idea of what they wanted and how they were going to get there."

"The movement was a little dysfunctional," agreed Bill Lazar, president of the Portland-based Lazar Foundation. "Things were happening quickly. People were speaking with many voices and many tongues. We thought the best thing to do was to jumpstart it and get out of the way."

In January of 1991, Lazar called Bonnie Phillips of Pilchuck Audubon at her home in Stanwood, Washington, and asked her to come to Portland for a meeting about forming a new organization that would work in Washington, D.C., to represent grassroots forest protection groups in the Northwest. "I was already overwhelmed," Phillips recalled. "But I understood the need. Grassroots groups had no power."

Out of the January meeting came the Western Ancient Forest Campaign, created to build a national constituency for saving ancient forests through permanent legislation. To assure geographic representation, Lazar asked Phillips, Monteith, Julie Norman of the southern Oregon group Headwaters, and Tim McKay of the Northcoast Environmental Center in Arcata, California, to serve as the new organization's board of directors. Monteith left the Oregon Natural Resources Council, his home for 17 years, to become the campaign's executive vice president.

A NEW PLAYER IN TOWN
In April of 1991, WAFC hired lobbyist Jim Owens to become the new organization's Washington, D.C.–based campaign director. Owens had lobbied successfully for designation of the Smith River National Recreation Area in northern California. No one in the Northwest wanted the job; the joke was that because it required the successful candidate to live in the nation's capitol, anyone who applied would have to be rejected on grounds of insanity.

The WAFC board of directors saw a need to make grassroots groups comfortable with the new D.C.–based campaign. But there wasn't much time. "The funders wanted to move quickly," Phillips said. "They felt there was no mechanism in place and it would take too long. I made sure we had one good grassroots group for each one of the seven national forests in Washington. But we never came up with a decision-making process to answer the question, How does Jim Owens know what to say on behalf of the grass roots?"

"We had no sense of democracy or process of any kind, but we figured the four of us could reassure everyone of the opportunity and its remarkable potential," Monteith recalled. "Eventually we'd work on democracy, but right now we had a war to fight."

Owens hit the ground running in D.C. One week after he opened the office, he sent activists in the Northwest a complete briefing paper on the politics of ancient forests inside the Beltway. At the same time Fran Hunt, a lobbyist for the National Wildlife Federation, and Kevin Kirchner, the Sierra Club Legal Defense Fund's new D.C. lobbyist, had been deployed to work full-time on forest issues. A new cast of characters was emerging. Not only was the forest campaign getting funding, it was gaining prominence and attracting new members to the national groups.

But the nationals initially fought funding for the Western Ancient Forest Campaign, which they saw as competition for foundation dollars—and as evidence of their own failure to advance the ancient forest agenda. It took a year of hard work before Owens gained acceptance within the conservation establishment's inner circle.

START-UP PAINS
The campaign suffered another setback in its first year, this one over money and lobbying. Because WAFC did not yet have tax-exempt status, Headwaters had agreed to be the campaign's fiscal sponsor. That

meant the Headwaters board had to be intimately involved in WAFC's financial affairs—a situation that created escalating tension between Monteith, WAFC's chief fundraiser, and Norman, the president of Headwaters.

Monteith threw himself into an aggressive fundraising campaign. Over WAFC's first 14 months, he raised nearly $1 million in foundation grants. Meanwhile, Owens was lobbying Congress hard on behalf of the Jontz Ancient Forest Protection Bill. This made Norman nervous. She and Monteith disagreed on how much money the campaign could spend to lobby Congress under tax laws governing nonprofits. By the summer of 1992 the Headwaters board was refusing to release money to cover the campaign's expenses, precipitating a temporary cash flow crisis. In September of 1992, Norman alerted funders to her concern.

At a November 1992 board meeting, both Norman and Monteith resigned from the WAFC board. The hard feelings between them persisted long afterward. "It was horrible," Bonnie Phillips said. "Both of them showed a great deal of class in not having this explode within the environmental community."

Norman refuses to discuss the episode. But Phillips says that, in spite of everything, Monteith got WAFC off on the right foot. "I am eternally grateful to James Monteith. He was the only one with enough vision and insight to see how to make it happen."

The Western Ancient Forest Campaign became a home base for visiting forest activists. They brought their maps and photographs and their passion for the forests to the nation's capital and tried to communicate that passion to congressional staffers who had never seen an ancient forest.

THE BIG TIME

But the foundations still weren't persuaded that all the pieces were in place for an effective national campaign. Pete Myers, of the W. Alton Jones Foundation, obtained a timber industry video that employed sophisticated television ads to counter the ancient forest message. Alarmed, Myers commissioned an outside analysis to determine where the ancient forest campaign stood.

Soon after, the foundations created yet another new D.C.-based organization, Americans for the Ancient Forests, to mount a national media campaign. They hired Bob Chlopak, a Washington insider who had worked for the Democratic National Committee, and gave him a budget of $1.5 million to run it.

Chlopak retained a high-powered public relations firm to produce radio spots on the logging of the last ancient forests, featuring the strains of a harmonica and the whine of a chainsaw. He sent out sophisticated press packets aimed primarily at the national media.

Chlopak had excellent access to Democratic leaders in Congress. He joined Owens in lobbying for passage of the Jontz bill. But the entry of big-time Beltway politics into the campaign rubbed some grassroots groups back in the Northwest the wrong way. They considered Chlopak, and to a lesser extent Owens, outsiders. And some of them were chafing under the controlling hand of their Pew patrons.

GOING ALL OUT

A Voice in Washington

Save America's Forests was already in business when the Western Ancient Forest Campaign arrived in town in mid-1991. If the national groups gave WAFC the cold shoulder, WAFC in turn spurned these penniless, rough-around-the-edges upstarts. Carl Ross, co-founder of Save America's Forests, said Jim Owens told him in an early meeting that he wouldn't help him, but he would use his organization shamelessly for his own ends.

By then Save America's Forests had built a loose-knit coalition of several hundred groups and businesses that worked on forest issues. Save America's Forests became a crash pad for itinerant activists. "We were a hand-to-mouth operation," Ross said. "We went out and got discarded furniture from in front of police stations. We got used computers. We stretched our bills out." When the money dried up, they took cash advances on Mark Winstein's credit cards to pay the rent.

Its pecuniary state didn't stop Save America's Forests from throwing everything it had at campaigns it considered crucial. In 1992, when Jim Jontz faced a rough reelection campaign in Indiana, the office emptied out as the entire staff went to work on his campaign.

While the Western Ancient Forest Campaign focused on the old-growth forests of the Pacific Northwest, Ross and Winstein worked tirelessly to bring the various regions of the country and the disparate groups in D.C. together on forest issues. At the time, the forest campaign was split regionally. "Each region thought its own campaign was the most important," Ross said. "The Northwest had the biggest trees; the Northern Rockies had the biggest roadless areas."

Late in their second year, with $1,000 in the bank, Ross and Winstein got word that an unacceptable Montana wilderness bill was nearing passage in Congress. The Senate version, sponsored by Max Baucus, a Montana Democrat, and Conrad Burns, a Republican, proposed to protect 1.1 million acres of rocks and ice while releasing 4 million acres of roadless national forest land for logging. Save America's Forests spent its last $1,000 putting out a postcard mailing all over the country, telling members to urge their representatives in Congress to defeat it.

The Baucus–Burns wilderness bill did go down to defeat. But after the Montana campaign, Ross and Winstein were flat broke. "In the winter of 1992," Ross said, "we sent out a little postcard to our members printed on a dot-matrix printer saying, 'We desperately need your help. Can you send us $100? If you don't send us money, we can't pay our rent and we won't survive.'" The mailing raised $15,000. Save America's Forests was rescued from extinction.

The push to get a strong Northwest ancient forest bill through Congress ended in 1992. The Jontz Ancient Forest Protection Act never gathered enough momentum to overcome the Northwest congressional delegation's opposition. On June 17, 1992, another strong ancient forest protection bill came close to passage in the House Interior Committee, which was chaired by Democratic Representative George Miller of California. Environmental lobbyists believed they had the votes for passage, but at the last minute House Speaker Tom Foley, a Democrat from eastern Washington, pulled the plug. Foley sent his aide Nick Ashmore into the committee hearing room to speak privately with several committee members, and the slim margin for passage disappeared.

In November of 1992, Jontz was defeated for reelection. His bill died with his departure from Congress. The following January, with the election of a new administration, the action would move to the executive branch of government.

Jack Ward Thomas, a Forest Service wildlife biologist and chief architect of President Clinton's Northwest Forest Plan, became chief of the Forest Service in late 1993.

James Monteith, an early visionary in the forest protection movement, headed the Oregon Natural Resources Council from its inception in the 1970s until he left to help direct the Western Ancient Forest Campaign in 1991.

Andy Kerr, conservation director of the Oregon Natural Resources Council, plots strategy on the run during a lobbying trip to Washington, D.C. In the early 1990s, Kerr's uncompromising stance and mastery of punchy sound bites made him the best-known spokesman for the ancient forest campaign.

Senator Mark Hatfield, here with James Monteith at a 1988 meeting of the Oregon Natural Resources Council, was the timber industry's most powerful friend in Congress for 30 years.

© Elizabeth Feryl

© Elizabeth Feryl

© Elizabeth Feryl

U.S. District Judge William Dwyer in Seattle played a crucial role in the campaign to save ancient forests when he issued a series of injunctions that in effect placed the forests under the protection of the federal courts for five years.

Julie Norman, president of the southern Oregon environmental group Headwaters, spoke up for protection of all remaining old-growth forests and roadless areas at President Clinton's Northwest Forest Conference.

Lou Gold, sage of the Siskiyous, traveled the country with a slide show describing the beauty of the Siskiyou old-growth forests and the imminent threat facing them under Forest Service logging plans.

Vic Sher, managing attorney in the Seattle office of the Sierra Club Legal Defense Fund, helped map the pathbreaking litigation strategy that won injunctions blocking continued logging of old-growth forests inhabited by the northern spotted owl.

Indiana Democratic Congressman Jim Jontz took on the challenge of introducing a strong ancient forest protection bill after touring an Oregon old-growth forest in 1989.

© Sky Shiviah

© Elizabeth Feryl

On Dec. 16, 1995, Tim Ream broke bread to end a 75-day fluids-only fast outside the federal courthouse in Eugene, Oregon. Ream fasted to draw attention to the salvage rider and to demand open public debate about "logging without laws."

Jeff DeBonis, a timber sale planner on the Willamette National Forest, founded a dissident group called the Association of Forest Service Employees for Environmental Ethics after seeing firsthand the effects of clearcut logging on federal land in Western Oregon.

© Elizabeth Feryl

Brock Evans (at left, with Argon Steel of National Audubon and Rick Brown of the National Wildlife Federation at a meeting of forest activists in 1992) played an important role in Northwest environmental politics for nearly 30 years.

Tonia Wolf, an Oregon forest activist, felt the hostility of her rural neighbors as she worked in isolation to save the old-growth ponderosa pines of the Ochoco National Forest.

© Trygve Steen

Left: *Bonnie Phillips joined the Pilchuck Audubon Chapter in Everett, Washington, in the late 1980s and quickly became a power in Washington forest protection politics.*

Tim Hermach of Eugene founded the Native Forest Council *to promote zero cut on national forests and published the tabloid* Forest Voice *to publicize the destruction caused by clearcutting in the Northwest.*

Mitch Friedman, a former Earth First! activist, founded the Greater Ecosystem Alliance (later renamed the Northwest Ecosystem Alliance) in Bellingham, Washington, to work for protection of large roadless areas in Washington and British Columbia.

Jim Britell of Kalmiopsis Audubon in Port Orford, Oregon, brought East Coast political street smarts to the Northwest ancient forest campaign.

Jim Rogers, a former timber cruiser, founded Friends of the Elk River to protect a matchless salmon stream on Oregon's South Coast.

Four prominent forestry experts known as the Gang of Four (from left: John Gordon, dean of the Yale University College of Forestry; Jack Ward Thomas, senior Forest Service wildlife biologist; K. Norman Johnson, Oregon State University forestry professor; and Jerry Franklin, University of Washington forest ecologist) delivered to Congress a menu of options for protecting spotted owls, marbled murrelets, and coastal salmon runs.

Valerie Johnson of the Oregon Lands Coalition, a passionate advocate for timber workers in the early 1990s, entered the lion's den when she agreed to speak before her adversaries at an environmental law conference in Eugene.

Forest activists from across the nation came to Oregon to plan strategy at a conference organized by forest economist Randal O'Toole in early 1993.

U.S. Senator Slade Gorton, a Washington Republican, shows off a plaque from the Northwest Forestry Association expressing its appreciation for "10,000 acres" of old-growth timber Gorton helped deliver to the industry through his support of the 1995 timber salvage rider.

Chapter Nineteen

Salmon Are an Old-Growth Species

The life cycle of the wild Pacific salmon is one of the great mysteries of nature. Spawned in cold mountain streams or lakes, the salmon smolt is imprinted with the memory of its birthplace. Young salmon carry that memory with them as they float downstream with the current, spend their adult lives at sea, and finally return to the exact bed where they were hatched, there to spawn and die. Salmon are as much a part of the Northwest's natural heritage as its great conifer forests.

Historically, the lower reaches of streams provided the most productive salmon spawning habitat. But heavy logging on downstream private lands throughout the 20th century steadily pushed salmon into the headwaters of streams on public land. By the 1980s, streams on both public and private land across the Northwest had been trashed. Logging and careless road-building on unstable soils had triggered landslides, burying salmon spawning areas in silt. Removal of large conifers along streambanks had deprived fish of resting pools and cooling shade.

East of the Cascades, logging and road-building, livestock grazing along streams, and large withdrawals of water for irrigation all contributed to severe stream degradation. Entire stocks of salmon and steelhead that had once spawned in Northwest streams were lost, a natural bounty squandered.

Yet despite growing documentation of the damage, federal and state forestry officials dragged their feet on protecting habitat for salmon and steelhead throughout the 1970s and 1980s. Ranchers' and farmers' groups fiercely fought restrictions on their grazing privileges and water rights. Timber companies wanted the big conifers that grew on valley bottoms, near streams.

Federal and state fisheries biologists in the Pacific Northwest seethed in silence over the loss of unique salmon and steelhead stocks and the damage inflicted on their habitat. In 1991, as irrefutable evidence of stream degradation and salmon declines accumulated, they broke their silence. The plight of Pacific salmon spilled over into the evolving forest protection debate—and transformed that debate virtually overnight. *165*

THE OREGON RIVERS COUNCIL

Bob Doppelt, Chicago-born and educated at Lewis & Clark College in Portland, forsook a career as a counseling psychologist to become a river rat and outfitter in Oregon. By the mid-1980s, his customers were beginning to complain about poor fishing on Oregon's Rogue and Deschutes Rivers and on the Salmon River in Idaho. Doppelt began thinking about the need to protect the wild, free-flowing rivers of his adopted state.

On a float trip through the Grand Canyon in 1985, he read *Encounters with the Archdruid,* John McPhee's classic portrait of conservation legend David Brower, which described Brower's unsuccessful battle against the Bureau of Reclamation's Glen Canyon Dam. Soon after his return he contacted two friends about starting a river protection group. They liked the idea. So did Senator Mark Hatfield. "Hatfield was looking for a legacy, and he knew the old-growth battle would get worse," Doppelt recalled. Protecting rivers seemed less controversial than protecting valuable commercial forests. In 1987 the Oregon Rivers Council, a coalition of 28 groups ranging from the Oregon Kayaking and Canoe Club to the National Wildlife Federation, made its debut on Oregon's environmental scene.

The National Wild and Scenic Rivers Act, passed by Congress in 1968, provided a vehicle for protecting free-flowing river sections from dams and destructive development. In 1988 the council, working closely with the Sierra Club and with Hatfield, won passage of the Oregon Omnibus Wild and Scenic Rivers Act, the first-ever comprehensive statewide rivers protection act passed by Congress. The 1988 bill protected 40 Oregon rivers and river sections in their free-flowing state—a total of 1,500 river miles and 500,000 acres of adjacent land—and required federal agencies to develop plans to preserve the wild, scenic, and recreational values of these areas.

Getting a bill through Congress and getting the agencies to take it seriously were two different things, however. By the early 1990s the Forest Service and Bureau of Land Management still were dragging their feet on writing plans to protect the designated streams from harmful logging, livestock grazing, and development. They had taken no steps to limit damage on private land bordering protected streams. Doppelt realized he had underestimated the agencies' ability to stall and finesse. And most of the state's rivers, those left out of the bill, still had no protection.

"I started wondering, What have we accomplished for fish?" Doppelt said. He began talking to fisheries biologists about what true protection of river systems would require.

THE ANDREWS WORKSHOP

In October of 1990, Doppelt and Charlie Dewberry, the council's recently hired fish habitat specialist, organized a workshop at the H. J. Andrews Experimental Forest near Blue River, Oregon, to discuss fish protection. They invited many of the nation's top fisheries and aquatic biologists. Most of the invited scientists subscribed to a school of thought on stream protection known as the "river continuum concept." An outgrowth of a six-year National Science Foundation project, its premise was that a river's functions could be understood only by studying its entire ecosystem, from headwaters to estuary and from floodplain to ridgeline.

To Doppelt's amazement, almost everyone accepted the invitation. Fifteen of the nation's leading experts on rivers and fisheries attended, including prominent Forest Service research biologists Jim Sedell and Gordon Reeves. "When we asked why they would come to a meeting called by a relatively small river conservation group, they said it was because no one had asked them to help put their research into policy form before," Doppelt said. "They had written a report for the National Science Foundation and it had sat on a shelf."

The biologists were sharply critical of fish protection standards in the Forest Service's new national forest plans. They said the 100-foot unlogged buffer strips the plans required along major fish-bearing streams were inadequate. They said the plans also should require buffers along streams with no fish and along streams that flowed only part of the year as well, because those smaller streams carried sediment downstream to where the fish were. They said entire floodplains, not just narrow strips along streambanks, should be considered in aquatic conservation plans. They talked about the need to protect the refugia—the last best habitat for fish. Jim Sedell came up with the slogan, "Protect the best, restore the rest."

After the meeting, Doppelt convened a team of Oregon fisheries biologists, who drew rough maps of the most intact watersheds remaining on the Pacific Coast. Doppelt laid them over a map of the wild and scenic rivers protected by the Oregon Wild and Scenic Rivers Act. There was almost no overlap.

The Andrews gathering was to prove a seminal conference—one of the first gatherings at which leading aquatic scientists from federal and state agencies and universities discussed their vision of watershed protection in policy terms. It jelled professional opinion about what needed to be done. The principles articulated during the two-day meeting—protect riparian areas and key watersheds, protect the best refugia, don't just put a Band-Aid on places that are hemorrhaging—soon became the standard for stream protection across the Northwest. Out of them came the Rivers Council's aquatic conservation strategy, federal stream protection standards for salmon, steelhead, and bull trout, and the concepts that would provide the foundation for President Clinton's Northwest Forest Plan in 1993.

In 1993, Doppelt changed the name of his organization to the Pacific Rivers Council to reflect its expanding range of concern.

SALMON AT THE CROSSROADS
On the heels of the Andrews conference, in March of 1991, the American Fisheries Society published a startling report, "Pacific Salmon at

the Crossroads," by fisheries biologists Willa Nehlson, Jim Lichatowich, and Jack Williams. The three compiled the report from field data gathered by fisheries biologists all over the country. The Crossroads report warned that 214 runs of naturally spawning Pacific salmon were in decline and at risk of extinction. It said many factors, including hydroelectric dams on the Columbia River and overfishing in the ocean, were responsible for this crisis. But it laid a large part of the blame on habitat loss and timber operations, especially in undammed streams where coastal coho salmon spawned.

The report's release prompted a major story in the *New York Times*. Soon after, the Washington, Oregon, and California chapters of the American Fisheries Society did their own studies of Pacific salmon runs. They identified still more stocks in decline. The 30-page report reached many of the same conclusions biologists had agreed upon at the Andrews conference. It stressed that wild salmon stocks must be preserved to maintain the natural genetic diversity that would allow them to survive ecological disturbances and climatic changes. And it called for "a new paradigm that advances habitat restoration and ecosystem function."

GANG OF FOUR

In 1991, ancient forest legislation was going nowhere in Congress. Jim Lyons, staff forester for the House Agriculture Committee, came up with an idea to get things moving by providing members of Congress with a menu of options from which they could build forest protection legislation.

Lyons knew Forest Service wildlife biologist Jack Ward Thomas, University of Washington forest ecologist Jerry Franklin, and Yale University Forestry Dean John Gordon from their days together on the Society of American Foresters old-growth study team in the mid-1980s. He knew Norm Johnson, the Oregon State University forest economist who had developed the computer program used in national forest planning to project timber yields. Lyons persuaded Harold Volkmer, the Missouri Democrat who chaired the forestry subcommittee of House Agriculture, to appoint the four to a new team that would develop options for protecting owls and other old-growth species. Volkmer told the team, "Don't surprise me with some damn fish."

The new team, immediately dubbed the Gang of Four, commandeered a large convention hall in Portland and enlisted scientists and resource specialists from all over the Northwest for the crash project. Bob Doppelt saw his chance. He called Norm Johnson and invited him to come to Eugene and have a look at his watershed maps. Doppelt put a mylar map of old-growth reserves developed by spotted owl biologists on top of the map of key watersheds. This time, there was a 60 to 70 percent overlap. "We said, 'Of course the best habitat for the owl is going to be the best habitat for the salmon,'" Doppelt recalled. "It's the last intact forest. It's the roadless areas, primarily." Johnson, intrigued, asked Doppelt to suggest some fisheries biologists who could confirm the information. Doppelt put him in touch with Gordon Reeves and Jim Sedell. Sedell and Reeves, two of the Forest Service's strongest advocates for protection of fish habitat, joined the team, making it the Gang of Four Plus Two.

Reeves had recently done battle with the national forest side of his agency over two proposed timber sales in the North Fork of the Elk River on Oregon's South Coast. His research in the North Fork since 1985 had led Reeves to conclude that this stream produced more coho salmon per mile than any other coastal stream outside Alaska.

In August of 1990, the Siskiyou National Forest advertised two sales in the high reaches of the North Fork watershed. Jim Rogers of the environmental group Friends of Elk River sued to stop the sales. The Forest Service auctioned them anyway.

When Reeves learned his own agency planned to log in the North Fork watershed, he warned the acting Siskiyou forest supervisor that cutting trees on its steep, unstable soils would harm the North Fork's world-class fishery. In January, recognizing it had a losing case on its hands, the Siskiyou National Forest withdrew the sales.

Jim Sedell had recently conducted an important research project focusing on the loss of salmon habitat in the Upper Grande Ronde River of northeastern Oregon, a critical spawning area for endangered Snake River spring chinook. Between 1957 and 1989, numbers of adult spring chinook in the 240,000-acre basin had dropped from about 3,000 to fewer than 400.

Sedell and a colleague counted the number of large pools in the Upper Grande Ronde and compared their 1991 findings with those from a similar survey done 50 years earlier. They found the number of deep pools, where salmon rest on their return journey to spawn, had declined by 59 percent as sediment from logging, grazing, and roads washed into the river. The findings provided some of the most solid evidence yet that land management activities were contributing to the salmon's demise.

THE WATERSHED OPTION

At the Portland convention center, 200 scientists and resource specialists spent several weeks poring over maps, transparencies, and field notes. Finally, a watershed option took shape. It defined 137 "key watersheds" critical to the survival of Pacific salmon, from the Canadian border to San Francisco Bay and east to the Snake River in Idaho. Some of these watersheds provided habitat for threatened fish stocks. Others contained exceptionally high-quality habitat and pure water. Within all of them, the scientists proposed removing or storm-proofing old logging roads to prevent erosion, logging on a 180-year rotation to avoid disturbing recovering soils, leaving wider unlogged buffers along streams, and keeping roads out of roadless areas. This watershed option quickly became the new standard in the evolving forest discussion.

On July 24, 1991, the Gang of Four released its report to Congress. It revealed that protecting salmon would carry a high price tag. Under even the least restrictive watershed option, the annual timber yield from federal lands in the spotted owl region would decline from 2.6 billion board feet to 1.5 billion board feet.

But political opposition to the concept was muted. Salmon, unlike spotted owls, were a resource the Northwest valued and identified with. Salmon also produced jobs—in commercial and sport fishing and in coastal fishing communities.

Within the top levels of the Forest Service, the implications of the Gang of Four report ticked like a time bomb with a short fuse. The agency appointed two task forces to review salmon protection measures in the new forest plans. The review was overdue. Each national forest had been left to its own discretion on how much protection to provide for fish in the new forest plans. Not surprisingly, the plans, when they finally came out, varied widely.

In August 1991, a regional panel reported that the new plans were not specific enough to determine whether or not they would protect the long-term viability of native fish runs. In October of 1991, Jeffrey Kershner, national manager of Forest Service fish habitat programs, strongly endorsed the Gang of Four's fish protection measures, saying they would provide "a strong basis for a conservation strategy" for sensitive wild fish across the region.

There was no way out of it. Like it or not, the Forest Service would have to start taking fish protection seriously in the owl forests west of the Cascades.

RETREAT ON THE GRANDE RONDE

East of the Cascades, in the realm of the Snake River salmon, the Forest Service continued to stall on salmon protection, even with the full power of the Endangered Species Act breathing down its neck. Though dams on the Columbia and Snake Rivers were largely responsible for decimating the wild Snake River runs, Jim Sedell's research on large pools and other studies had documented the heavy toll exacted by logging, livestock grazing, and road-building.

The listing of the Snake River chinook and sockeye salmon appeared imminent when Senator Mark Hatfield convened a salmon summit in October of 1990 to try to head off legal gridlock over wild salmon. He asked federal agencies to agree to voluntary salmon-protection measures. Participants included not only state and federal agencies but also the Indian tribes of the Columbia Basin: the Confederated Tribes of the Warm Springs, the Yakama Indian Nation, the Confederated Tribes of the Umatilla Indian Reservation, and the Nez Perce.

These tribes had harvested the abundant salmon of the Columbia and Snake Rivers for commerce, subsistence, and spiritual ceremonies over many thousands of years. Though their best fishing places had been drowned by Columbia and Snake River dams, they retained treaty rights, upheld by the federal courts, to fish for salmon at usual and accustomed areas. The question by 1990 was whether or not there would be any fish left in the river for them to take.

At Vey Meadow in northeast Oregon, the Grande Ronde flows out of the logged, mined, and grazed Wallowa–Whitman National Forest across a broad valley on its way to its confluence with the Snake. Vey Meadow lies within the 6.4-million-acre territory the Confederated Tribes of the Umatilla ceded to the U.S. government in 1855. Fallen logs and snags are few and far between in this stretch of the river, and the shading willows are gone, a casualty of cattle grazing. Without shade, summer temperatures can exceed a fish-killing 70 degrees Fahrenheit.

When he was a boy growing up on the Umatilla Reservation, Michael Farrow came to Vey Meadow to learn how to hook a salmon. But when the number of spawners began to decline sharply in 1977, the tribe closed its own Grande Ronde salmon fishery. Farrow, who eventually became the director of natural resources for the Umatilla Tribes, regretted that his own sons had never fished the Upper Grande Ronde.

In 1991, the Forest Service agreed to participate with biologists and hydrologists from the Umatilla and Nez Perce tribes, the Columbia River Inter-Tribal Fish Commission, and the state of Oregon in developing a restoration plan for this critical spawning area. The resulting plan to bring salmon back to all the spawning streams of the Upper Grande Ronde was a model, one Farrow believed should be adopted throughout the Blue Mountains.

It recommended establishment of protective stream buffers, restoration of native plant communities in floodplains, the return of woody debris to the river channel, and reestablishment of the river's natural course. It set forth processes for cleaning up mining wastes, reducing road densities, and restricting or prohibiting livestock grazing near streams.

Farrow promptly implemented the recommendations on the Umatilla Reservation. Among other changes, the tribe stopped cutting trees larger than 16 inches in diameter along salmon streams and prohibited logging on slopes greater than 35 percent. But the Forest Service lacked the political will to follow through. Though the Wallowa–Whitman National Forest supervisor agreed to the tough new standards, ranchers and timber companies opposed it, and in May of 1992, Forest Service Regional Forester John Lowe killed it.

In 1994, the Forest Service offered a much weaker Upper Grande Ronde plan. Farrow sent a scorching letter to the local district ranger, asserting that the agency's new plan violated the federal government's trust obligation to tribes in the basin.

"The spring chinook population in the Upper Grande Ronde is no longer strong enough to withstand the political machinations that the La Grande District has allowed during the last two years," he wrote. "These fish can no longer wait for you to attempt to gain political consensus. The compromises made in the draft conservation strategy, and the 97 years it has taken the U.S. Forest Service to begin planning for watershed conservation, will combine to result in the loss of these precious and ancient fish."

Chapter Twenty

The Forgotten Forests

In the early 1990s, as the owl wars raged west of the Cascades, a quieter and more complex forest drama was building over the great pine forests of eastern Oregon and eastern Washington.

Like the old-growth forests of the rainy Pacific slope, the open, arid forests of the Intermountain West had been transformed by a century of overcutting. But these forests had no spotted owl—no single species closely associated with all forest types east of the Cascades—to represent them in court. And the selective logging typical on these forests wasn't as visually shocking as the stark geometry of westside clearcuts.

Eastside forest activists, thinly scattered across a vast region, had to devise a different strategy if they hoped to save the last of the stately old-growth ponderosa pine and western larch. In 1992, after several years spent laying the groundwork, they made their move.

The forests of the east side were even more fragmented than those west of the Cascades. Giant pines had been logged for railroad ties, for timbers to shore up mine shafts, and for log cabins to house the miners, ranchers, and loggers who settled this country of harsh climate and scarce water. In time, a timber industry grew up, focused on the big yellow-belly ponderosas, so named for their fine yellow-hued wood. High-grading—the practice of taking the most valuable pine and larch and leaving the less valuable conifer species behind—was so visible that by the 1990s the Forest Service itself was forced to acknowledge what was written across the landscape.

In the 1980s, when national forest planners east of the Cascades conducted inventories of old growth, they discovered they had far less than they had believed. On central Oregon's Deschutes National Forest, where the new inventories showed a 40 percent disparity, the agency was forced to make steep reductions in logging levels.

In 1989, the National Audubon Society reached cooperative agreements with national forest supervisors in eastern Oregon and eastern Washington to conduct updated, on-the-ground inventories of old-growth stands east of the Cascades and field test the agency's own reports. The unusual arrangement, part of Audubon's national Adopt-a-Forest program, would give the Forest Service its first credible information on the extent of eastside old growth. And it would give conservationists ammunition to launch an effective eastside forest protection campaign.

A handful of eastside activists had worked tirelessly since the 1970s to protect the roadless areas of eastern Oregon and eastern Washington. They won an important victory in 1984 with designation of the 121,400-acre North Fork John Day Wilderness, which preserved habitat for large herds of deer and elk and a free-flowing salmon stream in the rugged Blue Mountains. But by the close of the 1980s, most forests east of the Cascades remained open to logging and livestock grazing.

Volunteers in the Audubon forest mapping project ventured into remote draws and rugged canyons, often on foot or horseback, to look for pockets of old-growth ponderosa pine, western larch, and, on wetter sites, Douglas-fir and white fir. They used aerial photos, logging records, and other Forest Service data to narrow their search. They explored valleys that logging roads had not yet reached. What they found revealed not only the scarcity of old growth but also the fragmented condition of the heavily roaded eastside national forests.

A FOREST HEALTH "EMERGENCY"

In the late 1980s spruce budworms, pine bark beetles, and Douglas-fir tussock moths began munching their way across 2 million acres of the Blue Mountains in northeastern Oregon. A crisis mentality gripped the Forest Service with the first reports of this "forest health emergency" east of the Cascades.

The reasons for the epidemic of defoliating and tree-killing insects were complex. Fifty years of fire suppression and a century of high-grade logging and livestock grazing had dramatically altered the composition of the eastside forests. In many logged areas, old-growth ponderosa pine, naturally resistant to insects and fire, had been replaced by dense stands of Douglas-fir and white fir, species more vulnerable to both.

From an ecological perspective, the insects were merely doing their job by thinning out these weaker trees. But in their wake they left ghostly stands of dead spires, which alarmed motorists driving along Interstate 84 through the Blue Mountains.

Fire too was a natural forest shaper east of the Cascades. Frequent natural ground fires had created the open, parklike ponderosa pine stands. Before the arrival of white settlers, native people had employed fire actively to open the forest and create habitat for game. But in the mid-20th century the Forest Service began an aggressive, almost religious campaign to snuff out forest fires. Smokey Bear drove home the message that fire, all fire, was bad for forests and wildlife. By the 1980s, fire had been excluded for so long that the forest floor in some areas was piled with dead wood—potential fuel for major stand-replacing wildfires—not only in eastern Oregon and eastern Washington but across the Intermountain West.

NO SILVER BULLET

Boyd Wickman, a Forest Service research entomologist, studied cycles of insect infestations in the forests of the Intermountain West for 25 years and in California for 10 years before that. In 1991, in a paper prepared for a research institute, Wickman warned that forest managers might have to start over to erase the mistakes of a century.

Each piece of the solution—prescribed fire, biological control of insects, and conversion of overstocked forests through thinning—would carry heavy costs and high risks, he said. Moreover, truly restoring the forests would require conserving virtually all remaining old-growth ponderosa pines in the Blue Mountains, both for their genetic traits and as a source of seed to grow healthy new pine forests.

"We will not achieve healthy forests overnight and there are no silver bullets," Wickman wrote. "We must now pay for the billions of board feet of cheap pine logged earlier in the century. We will pay and pay and probably see little or no return on our investments in our lifetime."

Wickman's paper never was formally released by the Forest Service, and Wickman's message that the remaining old-growth pines should be preserved fell on deaf ears. The Forest Service was slow to embrace the concept that fire was not the enemy in these forests or the notion that insect infestations were part of a natural cycle. Forest managers could not bear to see diseased trees "go to waste" in the forest when some of their commercial value could be salvaged by logging them.

In late 1991 the Portland regional office of the Forest Service launched a massive salvage logging campaign to cut as much of the dead timber as possible, as quickly as possible. The rush to salvage won strong support from the timber industry and from members of the Northwest congressional delegation. Platoons of Forest Service employees from forests west of the Cascades were detailed to eastside forests in a crash program to help lay out the sales.

But the loaned timber sale planners were not familiar with the ecology of Blue Mountain forests. Because most of them had no opportunity to get out on the ground during the winter, they marked sales on maps, using outdated forest inventories. Many of the "salvage" sales they laid out contained mostly healthy old-growth trees.

BLUE PAINT ON BIG TREES

In 1991, Karen Coulter moved with her partner, Asante Riverwind, and her young son, Sasha, from Washington to 40 acres of backcountry near the tiny eastern Oregon community of Spray. They lived in a yurt without running water or electricity at the edge of the Umatilla National Forest, raised goats and chickens, and kept three horses for exploring the forest at their back door. By candlelight and oil lamp, Coulter put out a newsletter, *Pacific Mountain Wildcat,* on a manual typewriter, alerting others to logging activity in northeastern Oregon.

Coulter, a longtime Earth First! activist, had decided to try to work within the mainstream to protect the forests. More than most activists, she and Asante tried to live their principles—to live lightly on the land and in harmony with their rural neighbors and local Forest Service officials. In 1992, Coulter got a seasonal job conducting a rare plant inventory for the Umatilla National Forest. At the same time, she was mapping old growth as an Adopt-a-Forest volunteer.

Coulter spent the summer of 1992 roaming the mountains and canyons of the national forest's Heppner District. In her explorations, she discovered groves of old-growth ponderosa pine in canyons the Forest Service had seldom visited. She fell in love with the old pine and larch and the creatures of the Blue Mountain forest. Her survey revealed something else: large, sound trees marked with blue paint, indicating they were to be cut as part of so-called "salvage sales" in areas infested with insects.

She and Asante obtained Forest Service studies by entomologists and forest ecologists. They read up on the role of insects in eastside forests. They concluded that many of these stands did not need salvaging. Coulter took her information to Delanne Ferguson, the Heppner district ranger, who sent a silviculturist into the field to verify her report. As a result of Coulter's on-the-ground work, Ferguson ordered changes in the district's salvage logging plan to reduce the number of sound, healthy trees removed.

Progressive district rangers like Ferguson were eager to move beyond politically driven "salvage logging" and begin practicing true forest restoration. They had drawn up plans for using prescribed burns to remove dead wood, breaking up soils compacted by grazing and logging, and repairing damaged streams. But though many eastside forests desperately needed this kind of long-term restoration, Deputy Northwest Regional Forester John Lowe told them it would be tough to justify the cost to Congress. At appropriations time, it was far easier to get money for salvage sales that benefited mills and local communities than for costly projects to heal damaged forests.

NO PLACE TO HIDE

The forest activists who took part in the mapping of eastside old growth meant everything to the campaign that was slowly taking shape in eastern Oregon and eastern Washington. They were its eyes and ears and its sturdy legs.

"Our people have been on every unit of every sale," said Judith Johnson of National Audubon, who coordinated the eastside surveys. "It's been an education for the people in the ranger districts. They've had to walk these units too. Suddenly they've had to focus on old growth, riparian zones, and wildlife. The whole process has enabled Forest Service employees to do their jobs better."

Yet eastside activists knew they couldn't count on political support for saving forests, either in Congress or in their own communities.

Environmentalists east of the Cascades walked a precarious line. Unable to hide behind the anonymity that cities offer, they were highly visible in isolated communities that lived by logging, grazing, and farming. Their allies were hundreds of miles away. Their adversaries stood next to them in line at the grocery check-out stand.

Living in conservative rural communities required them to eschew the deliberately inflammatory rhetoric of their city cousins. "You're more circumspect," said Tonia Wolf, a central Oregon activist. "I'm really aware of the consequences of the requests that I make. I have to keep checking my position to make sure I'm not on some self-indulgent trip."

Wolf worked to protect the wildlife and old-growth pines of the Ochoco National Forest. Like many eastside activists, she saw herself as the last line of defense against overcutting and overgrazing on public lands. "I'm the only one doing this on the Ochoco," she said. "If I leave it, it will die." Not just the campaign, she said. The forest itself.

Environmentalists had few congressional allies east of the Cascades. Their most influential adversary in the early 1990s was Democratic House Speaker Tom Foley, who represented an eastern Washington district. On matters affecting his home turf, no one in Congress would take Foley on.

During his long tenure in Congress, Foley had made no secret of his support for the timber industry. In 1976, during debate over the National Forest Management Act, Foley argued against an economic test for logging of "marginal lands"—those where the costs of selling timber might exceed returns to the federal treasury. He warned that such a test might bar logging "in great portions of the national forests"—including the Colville National Forest in his own House district.

In May of 1992, Foley announced that he would not support legislation to protect eastern Washington's old-growth forests. At the time, roads and clearcuts were carving the Colville at an unprecedented rate. The Spokane-based Inland Empire Public Lands Council launched a high-profile campaign to hold Foley's feet to the fire. In June, eight billboards appeared in the Spokane area featuring a photo of a large, freshly logged clearcut and the message: "Your Colville National Forest: A clearcut shame!"

NOT ENOUGH HABITAT

The first attempt to save eastside old growth through the federal courts failed. In 1989, the Natural Resources Defense Council, the Oregon Natural Resources Council, and other groups filed suit against the Forest Service charging that the Winema National Forest's 1987 draft forest plan violated the National Forest Management Act. They said the Winema, in southern Oregon on the eastern slopes of the Cascades, had disregarded studies by the Forest Service's own biologists, failing to set aside enough habitat for five sensitive species: the pine marten, the pileated, three-toed, and black-backed woodpecker, and the northern goshawk. A federal magistrate eventually upheld the plan's legality. But the campaign on behalf of eastside forests was just beginning.

The field reports from Audubon Adopt-a-Forest volunteers showed that logging had reduced the extent of old growth outside wilderness areas on the east side by at least 80 percent. They also revealed that planners had engaged in what amounted to a paper exercise in order to comply with a federal wildlife protection law.

To accommodate species associated with old growth, like the gos-hawk and woodpecker, they had laid out small old-growth reserves in a grid across the landscape. But at least 20 percent and possibly as many as half of these reserves didn't even contain old growth. Many had been logged in the 1980s. Where reserves did not meet the biological defi-nition of old growth, planners had labeled them "capable" old growth, on the theory that someday, if left alone, they might produce suitable habitat.

The agency's own research biologists had concluded that old-growth areas set aside for wildlife were far too small and that much of the habi-tat within them would not support old-growth species. For instance, a study by Forest Service research biologist Evelyn Bull revealed that nesting pileated woodpeckers needed four times as much protected habitat as the agency had set aside for them. When Audubon survey-ors looked around for replacement old growth within a five-mile radius of these wildlife reserves, in many cases they found it simply did not exist.

The Forest Service was not eager to release this new survey data. But it was quickly forwarded to Nathaniel Lawrence, a lawyer at the Natural Resources Defense Council in San Francisco. Forest activists now had the documentation they needed to move their campaign east.

President Clinton and Vice President Gore listen intently as forest ecologist Jerry Franklin (at left, back to camera) explains the principles of "new forestry" at the Northwest Forest Conference, held in Portland on April 2, 1993.

PART FIVE

THE CLINTON SOLUTION

1993–94

"We need to protect the long-term health of our forests, our wildlife, and our waterways. They are a gift from God and we hold them in trust for future generations."

—BILL CLINTON, *April 2, 1993*

"I became convinced we could not get a higher yield that was legally and scientifically defensible in the court."

—BILL CLINTON, *July 1, 1993*

"I miss George Bush."

—ANDY KERR, *November 1993*

THE ELECTION OF BILL CLINTON and Al Gore in November of 1992 should have been good news for ancient forests. Northwest activists were encouraged when the new administration recruited members of national conservation groups to fill key posts in environmental and natural resource agencies. The euphoria was short-lived; in March of 1993, a week before President Clinton held a promised forest summit in Portland, he backed away from a promise to reform the federal livestock grazing program under pressure from western senators.

The Northwest Forest Conference brought Clinton, Gore, and a large contingent of Cabinet members together with hopefuls and cynics for a long day of dialogues about the fate of Northwest forests and the

Northwest economy. Clinton appointed a scientific panel to develop the first "ecosystem management plan" for federal lands. The weight of science now argued for further sharp reductions in logging to protect salmon, forest-dwelling murrelets, and other old-growth species in addition to the northern spotted owl. The plan Clinton ultimately chose, Option 9, was a flawed compromise. It reduced timber sale levels and strengthened protection for salmon. But it also reopened some old-growth forests to modified clearcutting and permitted some level of logging across the landscape.

The administration successfully pressured grassroots groups to accept Option 9 and allow some court-blocked sales to go forward before it was adopted. This precipitated a donnybrook within the ranks of Northwest forest activists over tactics and fundamental principles.

As this lesson in realpolitik split the forest preservation movement, the Forest Service struggled to reinvent itself as an ecologically responsible agency. The administration, facing new lawsuits over salmon and eastside old-growth forests, launched a project to solve its problems by transplanting ecosystem management east of the Cascades, where both the forests and the culture were less forgiving.

Chapter Twenty-One

Presidential Politics

In the wake of the God Squad debacle, in the middle of a reelection campaign, and with the Rio Earth Summit looming, President George Bush needed something to polish his administration's tarnished environmental record.

George Bush had promised during the 1988 campaign to be "the environmental president." No ideologue on environmental issues, he had restored credibility to the Environmental Protection Agency and the Fish and Wildlife Service, badly damaged by the Reagan administration's frontal assault on environmental laws.

But whatever Bush's good intentions, they had been undermined by right-wing factions within his administration, including Vice President Dan Quayle, White House Chief of Staff John Sununu, and the crew at the Interior Department under Interior Secretary Manuel Lujan. In mid-1992, as the administration became more deeply mired in political quicksand over management of Northwest forests, Bush moved to control the political damage.

EMPTY PROMISES

On June 4, 1992, Forest Service Chief F. Dale Robertson stepped up to the plate when he announced his agency would abandon clearcutting as its preferred method of logging and begin practicing "ecosystem management" on its lands. Cy Jamison, director of the Bureau of Land Management, chimed in with a vague promise that his agency would adopt a policy of "total forest management."

The politically timed and largely symbolic announcements came on the heels of Bush's announcement earlier in the week that the United States would contribute $150 million to help save the world's forests. Bush clearly hoped that would defuse criticism that the United States had no moral standing to deplore deforestation in the tropical rainforests while it continued to clearcut its own virgin forests.

But any goodwill the shift might have bought Bush was quickly erased a week later, when the *New York Times* published satellite photos from the National Aeronautical and Space Administration. The images, each depicting about 1,000 square miles, contrasted the view of a tropical rainforest and a section of the Mount Hood National

Forest from outer space. They revealed the Northwest forest canopy to be far more fragmented by clearcut logging than the tropical rainforests of Brazil.

"It appears that much of the forest has been literally cut to pieces," Compton J. Tucker of NASA's Goddard Space Center told Timothy Egan of the *Times*. The diversity of animal and plant species needed to maintain a healthy forest ecosystem was bound to be compromised by such extensive logging, Tucker said.

DISGRACE AT RIO

The Bush administration's refusal to commit to meaningful controls on development disgraced the United States before a global audience at the United Nations Conference on Environment and Development, a gathering of heads of state from around the world in Rio de Janeiro. Vice President Quayle set the stage for the debacle in April, when his Council on Competitiveness launched an attack on the international biodiversity convention.

The council, an industry-dominated group bent on eliminating federal regulations protecting health, safety, and the environment, warned that the treaty scheduled for adoption in Rio threatened the U.S. economy and biotechnology industries. U.S. negotiators pressed for elimination of a global list of threatened species and imperiled habitat from the treaty. Representatives of more than 200 countries, many of them fearful of economic sanctions, bowed to U.S. pressure.

At Rio, despite the best efforts of EPA administrator William Reilly, the chief U.S. negotiator, Bush backed off from signing even the weakened biodiversity convention. Indeed, it was only at the last minute that Bush agreed to attend the Earth Summit. In the end, 165 heads of state, representing all but one of the world's industrialized nations, signed the treaty. George Bush's was the missing signature.

A CLEAR CHOICE IN '92

Bush's ineptitude, and the political agenda of the Interior Department, which hoped to preside over the dismantling of the Endangered Species Act, had kept the forests of the Pacific Northwest locked up in court for nearly his entire term. At the 1992 Republican National Convention, which was dominated by the GOP's right wing, Bush had nothing to gain by talking about his environmental achievements.

However, the ticket that emerged from the Democratic Convention in New York City guaranteed that the environment would be an issue in November, at least in the nation's northwest corner. Arkansas Governor Bill Clinton's environmental record was not well-known outside his state. But when Clinton tapped green U.S. Senator Al Gore of Tennessee as his running mate, voters were handed a clear choice.

Environmentalists in the Northwest had every reason to rejoice over Gore's presence on the ticket. Gore had recently published *Earth in the Balance,* a manifesto on the global environmental crisis that sounded

the alarm on global warming, ozone depletion, and worldwide deforestation. He had led the congressional delegation to the Earth Summit. In his book, Gore called for the United States to lead by example
in ending global deforestation.

"In the United States, particularly in heavily logged regions like the
Pacific Northwest and Alaska, there is a renewed assault on the great
stretches of temperate rainforest that are so important to us," he wrote.
"In national forests throughout the country, logging roads are being
built in order to facilitate the more rapid logging, even clear-cutting,
of public lands under contracts that require the sale of the trees at rates
far below market prices."

Gore even boasted that he had "helped lead the successful fight to
prevent the overturning of protections for the spotted owl": "In the
spirited Senate debate, it became clear that the issue was not just the
spotted owl but the 'old growth' forest itself. The spotted owl is a so-
called keystone species, whose disappearance would mark the loss of
an entire ecosystem and the many other species dependent upon it.
Ironically, if those wishing to continue the logging had won, their jobs
would have been lost anyway as soon as the remaining 10 percent of
the forest was cut."

ON THE CAMPAIGN TRAIL

Bush promptly nicknamed Gore "Mr. Ozone" and started ridiculing
his environmental doomsday rhetoric on the stump. Clinton reacted
by trying to soft-pedal his running mate's reputation as a radical environmentalist. Gore began backing away from his own printed words.
In a debate between the vice-presidential candidates, Quayle accused
Gore of calling for a $100 billion global Marshall Plan to solve Earth's
environmental crises, with the United States and other prosperous
industrialized nations footing the bill. Gore denied his book had advocated that and ducked the opportunity to defend the book's themes
before a national TV audience.

Bill Clinton's own environmental record as governor was not
stellar. In the 1970s, timber companies had begun rapidly converting the virgin mixed hardwood-and-pine forests of Arkansas to pine
plantations. Hardwood species most valuable for wildlife—hickory,
pawpaw, and persimmon—were routinely poisoned to keep them from
competing with pine. Weyerhaeuser Company and Georgia Pacific
Corporation became major players in this wholesale forest conversion
when they bought up a number of private land holdings in the state
and replanted them with pine.

In 1979, during his first term as governor, Clinton appointed a citizen task force on forest practices, which held hearings around the state
to discuss what should be done about the forest conversion problem.
But nothing came of the effort because in 1980, with substantial help
from the timber industry, Clinton was defeated for reelection. In 1983,
after he was reelected, Clinton gave the timber industry in his home

state a wide berth and threw himself into a campaign for school reform.

The timber industry in the Pacific Northwest saw little to fear in Clinton's record. While Clinton was governor, industry leaders pointed out, 80 percent of the Ouachita National Forest in Arkansas was allocated to timber production.

Clinton's record on other environmental issues was mixed. Although his administration's enforcement of clean water regulations against the poultry industry was lax, he did succeed in getting laws on recycling, solid waste treatment, and chemical right-to-know through the 1991 Arkansas Legislature.

During the 1992 presidential campaign, Clinton sent a carefully balanced message on the forest issue. In May, on a trip to Oregon, he called for quick completion of a spotted owl recovery plan and said he opposed amending the Endangered Species Act to give more weight to the economic costs of protecting species. In July, he promised a country "where we are pro-growth and pro-environment," while blaming log exports and mill automation for most of the woes of the Northwest timber industry. And in August he promised timber worker unions that, as president, he would hold a summit to find a solution to the timber impasse. Clinton gave lip service to protecting the environment, but his comments on the old-growth forest conflict indicated that his gut-level sympathies lay with workers displaced in a time of economic transition.

Bush chose the low road. On September 14, 1992, in a speech at a Colville, Washington, mill, he attacked environmentalists for using the Endangered Species Act to protect Northwest forests, called on Congress to pass Interior Secretary Manuel Lujan's repudiated owl plan, and threatened to let the act expire at year's end.

"I will not sign an extension of the Endangered Species Act unless it gives greater consideration to jobs, families, and communities," Bush vowed. "And I will not sign it without a specific plan in place to harvest enough timber to keep timber families working in 1993 and beyond. It's time to make people just as important as owls." Later that day he repeated the message at a mill in White City, Oregon.

The rhetoric may have won him some timber votes, but by that time even loggers and millworkers were skeptical. What had George Bush really done for them? The forests of the Pacific Northwest remained locked up by the federal courts.

At a rally in downtown Portland on the same day, Clinton barely mentioned ancient forests or timber jobs. But in timber-dependent Lane County, he kept a promise he'd made to organized labor. In the back yard of a Springfield millworker, he met for an hour with timber workers to hear their concerns. At the end of the hour he promised to hold a forest summit within the first 100 days of his administration to end the warring among federal agencies and get management of the national forests out of the courts.

Unlike Bush, Clinton did not play the demagogue. He never blamed environmentalists or the owl for the impasse. He took the longer view. The economic transition occurring in the Northwest, he said, was like others occurring all across the nation, even in his home state.

ENTER THE MARBLED MURRELET

Meanwhile, another forest bird stirred up new problems for George Bush.

On September 28, the U.S. Fish and Wildlife Service, under a federal court order, announced that it would list the marbled murrelet as a threatened species in Oregon, Washington, and California. The elusive, robin-sized seabird spends its life in coastal waters and nests in old-growth conifers up to 50 miles inland. Biologists believed the murrelet was even more dependent on old-growth stands than the spotted owl.

Forest Service officials in Portland were in denial about the plight of the murrelet. They remarked that the bird could just use the same habitat the Forest Service had already set aside for the spotted owl.

During the murrelet's summer nesting season, logging of murrelet habitat was barred. But in late September of 1992, at the end of the nesting season, and with the listing of the murrelet as a threatened species imminent, officials in the Forest Service's Northwest regional office allowed logging of murrelet habitat to resume. Trees fell within one of the most important murrelet sites on the Olympic National Forest, an area where biologists had counted 124 murrelet sightings in one 40-acre old-growth tract. Environmentalists denounced the incident, saying it constituted "blatant and calculated disregard" for the Endangered Species Act. And George Bush got another black eye.

KEEPING A PROMISE

Bill Clinton was elected with key support from Oregon and Washington. The week after the election, a gleeful Bruce Babbitt kept a speaking engagement at a water law conference at Portland's Lewis & Clark College. Babbitt, former Arizona governor and president of the League of Conservation Voters, already was rumored to be Clinton's top choice for Interior Secretary. As governors, Babbitt and Clinton had worked together to help found the Democratic Leadership Council, an effort to blend a liberal social agenda with conservative fiscal policies.

Babbitt promised confidently during his Portland appearance that the Clinton-Gore administration would restore environmental credibility to the federal government. He attacked the resource extraction industries for trying to subvert environmental laws and for their "record of abuse and excess." He praised the Endangered Species Act, calling it "the single most inventive and trail-blazing law of this century." It must never be weakened, Babbitt said.

On December 16, as the Clinton transition team began its work in Little Rock, Arkansas, Clinton's promise to hold a forest summit in the Pacific Northwest was high on the agenda. Tom Tuchmann, forestry staffer for the Senate Agriculture Committee, was summoned to Little

Rock to head the Clinton-Gore forest policy transition team and lay the groundwork for the summit.

Pressure from the timber industry and the Northwest delegation on the new president to keep his promise was intense. U.S. Representative Mike Kopetski, an Oregon Democrat, had written to the president-elect on November 5, urging him to begin planning for the summit immediately, rather than wait until after Inauguration Day.

THE GREEN DREAM TEAM

Clinton's appointments to key environmental and natural resource posts, heavily influenced by Gore, seemed to promise an administration that would be a green dream team. In spite of themselves, environmentalists were swept up in the optimism that infused the transition and the early weeks of the administration.

As predicted, Babbitt became Interior Secretary and assumed primary authority over the embattled Endangered Species Act. Babbitt picked George Frampton, president of the Wilderness Society, as his assistant secretary of interior for parks and wildlife—an appointment that drew strong opposition from wise-use groups. For months after his confirmation, the administration kept Frampton under wraps.

Babbitt's other appointments also seemed to signal the greenest Interior Department in recent memory. Mollie Beattie, former deputy secretary of Vermont's Agency for Natural Resources, won confirmation as director of the Fish and Wildlife Service. Jim Baca, New Mexico's progressive state land commissioner, was appointed to head the Bureau of Land Management. Several professional environmentalists were ensconced in less visible but influential advisory positions in the department.

Two of Gore's former Senate staff members and protégés, Katie McGinty and Carol Browner, won important posts. Browner, director of the Florida Department of Environmental Quality, was named administrator of the Environmental Protection Agency. McGinty was named to a newly created position, director of the President's Office of Environmental Policy. Her job was to coordinate the administration's environmental agenda across department lines.

As agriculture secretary Clinton chose Mike Espy, a former Mississippi congressman who had no background on forest issues. However, his choice for the key post overseeing the Forest Service was Jim Lyons, a man environmentalists trusted to do the right thing. It was Lyons who had written the 1985 Society of American Foresters report on old-growth forests. It was Lyons, as forestry staffer for the House Agriculture Committee, who had engineered the Gang of Four. There was every reason to believe Lyons would support a green resolution of the old-growth forest imbroglio.

Bob Doppelt, executive director of the Pacific Rivers Council, saw his opportunity to sell this new administration on watershed protection early. He met with Baca, the new BLM director, and with Lyons.

He pitched the Pacific Rivers Council's aquatic conservation strategy as a job-creating program. Not only would restoring battered salmon runs help revive the commercial and sport fishing industries, he said, taking out roads and culverts in key watersheds could also put unemployed loggers back to work.

"Jim got very intrigued," Doppelt said. "He is the one who called Katie McGinty. They had a major political problem on their hands with salmon, and they didn't want to go through this twice. The second they understood there were jobs associated with this, they were with us."

THE FIRST RETREAT

The honeymoon was to be of short duration. On January 20, 1993, during his confirmation hearing, Babbitt defended the Endangered Species Act before western Republicans. "When we start extinguishing links in the ecological web of the Western landscape, we take enormous risks and ultimately threaten our ability to live in harmony and productively in that environment," he said.

"You are walking right into the middle of a hornet's nest," warned Republican Senator Larry Craig of Idaho, one of the law's harshest critics. But Oregon's senior senator, Republican Mark Hatfield, gave Babbitt a surprise vote of confidence, saying he had the potential to become one of the nation's greatest Interior secretaries. Mark Rey, the timber industry's politically savvy D.C. lobbyist, praised both Babbitt and Espy and urged the Senate to confirm them. "Both have demonstrated knowledge and experience about natural resource issues, and they are expected to share President Clinton's dual concern for the environment and the economy," he said.

On February 17, in a speech to Congress describing his deficit-reduction plan, Clinton gave environmentalists reason to cheer when he vowed to stop selling federally subsidized timber, livestock forage, and hard-rock minerals. The new president promised he would push for a 12.5 percent royalty on precious minerals taken from federal land, a phase-out of timber sales that cost the federal treasury more to administer than they brought in, and an unspecified increase in the fee ranchers paid to graze cattle on federal land. Babbitt wasted no time announcing that he would prepare a bold proposal to reform the federal grazing program from top to bottom.

Western senators and governors who had delivered their states to the Democrats were livid. In mid-March, Democrats Max Baucus of Montana and Ben Nighthorse Campbell of Colorado demanded and got a meeting with Clinton and Gore. Afterward, Baucus said the president had "recognized the adverse impact that his plan would have on Montana and other Western states." Soon after that, a White House spokesman said the proposal to phase out subsidies would remain in the president's budget but that Clinton would allow Congress to delete it.

In the absence of White House support for a hard line, Babbitt was forced to backtrack on his pledge to reform the federal grazing program—just a week before Clinton's April 2 forest summit.

Clinton's reversal sent a message that on hot-button environmental issues with political consequences, he would not delegate decisions to Gore. Opponents of western public land reform gloated. "The gossip was that he'd write off the West and gain votes in California by going with the environmental community," Campbell said. "This disproves that. He's really willing to listen. And he doesn't want to hurt the West."

The administration's retreat on the environment had begun.

Chapter Twenty-Two

A Friendly Administration

The Old Ashland Armory hummed with high anxiety on the first week-end in February 1993, as forest activists from Southeast Alaska to the Sierras converged on the college town of Ashland, Oregon, for an urgent strategy session.

Julie Norman, president of the environmental group Headwaters, was nervous. She knew the ancient forest movement had reached a critical juncture. A dozen years of Reagan-Bush had forced activists to become effective political adversaries. The Clinton administration was just two weeks old, but already the political climate was shifting. The question on her mind, on everyone's mind, was how the Northwest's old-growth forests would fare with this new "friendly" administration.

In organizing this conference, Norman had taken a risk. Most gatherings of forest activists were tribal affairs, where tree huggers could let down their guard, trade tactics, party, argue, commiserate, and reinforce each other in the work they all shared: saving the forests, if necessary one tree at a time.

But this year her intuition told her the tribe needed to hear new messages, new voices, if it was to save itself from a growing insularity. She had invited Agnes Tao-Why-Wee Pilgrim, the oldest known descendant of the Takelma people, to speak about the Native American relationship with the forest. She had asked Jennifer Belcher, the newly elected Washington state commissioner of public lands, to deliver straight talk on tactics.

Logging contractor Tom Hirons, a wise-use leader who harbored an inchoate desire to reach out across the chasm that divided him from environmentalists, would be speaking. So would Denny Scott, a national officer in the United Brotherhood of Carpenters and Joiners. Scott had made the tough decision to explore with environmentalists the possibility that labor and the environmental movement might share common ground in the coming showdown. It was a bold step; until now, unions had allied themselves with timber companies in the campaign to keep federal timber flowing to Northwest mills.

Norman had tacked a number of banners to the walls that conveyed her own philosophy. The one that seemed most relevant today was from

Terry Tempest Williams, the Utah writer and naturalist: "We must be compassionate and fierce at once."

As one of the few women to hold a leadership role in the forest preservation movement, Norman had held her own with her male compatriots and had made Headwaters a major player in the ancient forest campaign. For 10 years she had immersed herself in learning everything she could about the federal timber sale programs that were steadily eating away at unprotected wilderness on federal land in southwestern Oregon. Because of Julie Norman and others like her, the environmental movement had grown in sophistication and scope. It had learned the uses of science and law in protecting wild forests. It had attracted national support.

After so many years, forest activists were skilled adversaries. But they had not succeeded in broadening their political base at home. Their movement had grown inbred. It was unprepared for Bill Clinton and the challenge his young administration posed.

UNFAMILIAR TERRITORY

In two months the new president would keep a promise to organized labor by holding a summit in the Northwest to end the forest gridlock. Labor and industry groups were sounding more upbeat than they had under four years of George Bush. Without a shared vision and a unified strategy, Norman feared the campaign that had consumed the people gathered in this old armory could finally fail and the forests become mere chips in a bigger game of presidential politics.

If the shape of a compromise was not yet clear, most of the players who would forge it were in place. The team would include Vice President Gore, Assistant Agriculture Secretary–designate Jim Lyons, Office of Environmental Policy Director Katie McGinty, and, from Interior Secretary Bruce Babbitt's staff, Tom Tuchmann, Will Stelle, and Tom Collier, Babbitt's chief of staff. They were all smart, knowledgeable, and environmentally progressive. They had Clinton's ear. But Clinton himself was a moderate on environmental issues. What role Gore would play in organizing this conference was unclear.

Clearly the movement had arrived at a political crossroad. For three years, since 1990, it had been able to stave off harmful riders. But environmental lobbyists hadn't managed to build congressional support for ancient forest protection legislation. Some grassroots activists said lobbyists for the national conservation groups hadn't really tried. Now Democratic Representative Jim Jontz of Indiana, who had stepped forward to carry their banner, was out of office, defeated by wise-use groups that had mobilized to support his Republican opponent. Also gone, his career ruined by a sex scandal, was Democratic Senator Brock Adams of Washington, the movement's lone Senate supporter within the Northwest delegation.

Environmentalists' court victories had breathed new life into the wise-use movement, which was borrowing some of their own tactics—

grassroots organizing and quick-response press releases and news conferences—to argue that environmentalists were destroying a way of life.
The forest preservationists were on the defensive politically, accused of
callous indifference to the plight of unemployed loggers.

Several D.C. environmental lobbyists had flown west to be in this hall
today. They had a message for the battle-worn ground troops: Overnight,
the world had changed. And so must their movement.

THE CHALLENGE

"You are a group of people who have changed history," said Jim
Owens of the Western Ancient Forest Campaign. "You've taken this
issue across the nation. The president has given the signal that this is
going to be his top environmental priority. But we're in a new political environment. Twelve years of Bush and Reagan have caused us to
be very defensive. Now the challenge is to move forward, to identify
the paths of progress, to figure out how to work with a friendly
administration."

Owens urged the activists to help educate new members of Congress
and to work with governors and friends in the administration. Most
of all, he said, they must help reduce the polarization in the Northwest
by reaching out to new audiences: retired citizens, nurses, church
groups. "We need to refocus our energy," he said. "We have common
shared values. Why do we live here? We want the trees on the hill, the
fish in the streams. We can't get a bill passed that achieves our goal until
we change the political environment in these communities. The members of Congress like to be green, but we need to help them, because
the environment they operate in is not green."

Kevin Kirchner, a lobbyist for the Sierra Club Legal Defense Fund,
warned the activists not to pin all their hopes on continued court injunctions. "The courts have served as a backstop, but there's no way we can
sue over every timber sale," he said. "The courts ought not be an agent
for social change but a brake on environmental destruction."

Jim Britell, the street-smart conservation director for Kalmiopsis
Audubon on the southern Oregon Coast, had some harsh words for
his friends in the movement. "Many of you are apolitical," he said. "You
don't vote, don't give money." He lectured them for letting Jim Jontz
take the fall for them. About 30 environmentalists, Britell among them,
had gone to Indiana to canvass and raise money for Jontz. It hadn't
been enough.

"Embracing environmentalism cost Jontz 200,000 votes," Britell
admonished. "If we want access, we can give money, we can volunteer,
but somehow we have to pay our way. We have to find our roots, with
the labor movement, with the populists, with the Democrats. Let's
learn the proper lesson from our experiences."

Even Andy Kerr, veteran conservation director for the Oregon
Natural Resources Council, who had cultivated an image as the
movement's attack dog, tried to get into the spirit of the occasion with

a new, more conciliatory speech. "We can't afford to leave part of our society behind," he said. "It is not only bad economics, it is unjust."

LABOR MAKES AN OVERTURE

Since 1989, organized labor had made common cause with the timber industry on forest policy, even agreeing not to oppose the export of raw logs and U.S. jobs overseas in exchange for industry clout and access to the Bush administration. It hadn't bought workers much. Denny Scott began his remarks by pointing out that Clinton owed labor a favor. It was the unions, he noted, that had won his promise to convene the upcoming summit.

Clinton's careful campaign posture, in which he called for an end to forest gridlock but avoided taking sides, had won him broad support in the Northwest, where most people were weary of the owls-versus-loggers debate. "I believe it helped him carry Oregon and Washington," Scott said. "It was an astute move; he could talk about the disarray in the agencies without discussing the substance of a resolution. We take partial credit for Clinton's win. But now Governor Clinton has become President Clinton and we're faced with the reality of a summit."

Organized labor had done its grieving, Scott said. It was ready to come out in favor of protecting old growth—but only if a way could be found to get some younger timber moving out of the woods quickly. He urged environmentalists to help craft an old-growth plan, hammering out principles with key parties behind closed doors, deciding what they were willing to give up and what they would fall on their sword to protect.

"The ancient forest campaign has a decision to make: Whether to enter the impure water of political negotiation and compromise," Scott said. "You won't have the opportunity to stay at arm's length and let others develop a compromise. It's my view that you, like us, should be directly involved in the process."

A TOUGH SELL

But the audience for this message of realpolitik was a tough sell. Many of the assembled activists had devoted 10, 15, even 20 years to the ancient forest campaign. Most of them advocated for forest protection as unpaid volunteers or underpaid directors of small nonprofits. Some had arrived at middle age without house, children, or money in the bank, foregoing the ordinary rites of passage in their single-minded devotion to saving forests.

Their lives were far from glamorous. They skirmished constantly with bureaucrats in the Forest Service and Bureau of Land Management who had dug in their heels to resist change. Appealing timber sales, driving logging roads, and trying to keep track of a hundred front lines in the battle for the forests was full-time work. If they lived in rural areas, they saw their failures every day in the denuded hills around them.

Each person in the room had sacrificed to protect the forests. In return, the work of saving the forests had given their lives purpose. They could be forgiven for not being receptive to the message that Bill Clinton's election meant not victory, but more compromise.

As for outreach, forest activists had been vilified, threatened, and ostracized for their role in shutting down the forests. Though some rural activists had reached an uneasy accommodation with loggers and millworkers that allowed them to live side-by-side in small communities, their values and world views remained far apart. Tree huggers had developed the protective armor they needed to survive in rural outposts. It was hard to see how they could make timber workers their political allies.

A more complicated dynamic was at work as well. Politicians tended to group environmentalists with advocates for workers' rights, civil rights, and social justice under the progressive Democratic umbrella. Yet the two movements sprang from different origins. The labor movement, born out of the mobilization of exploited workers, had achieved its power through often-bloody political confrontation. The early nature conservation movement was a movement of the privileged and politically influential. Its leaders, many of them Republicans, hobnobbed with presidents. In the Northwest, the labor and conservation movements seldom had been natural allies.

The environmental movement reborn on Earth Day 1970 was more egalitarian. Yet many forest activists still felt more comfortable communing with the forest than communicating with their working-class neighbors, more confident taking on federal agencies than engaging the political system directly by campaigning or running for office.

As Andy Kerr once said when accused of lacking compassion for timber workers: "We're not humanitarians, we're environmentalists."

The forest protection movement's reliance on a mix of passion, science, technical mastery, and political pressure had served it well during the Reagan-Bush years. But a moderate Democrat with traditional ties to labor and human rights groups was now in the White House. Could the movement survive in this new political climate?

As activists debated strategy, they chose not to grapple with the need to broaden their political base directly. Instead, a consensus emerged: They would fight to save all the old growth, all the roadless areas, all the pristine salmon streams. On that, compromise was impossible.

Moreover, they were now ready to raise the ante. It was time to confront the new administration with the need to protect forests on the other side of the Cascades.

EXPANDING EAST

On March 30, three days before Clinton's forest summit, activists armed with the Audubon Adopt-a-Forest surveys and a sheaf of Forest Service wildlife studies held a press conference in Portland. Nathaniel Lawrence, a lawyer for the Natural Resources Defense Council, announced that he had formally petitioned the Forest Service on behalf of 22 environmental groups to stop cutting old-growth forests east of the Cascades until it developed adequate standards for protecting wildlife.

"There isn't any westside solution that stands by itself," Lawrence said. "The administration may be tempted to fix the problems of the west side on the back of the east side." In fact, logging already was increasing in the pine forests east of the Cascades.

It was a preemptive strike. The Clinton administration had refused to put eastside old growth on the agenda at its forest conference. Now Clinton would be forced to deal with the issue, or forest activists would see him in court.

Chapter Twenty-Three

Summit in Portland

On April 1, 1993, Bill Clinton, hatless in the rain, made his way through a throng of supporters outside the Benson Hotel in downtown Portland. His step had a confident bounce. In the third month of his administration, the new president still believed all things, even the conflict over old-growth forests, could be resolved if the right people were brought to the table. Tomorrow, at his promised Northwest Forest Conference, the process would begin.

Clinton was committing extraordinary resources to the daylong event. Among those in attendance would be Vice President Al Gore, Interior Secretary Bruce Babbitt, Agriculture Secretary Mike Espy, Labor Secretary Robert Reich, Commerce Secretary Ron Brown, Environmental Protection Agency administrator Carol Browner, and Alice Rivlin of the Office of Management and Budget.

They would sit around a vast conference table with scientists, environmentalists, economists, timber industry executives, small business owners, labor union representatives, loggers, local officials, and tribal leaders—even a Roman Catholic archbishop. They would discuss problems and solutions. Conspicuous by their absence would be members of the Northwest congressional delegation. This was to be an administration show all the way.

The announced purpose of the event, a combination teach-in and regionwide town hall meeting, was to give the new administration guidance as it began crafting a solution to the forest impasse. Equally important to the new administration was to place the new president squarely in the middle of the forest debate. In a region that had helped him defeat George Bush, it was important not to take sides or fix blame.

The new president promised that he would exert leadership and not let the conflict continue to fester as his predecessor had. Breaking legal gridlock, he said, would require the federal agencies involved in the forest impasse—the Forest Service, BLM, Fish and Wildlife Service, and National Marine Fisheries Service—to work together, not at cross-purposes. With the God Squad spectacle still a vivid memory, it was an appealing idea to just about everyone except wary environmentalists. Legal gridlock, after all, was what had kept the federal timber sale program tied up in court during most of the Bush administration.

Clinton made it clear that this situation would not continue under his administration. Letting the courts continue to direct management of 24 million acres of federal land on narrow legal grounds would not lead to the regionwide resolution he was convinced the people of the Northwest hungered for. "I think most people are truly tired of fighting the battle in the way we've been fighting it," he said on the eve of the conference.

Before accord could be achieved, the administration faced the immediate challenge of adopting a forest management plan that would satisfy the letter and spirit of the nation's environmental laws. But Clinton said the ultimate decisions facing the region were much broader: "What do we want Oregon, Washington and California to look like? And how important is it to save some of the old-growth forests forever?"

DESPERATELY SEEKING BALANCE

After weeks of suspense, the conference had been organized hastily to capitalize on Clinton's April 3 meeting with embattled Russian president Boris Yeltsin in Vancouver, British Columbia. The new president was about to make his debut on the international stage, where the stakes were high and success far from certain. But here, in this wet, quixotic corner of the country, was a problem he ought to be able to master. Here was an issue on which the federal government could and should take the initiative.

In late March, the administration's forest team dispatched Babbitt and Espy on high-profile advance trips to the Northwest. Espy took his first walk in an old-growth forest and pronounced himself in awe of "God's work." Babbitt toured sawmills and met with timber workers. He declined to say whether he supported saving any old growth at all. What impressed him most on his Northwest swing was a meeting held by a group called the Applegate Partnership on the bank of the Applegate River in southwestern Oregon.

The Applegate Partnership, only a few months old, was the kind of effort almost everyone applauded. It began when a few people who shared little but the 500,000-acre Applegate Valley began meeting to discuss threats to their valley—the wildfires that raged through the rugged mountains periodically, threatening rural homes; the fragmentation of the watershed's old-growth forests by logging; and the impact of logging, road-building, and farming on native fish runs.

The group included a few property owners with environmentalist leanings, the owner of a helicopter logging company, a timber association representative, and a community organizer who saw the Applegate's potential as a model for sustainable forestry. It grew to include farmers and Forest Service and Bureau of Land Management officials.

The alliance kept its experiment in consensus-building a secret until local newspapers broke the story. Within weeks, the White House was calling.

Babbitt sat enthralled on a Saturday afternoon as he listened to speaker after speaker discuss the need to restore the Applegate watershed and manage all of its natural resources sustainably. Afterward, he proclaimed the Applegate Partnership the wave of the future.

"I may be witness today to a very important beginning," he said at an impromptu news conference. "It's important to know there are a few places on this battlefield where people have put down their weapons and started talking to each other."

The administration's desire to strike a balance and work toward consensus also drove selection of the 52 invited speakers who would make up the three conference panels. Organizers chose the panelists carefully, with an eye to avoiding advocates of extreme positions. When the list of speakers was released, only days before the conference, Andy Kerr of the Oregon Natural Resources Council wasn't on it. Environmentalists protested. Despite his combative, hard-line position on forests, or perhaps because of it, Kerr had become a national and highly visible spokesman for the ancient forests. Someone explained to the administration that it could not have a forest conference without Andy Kerr. His name was added at the last minute. When the Oregon Lands Coalition protested that it wasn't represented, Jackie Lang, the coalition's articulate spokeswoman, also got an eleventh-hour invitation.

But even as the administration worked to position itself at the center of the issue, behind the scenes its options for finding a solution Clinton could sell as "balanced" were narrowing.

THE SAT REPORT

On March 19, the administration delivered a little-noted but enormously significant document to Judge William Dwyer: a massive report prepared by a 24-member scientific panel headed by Jack Ward Thomas. The Scientific Assessment Team (SAT) report offered the first look at the consequences of true ecosystem management. A few people, including Thomas, recognized it as a preview of the plan the Clinton administration would have to assemble after the drama and hoopla surrounding the Forest Conference subsided.

The Forest Service had asked Thomas to oversee preparation of the SAT report in response to an order from Judge Dwyer in the ongoing lawsuit against the Forest Service over owl protection. Dwyer had directed the agency to move beyond owls and to develop a plan that would also protect 32 other sensitive species associated with old-growth forests, including the marbled murrelet, recently listed by the Fish and Wildlife Service as a threatened species. In effect, Dwyer had ordered the Forest Service to write not an owl plan but an ecosystem plan.

At Thomas's suggestion, the SAT scientists expanded their inquiry. They attempted to assess the status of no less than 667 species of animals, plants, and fungi and predict how various levels of logging would affect each one. It was an unprecedented effort to measure human impacts on biological diversity.

The SAT report's bottom line was sobering: Saving owls, murrelets, salmon, and other old-growth species would require further restrictions on logging across the landscape. In the Oregon Coast Range it would require an end to the logging of old forests. Though the report did not specify how much timber could be cut under this scenario, insiders knew annual timber sales in the owl region would drop to about 1 billion board feet—a 75 percent reduction from near-record levels of the late 1980s.

Forest Service Chief F. Dale Robertson quickly distanced himself from the findings. "This is a scientific report prepared in response to a court order; it is not a policy statement," he said. The chief added that the team had been created to answer questions from Dwyer "raised by actions taken by the previous administration."

With hardly a break, Jack Ward Thomas then began working on President Clinton's new forest planning project, his fourth in four years.

A PERSONAL REQUEST

By now Thomas was physically, mentally, and emotionally spent. Special assignments from the Bush administration had taken him away from his home in La Grande and his work with the elk herds of the Blue Mountains too frequently since 1989. He had headed three scientific panels, each with a high-priority task to complete and an impossible deadline for doing it. He routinely received death threats, both at home and at the office. But what only those close to him knew was that for the past several months, he had also been living with personal tragedy. His wife Margaret was dying of colon cancer.

Clinton had personally asked Thomas to head this new crash project to help him develop what would become the president's Northwest Forest Plan. Thomas recalled later that the president said to him, "I know you have caught incredible personal hell on this and I appreciate it. And I'm going to have to ask you to go into the breach one more time."

"What could I say?" Thomas asked later. "There's such a thing as duty."

PRE-SUMMIT HYPE

As the day of the forest conference approached, the level of hype surrounding it reached all-out frenzy. Portland became a vortex of pro-timber rallies and pro-forest rallies, dueling press conferences, and missives from White House advance teams. Environmentalists organized a huge rock concert at Portland's Tom McCall Waterfront Park on the eve of the conference. The early spring rains were unrelenting; 50,000 concert-goers who came to hear Carole King, Neil Young, and David Crosby huddled in a downpour and 45-degree temperatures.

Timber industry groups were positively jaunty at a pre-summit press conference. They saw the event as their best chance to make their case to the new president and the American public.

There were indications that the new administration wasn't interested in using this national forum to hear the unvarnished truth. Clinton refused to put the log export issue or eastside forests on the agenda. The list of invitees itself raised some eyebrows: It was heavy on loggers, millworkers, corporate officials, and timber community leaders. Speakers were required to submit their comments in advance.

SOFTENING THE MESSAGE

On April 2, the police lines went up at dawn around the Convention Center, a new Portland landmark locals had nicknamed Twin Peaks for its two bottle-green spires. A soaking Oregon rain, the kind that makes Douglas-firs grow better in the Northwest than anywhere else, pelted the few sign-toting protesters who stood on the sidewalk hoping to get a glimpse of Clinton and Gore as they hustled into the building. In the foothills at the fringe of the city, heavy clouds off the Pacific Ocean dumped rain over the clearcuts, young plantations, and old-growth forests.

Kimbark MacColl, a respected Portland historian, had been asked to provide an historical overview of the timber industry in the Northwest. With other panelists, he was shuttled by bus to the Convention Center, where he handed over his prepared text. As he drank coffee in the lobby, Portland attorneys Jeff and Kristine Rogers approached him. The two, close friends of Bill and Hillary Clinton from college and law-school days, had worked closely with the White House on organizing the conference.

"They said, 'We'd like to discuss your talk.'" MacColl recalled. "They explained that the White House didn't want anything too sharp. It was 'work the land' rather than 'exploit it.'" Soon after, Dee Dee Myers, Clinton's press secretary, approached MacColl and asked him to soften his message. "I decided that when you're about to be raped, you might as well lie back and enjoy it," he said. "It was the first time I'd ever given an authorized speech."

TALKING TO THE PRESIDENT

Today the world would be watching the Northwest, if only through the jaded eyes of the White House press corps. Throughout the region, there was a sense that history was about to be made. It was as if the forest preservation campaign of two decades were culminating in one marathon seminar.

Reporters from around the world submitted to security checks and filed into the cavernous concrete basement vault that had been transformed for the day into a media center. Most of them would watch the eight-hour proceedings on small television sets, straining to hear over the din of conversation. Members of the national press corps filed their stories early, patching a few sound bites onto backgrounders prepared in advance. They wanted to get this exercise over with and move on to the main event, Clinton's Saturday summit with Boris Yeltsin.

The 54 invited participants and several hundred invited guests began filing into the blazing ballroom. It was hard not to be impressed, hard not to feel a stirring of hope, as environmental activists and loggers took their places around the big table with the likes of Babbitt, Browner, and Reich.

Clinton opened the session by speaking warmly of the timber workers he had met in Oregon the previous summer. "As I've spoken with people in the timber industry," he said, "I've been impressed by their love of the land." Then he stressed the need for the government to speak with one voice and for people on different sides of the issue to meet in a conference room, not a courtroom.

Oregon Governor Barbara Roberts, who had worked closely with the White House to make the conference a reality, offered a variation on her "playing the cards we've been dealt" message. "Your presence here is a testament to your willingness to find workable solutions," she said. "The real question facing Oregon and the nation is whether we can make change our friend and not our enemy."

It fell to Kimbark MacColl to deliver straight talk on what had brought the Northwest to this day. Even in its censored and sanitized form, his speech packed a wallop. He reminded the audience that the first white settlers had come to this raw corner of the continent seeking not natural beauty but new opportunities. "To them, nature was an obstacle, a rough world to be tamed, a wilderness to be cleared. Trees were barriers, or when felled, stumps in the farmer's or city builder's way."

The audience did not hear what he had planned to say next: "It could be argued that while the farmer came to settle and improve the land, the timber cutter came to despoil it. At least the farmer represented permanence while the absentee timber owners simply treated the region as a colony to be exploited. They came to cut and get out!"

Then, for eight extraordinary hours, under blazing television lights, each panelist said his or her piece to the president of the United States. Political reporter Jeff Mapes called the gathering a "dysfunctional family" of Northwest residents. But for today, members of this fractious family—even Andy Kerr—were on their best behavior. Apocryphal tales of mills closed because of the owl and loggers' families living destitute in the woods went unchallenged. The focus was on the future.

Clinton had done his homework. He talked knowledgeably about the economic transition the timber industry was experiencing in the Pacific Northwest, the influence of foreign competition, the cost to workers when large corporations restructure. Many speakers had positive stories to tell about surviving the transition from an economy based on liquidating old-growth forests for 2-by-4s to one based on making products from second-growth timber.

When it was Julie Norman's turn to address the president, she looked him in the eye and ticked off in a firm and resolute voice the terms of engagement grassroots forest activists in the Northwest had agreed upon for a resolution of the forest conflict: "We must disturb no more of the remaining refuges of biodiversity. We must establish reserves for suitable habitat for threatened species. They must encompass the eastside forests as well as the westside forests. The decline of our forests' health must be dealt with at its source. The future of both the environment and the economy lies in restoration and in second growth."

"To achieve this," Norman added, "will require nothing less than a revolution in the U.S. Forest Service and Bureau of Land Management."

BLAME ENOUGH FOR ALL

Jack Ward Thomas was on the final panel, the one dealing with solutions. He had already had his chance to speak to the president privately. He had agreed to help extricate Clinton from the mess he had inherited. Speaking from hand-scribbled notes, Thomas asked the president on this day for clarity in the midst of ambiguity.

"The focus of the National Forest Management Act is a tough call," Thomas said. "If you don't perform under that act, you have to go to the penalty box, which is the Endangered Species Act. We have a de facto policy of biodiversity protection for federal lands. If it's not so, we need to say that clearly. You command natural resource agencies that have incredibly talented people who can do incredible things when they understand their mission."

"All sides speak the word 'balance,'" Thomas said. "They all mean different things. That leads to misunderstanding. I think it means obey the law, then minimize the economic costs."

Moving to protection of ecosystems rather than single species "is not going to be simple, it's not going to be cheap," Thomas warned. "Ecosystems are not only more complex than you think, they're more complex than you *can* think."

The owl, said Thomas, was a fork in the road. "As we move on with the rest of our lives, we can't go back. There's no point in looking at the past except to learn from it. In the past is blame enough for all of us. In the future perhaps there will be credit enough to go around."

Clinton looked straight at Thomas and nodded, as if to say he got the message loud and clear.

Chapter Twenty-Four

Friendly Betrayal

Scientists began assembling in the pink marble U.S. Bancorp Tower in downtown Portland in late March of 1993. They had two months to produce a blueprint for the survival of the Northwest's old-growth forests and all the creatures that inhabited them. As if that weren't challenge enough, President Clinton wanted a plan that would allow federal timber to flow again, and soon.

The new team was not starting from scratch. This time, however, scientists were being asked to prepare an overtly political document. Though Jack Ward Thomas was in charge of the platoon of scientists working in Portland, Clinton's political operatives looked over his shoulder every step of the way.

THE FEMAT CHALLENGE

Initially, the Clinton administration envisioned a team of about 15. Assistant Interior Secretary George Frampton worked with Thomas to pick the core group. But as the scope and complexity of the task began to sink in, more scientists were enlisted. By the end, there were more than 100. Eventually, the unwieldy group was given an unwieldy name: the Forest Ecosystem Management Assessment Team, or FEMAT for short.

Everyone on the team was invited to take part in discussions, with final decisions left to Thomas's discretion. It was a heavy responsibility, even for someone with his knowledge and political acumen. He eventually named a core group of a dozen scientists to advise him on important issues.

Early on, the administration decided the scientists' work would be done in secret, without public involvement or press access. The reason offered was that time was so short they could not afford distractions. The shroud of secrecy surrounding the deliberations heightened media curiosity and fed the rumor mill.

The administration also made a fateful decision not to include line officers in the development of its new forest plan. Yet Clinton's top forest advisors in Washington, D.C., were briefed regularly. This fueled resentment in the agencies.

It was a full month before FEMAT had a charter. During this time, many decisions about how to proceed were made, changed, and changed again, according to a postmortem critique by key members of the team.

At the outset, some of the scientists believed they were supposed to develop a single conservation strategy that would become the president's plan. But the administration soon issued new marching orders, asking for a range of options from which Clinton could choose. That meant a less free-wheeling, more systematic analysis would be required.

The scientists began by reviewing all the previous studies that had brought the federal government to this moment. There were nearly 50. They singled out the ones that could pass muster scientifically for further consideration. Eventually, they chose eight options for detailed evaluation.

The first computer runs predicting timber harvest levels under the eight options jolted even Thomas. Protecting all those plants and animals, with a moderately high level of certainty that none of them would go extinct in the foreseeable future, meant that very little logging could occur in the owl region. "We were shocked there was so little wiggle room," Thomas said later.

In early May, the various FEMAT working groups presented their work to the full team during an all-day session in Portland. Several administration officials and government lawyers also attended. During the presentations, it became clear to Thomas that none of the eight options were politically viable. None articulated a core philosophy or vision of how the forests should be managed for future generations. More to the point, only two options would produce more than 1 billion board feet of timber, and both of those were likely to be rejected by Judge Dwyer. Others clustered at 600 to 700 million board feet. Option 1, the greenest, came in at just 200 million board feet—virtually a zero cut.

George Frampton also recognized that numbers like those wouldn't fly. "If that was to be the timber cut in the final alternatives, it wouldn't be acceptable," he said. He contends the scientists on the team knew it too. "They knew what the political margins were."

Rumors spread quickly. Timber industry lobbyists and their friends in Congress went straight to Tom Collier, Interior Secretary Babbitt's chief of staff. According to Frampton, Representative Norm Dicks, a Washington Democrat, delivered the administration an emphatic ultimatum: "We've got to have 2 billion board feet."

Thomas himself clashed with Collier a number of times. "We had our confrontation over the line between politics and science," he recalled. "They wanted an easy life."

OPTION 9

Thomas felt the weight of destiny upon him as he flew back to Portland in late spring of 1993 after yet another briefing in Washington, D.C. He had not gotten this far without political savvy. He knew he had to give the president an out. In the sealed sanctuary of the bank tower, he called his colleagues together. "We have to do better, guys," he said. "Who will help me try one more time?" Among those who stepped forward were his old buddies from the owl team, Eric Forsman and Charles Meslow, and University of Washington forestry professor

Jerry Franklin, the guru of new forestry. Franklin's moment had arrived. He agreed to take the lead in designing a new alternative.

Lately, Franklin had been touting "restoration forestry"—the theory that if dense second-growth forest plantations were aggressively thinned to reduce competition and open the canopy, they would acquire old-growth characteristics sooner, accelerating their use by spotted owls. Though some small-scale experimental sites had been thinned in this way, it would be decades before scientists knew whether restoration forestry could create forests that spotted owls actually would live in.

Still, Franklin's concepts pointed to a way out of the impasse, a way to leave habitat reserves open to some kind of management and to ratchet up the timber yield, however slightly. The scientists decided to write a new option that would allow thinning of trees up to 80 years old within old-growth reserves—*if* it would hasten the development of old-growth characteristics within these younger stands. They also decided to allow salvage logging in the reserves—*if* it could be shown to promote "forest health."

Under this option there would be no new inviolate reserves. And at least a quarter of the remaining old growth would stay in the "matrix," the area open to modified clearcutting. This was not what Julie Norman had had in mind when she said her piece at the Forest Conference.

It was a given that the plan would have to protect dwindling wild salmon runs if the administration hoped to stave off future endangered species listings. The scientists redrew the old-growth reserves, concentrating them in watersheds critical to the survival of salmon. They theorized that these reserves could do double duty as habitat for land species—spotted owls, marbled murrelets, and salamanders.

No logging or road-building would be allowed within these "key watersheds" until the agencies formally studied them. Roadless areas within key watersheds would remain roadless. Even small streams would be protected by buffer zones. It was a nearly total embrace of the watershed option developed by the Gang of Four the previous year.

To accommodate Bruce Babbitt's fascination with consensus groups like the Applegate Partnership, the team drew 10 enormous "adaptive management areas," ranging in size from 80,000 to 400,000 acres. Within them, foresters would be encouraged to conduct large-scale experiments in ecosystem management, with local citizens closely involved in designing the experiments.

Computer runs showed that by leaving 25 percent of the old growth in the matrix, and by allowing thinning and salvage logging even in the reserves, the federal agencies could sell about 1.2 billion board feet of timber annually.

The scientists christened this new strategy Option 9.

NO SURPRISE

To those following the evolution of the forest issue, this new timber yield figure was not a shock. "We all knew going in that an ecologically credible plan would not produce more than 1 billion board feet," Frampton said.

When Frampton got his first look at Option 9, he himself objected at first to allowing logging within forest reserves. Ultimately, though, Frampton signed off on Option 9. "I was persuaded," he said, "that the desire for certainty was not a scientific instinct but a political instinct."

Thomas knew Clinton would pick Option 9 because, among the options that could pass muster with Judge Dwyer, it was the one that would allow him to sell the most timber. He also knew the president had hoped for a plan that would allow him to sell much more. But Option 9 was the best he had been able to deliver. "Do I think there was false hope created? Yes," Thomas said later. "But no one should have been surprised by 1.2 billion board feet."

Thomas flatly denied that the Clinton administration had directed the outcome of the FEMAT process. "I never detected that they were trying to do anything but the right thing," he said. "One of the biggest lies to come out of this is that we were pressured to do Option 9." If anyone was putting pressure on the team, Thomas insisted, he himself was the culprit.

He recalled that late in the process, Katie McGinty, director of Clinton's Office of Environmental Policy, called him and said, "I hear you're being pressured to produce more timber. If there's one SOB putting pressure on you, I want to know who it is." Thomas's response was: "It's me!"

PLEASING NO ONE

By mid-June, rumors began circulating about a new option for westside forests that had been written on a fast track, with only cursory scientific review. As details of Option 9 began to leak out, intense political posturing began.

On June 21, House Speaker Tom Foley told reporters that Clinton's preferred plan had virtually no chance of winning congressional approval. "Many in Congress feel there has to be a plan which provides significantly larger than 1.2 billion board feet of allowable cut in order for any kind of forest products industry to survive on federal lands," Foley said.

The Oregon Lands Coalition, briefed in late June, fired off a press release denouncing Option 9 even before it was made public. "The President and his wet-behind-the-ears process people have made a fatal miscalculation," fumed Merrilee Peay of the Eugene-Springfield Yellow Ribbon Coalition. "They seem to think Middle America is going to stand by and allow a small group of elitists—career environmentalists—to decimate hundreds of small towns and thousands of small businesses."

Environmentalists for once held their tongues. Though they were apprehensive, without the actual plan and maps in hand, they could not say much that was substantive. Besides, their friends in the administration were acting as if they were about to hand them a huge victory.

On July 1, five weeks late, President Clinton unveiled Option 9 in a somber press conference fed by closed-circuit television to the Northwest. The president looked downcast and uncomfortable. With Vice President Gore and several Cabinet members and congressional Democrats flanking him, he apologized to the people of the Northwest for not offering a plan that provided more timber. He explained that his scientific and legal advisors had told him this plan was the best that could be managed under existing law. He blamed years of overcutting by previous administrations. He admitted that the timber industry would be disappointed with timber sale levels and that environmentalists would be disappointed because the plan lacked some of the protections they had sought.

Then he borrowed a line from Oregon Governor Barbara Roberts: "I can only say that as with every other situation in life, we have to play the hand we were dealt. We are doing the best we can with the facts as they now exist in the Pacific Northwest. If these were easy questions, they would have been answered long ago."

Interior Secretary Bruce Babbitt then made a promise he would live to regret. "I'm confident we can move 2 billion board feet into communities of the Northwest in the coming year," he said. "It's our intent to sit down with groups in the Northwest and ask them not to debate Option 9 but to talk about implementation."

The subtext was clear: Bill Clinton had done all he was going to do on behalf of the old-growth forests. He had done it reluctantly, to get the federal timber sale program out of the courts. Now it was time to mitigate the political damage.

That same afternoon, Babbitt and Espy stepped onto the tarmac at Portland International Airport with a clear mission from the White House: to sell the plan in the Pacific Northwest. "We are really hell-bent on implementation," Babbitt said.

READING THE MAPS

The first reactions from environmentalists were muted. Bob Doppelt of the Pacific Rivers Council, who deserved as much credit as anyone for the key watershed strategy in Option 9, was cautiously optimistic. "Not only do we support the scientific principles but we think this is a pretty good framework to begin to build a really solid resolution," he said.

The extent to which Clinton had compromised the old-growth forests took a few weeks to sink in. It was mid-July before the full FEMAT report and maps were available. When environmentalists finally got a chance to study them, they discovered that many prized roadless areas remained open to clearcutting. But it was summer, people were burned out, and the Northwest environment community offered no coordinated response to Option 9.

Jim Britell, conservation director of Kalmiopsis Audubon in Port Orford, Oregon, was one of the first to critique Option 9. In published articles and in formal comments to the government, he attacked its scientific underpinnings, the assumptions on which it was built, and the political motives that prompted the administration to choose Option 9 over Option 1, which offered a much higher level of certainty that most old-growth species would survive.

Some of the decisions the map-drawers made defied logic. The steep-sided watershed of Still Creek east of Portland, forested with natural stands of Douglas-fir, cedar, and hemlock 80 to 100 years old, is one of the last nearly intact valleys in the Mount Hood National Forest. When Regna Merritt of the Oregon Natural Resources Council studied the maps, she discovered that under Option 9 nearly all the watershed would be open to logging—logging that would be clearly visible from historic Timberline Lodge near the Mount Hood summit.

State and federal fisheries biologists considered the lower 11 miles of Still Creek so important to chinook salmon that they had invested nearly $350,000 in repairing the damage from old logging and road-building activities upstream in an effort to restore salmon spawning beds. There was a real risk that future logging on its steep slopes would trigger land-slides, wiping out that investment. Option 1 would have protected most of the watershed. Under Option 9, nearly all of it was in the matrix.

As they studied the maps, environmentalists found many similar compromises. An analysis by the Wilderness Society revealed that in the Gifford Pinchot National Forest, in the southern Washington Cascades, many roadless areas bordering wilderness had been left in the matrix, further fragmenting the forest, while some of the forest's most heavily logged lands were protected in reserves.

In the Siskiyous, Option 9 placed more than 30,000 acres of burned-over, heavily roaded BLM plantations in a reserve while leaving sev-eral pristine roadless areas open to logging. "I'm happy that this is an ancient forest reserve," Dave Willis of the Soda Mountain Wilderness Council said on a tour in September of 1993, as he gazed out at stump fields. "What I don't get is why they're going to cut ancient forests they already have in exchange for lands that might become ancient forest reserves someday."

SCIENTISTS WEIGH IN
In the fall of 1993, after the Clinton administration formally proposed the adoption of Option 9, scientists began to weigh in. Their verdicts, for the most part, were damning: They found the plan was based on untried scientific theories, posed unacceptable risks to salmon and marbled murrelets, and might not even assure the recovery of spot-ted owls.

The Wildlife Society criticized Option 9 for dumping the 50-11-40 rule, developed by the Interagency Scientific Committee in 1990 to assure that enough forest cover would be maintained to allow owls to disperse across the landscape. Instead, Option 9 relied on narrow for-ested stream buffers and small patches of trees in clearcuts to connect the old-growth reserves.

The 7,000-member Ecological Society of America and the American Institute of Biological Sciences, a federation of 50 scientific societies and 80,000 members, released a joint peer review of Option 9 in late October. The two prestigious panels gave the plan its due, noting that it "includes some important advances in the application of ecological knowledge to the management of forests."

But they concluded that it did not adequately reflect scientific uncertainties that could result in "a significant loss of biological diversity." Two other options offered much higher levels of protection for wildlife, they noted, and a third offered better protection for streams and aquatic life. They also questioned the proposal to allow thinning in naturally regenerated stands up to 80 years old within the old-growth reserves and to allow salvage of damaged timber within the reserves after catastrophic disturbance. Those practices, they said, "may cause disruption to a reserve that outweighs any benefit to its recovery."

The Pacific Seabird Group, a professional association of avian biologists, said Option 9 failed to protect critical and scarce old-growth stands for marbled murrelets on federal land within 25 miles of the ocean. They also warned that thinning in natural stands "could open up the canopy, allow access to predators, and thus create the potential for decreased reproductive success."

A BITTER DENOUEMENT

By the end of the FEMAT process, Thomas was physically and emotionally depleted. He had worked 94 straight days, 14 hours a day, taking only two days off when his wife became ill from chemotherapy. In all, he had given four years to the owl plans and their ecological offshoots.

On August 23, 1993, while attending a convention at the Portland Marriott Hotel with Margaret, Thomas reflected somewhat defensively on the job he'd just completed and the inevitability that the plan produced would further reduce logging on federal land. "Think of our mission. We had to deal with owls and fish and murrelets and the old-growth system and the economic issues. Before you know it, you're on the yellow brick road and you're on the way to the Emerald City again."

Thomas praised President Clinton for holding the forest conference and fulfilling his pledge to the Northwest. "He kept his promise. He did it right here in Portland, with his vice president and three or four of his cabinet members. He listened."

But he was weary of the polarization. "I am so tired of the goddam gladiators on both sides," he said. And he saved his harshest comments for environmentalists, his one-time allies.

"It would look like we'd be heroes to somebody. Now it's the environmentalists who accuse us of selling out," he said. "The timber industry has been more technically responsible and more honest in its response than the environmentalists. They don't make it a moral issue. In the end, I've had more respect for the industry people than some of the extremists in the environmental movement."

Chapter Twenty-Five

Splitsville

The mood within the forest preservation movement was bitter on the weekend before Thanksgiving 1993, as forest activists met in a stark Portland State University lecture hall for a blood-letting. This tense night found James Monteith and his old sidekick Andy Kerr on opposite sides of a debate over a recent compromise struck with the Clinton administration.

Reluctantly, and with much agonizing, the Oregon Natural Resources Council and most other plaintiffs in the long-running lawsuit against the Forest Service had succumbed to bullying from the administration. They had agreed to the release of 52 timber sales from their hard-won injunction. The administration had threatened to throw its support to a congressional rider shielding its new forest plan from legal challenges if they didn't go along.

For those who had lived through the 1989 Rider from Hell, it was deja vu all over again. The 1989 rider had forced the release of more than 1 billion board feet of timber from an injunction in this same lawsuit. Then, environmentalists had chosen the sales to be released with a gun at their head. This time, they had done it voluntarily. Critics of the compromise called it the Deal of Shame. It was a moment of realpolitik no one could have predicted.

SHOWING GOOD FAITH
The pressure began even before the administration unveiled Option 9 in July. Tom Collier, Interior Secretary Bruce Babbitt's chief of staff, urged environmental plaintiffs to agree to the release of 200 million board feet of timber from the injunction Judge William Dwyer had imposed in 1991. Collier's emissaries in the negotiations said cooperation would be a sign of good faith—a signal that environmentalists were committed to a peaceful resolution of the forest impasse. Not so coincidentally, springing some timber would also allow Babbitt to save face over his foolish promise to the timber industry that the administration could sell 2 billion board feet of timber in its first year.

Collier wielded a stick as well as a carrot. Without this "good-faith effort," he said, Babbitt would recommend to President Clinton that he support legislation declaring his new plan immune from legal challenges.

The threat infuriated grassroots groups. But lawyers at the Sierra Club Legal Defense Fund advised their clients to go along with the administration. Most lawmakers believed Option 9 was a tremendous victory for environmentalists, they warned. Refusing to cooperate might fuel the backlash against the Endangered Species Act. And now that a Democratic administration had adopted what appeared to be a balanced plan for solving the forest impasse, for the first time in years there was a real chance a rider could succeed.

Kevin Kirchner, SCLDF's lobbyist in Washington, D.C., was the source of some of these warnings. For four years he had succeeded in warding off another Rider from Hell. But Kirchner was convinced that Clinton's election, and the public perception that he had solved the forest crisis with Option 9, had changed the political dynamic on Capitol Hill.

Kirchner says he never recommended that the Deal of Shame be accepted. But he had no doubt that the threat of a rider was real. "Democrats on the Hill were still somewhat enamored of Bill Clinton, Al Gore, and Jack Ward Thomas. They said, 'You mean to tell us you want us to get to the left of Bill Clinton? No way.'"

MINIMIZING THE DAMAGE

Bonnie Phillips of Pilchuck Audubon was still smarting from the Rider from Hell, but a Senate staffer had convinced her that the votes were there for another rider in 1993. "It's the only thing that could have persuaded me," she said. "It was blackmail, pure and simple."

Phillips also perceived that energy was fast leaking out of the movement as burned-out activists looked for new challenges. "We have fewer people involved in forest issues than before," she said. "People are awfully tired. The attitude in Washington is, 'Clinton dealt with the issue. I can't believe you people are still complaining.'"

Once she made the decision that a rider was a serious threat, Phillips vowed that environmentalists would not repeat their experience of 1989. They would set strict ground rules on which sales they would release. If they had to do the dirty work, at least they could try to minimize the damage.

The plaintiffs told the administration they would consider only timber sales in areas slated for logging under Option 9. They would not look at sales in roadless areas, old-growth reserves, or key watersheds. The agencies would have to redesign the sales to increase stream protection. Environmentalists would retain their right to challenge Option 9 in court.

In the end they agreed to release only 83 million board feet of timber. But it wasn't the volume that was at issue; it was the precedent.

Larry Tuttle, the blunt and outspoken new executive director of the Oregon Natural Resources Council, opposed the Deal of Shame from the outset. "My argument was, At some point we're going to have to have a fight with this administration," Tuttle said. "If nothing else, that could have revitalized the movement."

Tuttle, a former banker and central Oregon county commissioner, went head-to-head with the Sierra Club Legal Defense Fund. At one point, he said, SCLDF attorneys Vic Sher and Todd True threatened to fire ONRC as a client if he refused to go along with the deal.

Melanie Rowland, a lawyer for the Wilderness Society, took a more pragmatic view. "It was clear to me that Congress was still not friendly to us, that the Clinton administration was critical. We had to have their support. If we didn't, I didn't see any way we could hold on to our victories."

"It was partly that we had to deal with this administration in a different way. We trusted some people, but they were now political animals in a very shaky administration. We had a need to seem flexible. What looks firm and principled in one situation looks rigid and uncompromising in another."

FACING THE TIGER

Those arguments held little sway on this November night, at a meeting called to vent passions over the Deal of Shame. James Monteith, who had left the Western Ancient Forest Campaign and started his own group, Save the West, reminded the partisan grassroots audience what the deal actually signified. "The political strategy of permanent protection has been our goal for 20 years," he said. Never before had forest activists been voluntary parties to the destruction of old-growth forests.

"The rider was our opportunity to turn around and face the tiger and fight to win," Monteith told the crowd. "Most of us felt the rider was a bluff, and if it wasn't a bluff, we thought we could defeat it. I don't sense that Babbitt is through with us, through with working us over to see what else he can get out of us."

"I have to refuse to accept this notion that we've lost the ability to defend against riders," agreed Lou Gold of the Siskiyou Project. "The ability to go to court and win means something only if we can defend against riders."

Other activists argued passionately that the plaintiffs had no right to give up the injunction. "The forests aren't ours to bargain away. They belong to the species who live there," said Asante Riverwind, who worked with his partner, Karen Coulter, to save forests in the Blue Mountains of northeastern Oregon. "We can't forget the power of the grassroots movement that got us here. We have to get away from a situation where a few people in a few environmental groups can be put in a room and blackmailed."

Jim Britell of Kalmiopsis Audubon accused his fellow activists of failing to adequately explain the Clinton plan to the public and the press. "The media don't understand that the Clinton plan cuts old growth," he said. "The people who are most radicalized about the Clinton forest plan are those who read it."

Tim Hermach of the Native Forest Council lambasted the movement for bowing to political pressure. "Bill Clinton today is between a rock and a sponge because of what we say and how we say it," he shouted. "They're our forests, they're our trees. Why are we on the defense? It's time to draw a line and say, 'Mr. Clinton, we're not moving. We're a rock, too.'"

Kerr defended his decision to deal against this hall full of frustrated activists. Babbitt was calling leaders of national environmental groups for support, he said. Some of the strongest friends of forest protection in Congress were saying they saw no way they could defeat a rider if the administration supported it.

"Once a rider starts, you don't control it," Kerr said. "I felt we did not have the power to fight the Clinton administration. I thought the threat was real and I still believe it was. It was an ugly, tactical decision to surrender some volume. . . . If a rider had passed we could have joined the blame game. That would have been politically the best thing to do, but I didn't think it was best for the forest. It's the most difficult piece of political calculus I've ever been involved in."

For Kerr of all people, it was a bitter lesson. Soon after, he moved with his wife, Nancy Peterson, to the small northeastern Oregon town of Joseph to get some distance, or so he thought, from the fractious internal debate.

A SLAM DUNK

In the spring of 1994, the administration submitted its final plan to Judge Dwyer. Responding to public comments, it had increased protection for small seasonal streams and had added some land to old-growth reserves, but Option 9 remained essentially unchanged. Just before Christmas 1994, Dwyer ruled that Option 9 complied with federal law—if only barely. "The question is not whether the court would write the same plan, but whether the agencies have acted within the bounds of the law," he wrote. "On the present record, the answer to that question is yes."

But Dwyer also noted that the administration itself had stated Option 9 would produce the highest sustainable timber levels of all legally acceptable options it had considered. "In other words, any more logging sales than the plan contemplates would probably violate the laws," Dwyer wrote. "Whether the plan and its implementation will remain legal will depend on future events and conditions."

The Clinton administration was jubilant over this narrow victory. Only three groups—Hermach's Native Forest Council, Monteith's Save the West, and the Forest Conservation Council—appealed Dwyer's ruling to the 9th U.S. Circuit Court of Appeals. They argued that it fell short of adequately protecting salmon, murrelets, and spotted owls. The case was still alive, but with the injunction lifted, the forests were unlocked and the administration was home free.

LOSING CONTROL

The acrimony dividing the environmental movement went deeper than the release of a few timber sales. The forest protection movement was being torn asunder by a debate about who controlled it—the uncom-promising grassroots activists who had created and sustained it out of their own deep commitment, or the national conservation groups and big foundations, latecomers to the campaign, which had close ties to the new Democratic administration and which now wielded so much influence.

In June of 1993, shortly after he became ONRC's executive direc-tor, Larry Tuttle received a lesson in the cost environmental groups might pay if they challenged the Clinton administration head-on over forest policy. Tuttle met with Tom Wathen of the Pew Charitable Trusts in New York to discuss the possibility of a Pew grant to support a major ONRC grassroots organizing effort. "We were going through an ago-nizing debate about our real relationship to our grass roots," Tuttle recalled. But Wathen told him, "No, that's not going to work."

What Pew was willing to support, Wathen said, was a monitoring program to ensure that the Forest Service and BLM followed Option 9. Wathen also told Tuttle that if he wanted Pew money, ONRC would have to enter into a written agreement with other groups funded by Pew that worked on forests.

Tuttle went back to Portland and told his staff, "I think we should run away from this money as fast as we can. We'd lose our indepen-dence." Andy Kerr and the ONRC board of directors disagreed. "Things blew up at that point," Tuttle said. After Tuttle left the following year, Kerr took over as executive director and accepted the Pew money.

Wathen, a lawyer, said it was obvious as soon as Option 9 was re-leased that it would survive new challenges because the administration had made a good-faith effort to adopt a legal plan. The question the new plan posed for foundations funding the ancient forest campaign, he said, was what to do next. "Option 9 changed the status quo. It didn't get us the inviolate reserves, so the question was, How do you improve it?"

The solution the foundations came up with was to fund an inten-sive monitoring program that would assure the agencies followed the new plan to the letter and document violations. "No one came up with a better solution," he said. No one, he added, was forced to take the money.

Tuttle traces the day environmentalists began to lose the ancient forest campaign to the day they allowed foundations to become major players. At that point, he said, they turned their attention from grassroots organizing to the technical and scientific arguments for forest preservation. "The question is whether the scientific approach to for-est protection helped us or hurt us. By directing organizational efforts away from the grass roots toward gathering facts, we drained all the passion out of the movement."

Not everyone agreed with Tuttle's view. But it was clear that in this new political era scientific and technical arguments alone would not save the ancient forests.

KNOW THINE ENEMY

The seeds of dissent sown in 1993 continued to germinate. In early March of 1995 at the annual University of Oregon Environmental Law Conference, environmentalists packed a huge University of Oregon lecture hall to watch Ron Arnold, the white-bearded founder of the wise-use movement, join two disaffected activists on a panel entitled "Foundation and Corporate Control Over Environmental Organizations."

Arnold, director of the Center for the Defense of Free Enterprise in Bellevue, Washington, had agreed to be on the panel after debating Tim Hermach on a radio talk show in New York City. He had gone away with a grudging respect for his adversary. "We disagreed on most issues concerning what the Earth is like and people's role in it," Arnold said. "But we had a good knockdown, drag-out debate. I respect an honest opponent that doesn't give us a lot of bullshit." The two had agreed on one thing, he added: "Something has gone wrong with corporate environmentalism."

The other panelists were Michael Donnelly, founder of Friends of the Breitenbush Cascades, who was deeply bitter about what he regarded as a co-optation of the ancient forest movement by the national groups, and Jeff St. Clair, editor of the leftist environmental journal *Wild Forest Review*. Both believed grassroots groups had lost their voice—and their edge—with the infusion of big foundation money.

Since 1990, Northwest environmental groups had come to depend heavily on foundation support. The Seattle-based Bullitt Foundation alone increased its support of Northwest environmental causes 15-fold between 1989 and 1995, from $300,000 to $4.5 million. Most of its grants went to support forest preservation work. Overall, foundation grants accounted for 80 percent of revenue to Northwest groups by the mid-1990s, up from 20 percent a few years earlier.

It was the large East Coast foundations that had come under fire from Donnelly, Tuttle, and St. Clair, however—especially the Pew Charitable Trusts. Dissidents hadn't forgiven Pew for funding what they regarded as a discredited lobbying and litigation strategy.

Of late, Arnold was portraying national conservation groups as the Goliaths and local wise-use activists as the Davids in the contest for the hearts and minds of the American people. In a 1994 report, *Getting Rich,* Arnold profiled the budgets, top salaries, major contributors, and investment portfolios of the 12 largest environmental organizations. He saw hypocrisy in the fact that the Wilderness Society invested in Caterpillar, Inc. Arnold focused particular attention on the Environmental Grantmakers Association, a 10-year-old coalition of 160 private foundations that provided most of the $340 million donated to environmental causes each year.

Jeff St. Clair questioned the propriety of environmental groups taking money from Pew, Rockefeller, or W. Alton Jones, all philanthropic subsidiaries of huge oil companies. "The environmental movement is now accurately described as just another cynical well-financed special interest group," he accused. "'Settle and move on' is their mantra."

These were not new arguments in the fractious ranks of the movement, although on this day they were put forth with a harshness seldom heard in public. But asking Arnold to join in the movement-bashing was an audacious move.

St. Clair defended the decision to invite Arnold onto environmental turf. "If we have any chance of prevailing as a political movement, we have to demystify the opposition," he said. "Who knows, we may even find some common ground, or a common enemy."

DIVIDE AND CONQUER

Before this sea of adversaries, Arnold, a stiff and aloof man, proceeded to attack the national groups by name and offer tips on where to get the goods on them. He suggested that grassroots activists could use the information in his report to achieve their own goals. "It's not a point of agreement," he said, "but a point of mutual utility."

As he recited the names of tax documents and reports, however, a lightbulb went off in the audience. Someone stood and demanded to know, "Are you here to divide and conquer?"

Then David Brower, elder statesman of the movement, stood and demanded of Arnold, "What do you want to see trashed next on the planet?"

"The idea that wise use is a bad thing," Arnold said lamely.

Environmentalists now went on the offensive. They demanded that Arnold explain his world view. "What you people do is come in and polarize communities," one woman in the audience declared.

Mitch Friedman stood to defend the role of foundations. In 1989, Friedman, a former Earth First! activist, had made a decision to become involved in two giant wildland projects, the campaigns to protect the Greater Yellowstone and North Cascades ecosystems. Foundation funding had allowed him to build the case with scientific arguments and computer-assisted mapping. "It wouldn't have happened without them," he said. "Don't throw the baby out with the bathwater. We need all the help we can get to counter the wise-use movement."

It fell to Lou Gold, grizzled protector of the Siskiyous, to bring the emotional debate to closure. Because he had traveled around the country with his slide show, building a base of 10,000 members in 45 states for protection of the Siskiyous, his organization, the Siskiyou Regional Education Project, had been free of outside pressure, Gold said.

"No foundation has twisted our arm, no national group has undercut us. When you have that relationship with place, and you have adequately communicated it, then no one can take that away. I don't want to spend all this time debating and second-guessing. I have a deep faith in our message."

Chapter Twenty-Six

Reinvention Blues

Chuck Hoyt, a longtime public relations officer in the Oregon office of the Bureau of Land Management, saw the shift coming in the days before Bill Clinton was elected president. As Lauri Hennessey, Hoyt's boss, recalls, "Chuck used to say, 'Nobody around here gets that the day after the election, we all have to go out and read *Earth in the Balance*.'" Sure enough, after the election, Hoyt could be seen poring through Al Gore's ecological opus in spare moments at the office.

Not everyone in the forest management agencies was so adaptable. The question, as the Clinton team mobilized to implement Option 9, was whether or not the agencies would fall in line with the administration's new vision.

Option 9 was, among other things, an effort to change the embedded timber culture of the Forest Service and the BLM, a culture nurtured for a half-century by the timber industry, members of Congress from both parties, and both Republican and Democratic administrations.

But the Clinton forces took on the task with more chutzpah than finesse, raising hackles among forest managers who were still in deep denial about the changes the federal courts and this new administration had foisted upon them.

A NEW CHIEF

Rumors had been circulating since early summer of 1993 that Assistant Agriculture Secretary Jim Lyons wanted Jack Ward Thomas to replace F. Dale Robertson as chief of the Forest Service. Robertson, who had risen through the Forest Service ranks as the supervisor of big-timber forests, was the personification of the agency's traditional timber-first orientation. He had shown little leadership during its turbulent transition. He had not embraced the Clinton administration's new ecosystem-based approach to forest management. Jack Ward Thomas, on the other hand, was the architect of that approach.

But there was a problem. Though Thomas had spent 27 years with the Forest Service, and had risen to become the agency's senior research wildlife biologist, he was not a member of the elite Senior Executive Service. The only way Lyons could make him chief was through a political appointment—a maneuver that met with stiff opposition among the agency's traditionalists.

The Senior Executive Service was a cadre of 6,800 high-ranking federal civil service employees. Its members were chosen by invitation from other members. They qualified for top posts in government by undergoing special training in the intricacies of administration and budgeting. Since 1978, Forest Service chiefs had been drawn from the Executive Service's clubby ranks. Even before that, new chiefs traditionally had been selected by their peers. To break that precedent, critics said, raised the specter of politicizing an agency that prided itself on professional leadership. In truth, however, few federal agencies are more intensely political than the Forest Service, especially in regard to how it chooses its chief.

As rumors of Thomas's imminent appointment flew in October of 1993, former Forest Service Chief Max Peterson wrote to Agriculture Secretary Mike Espy, Lyons's boss, urging him not to "politicize" the chief's position. If he did, Peterson warned, there would be nothing to stop some future administration from replacing Thomas with its own hand-picked chief, who might be far less qualified for the job. "We believe the proper management of natural resources requires a long-term view—not the shorter view often engendered by the political process," Peterson wrote. Seventy forest supervisors from around the country signed the letter.

Some who signed genuinely feared for the professional integrity of their agency if its chief served only at the pleasure of whatever administration was in power. But others objected to Thomas because his background was in wildlife biology, not timber. Though he was clearly a "career professional," in the hierarchy of national forest management he was an outsider. He had never put up a timber sale.

The flap over how the next chief would be chosen left both Thomas and Robertson twisting in the wind. In late October of 1993, as Lyons tried to get the paper work through the Office of Personnel Management to put Thomas in the job, things got so ugly that he was forced to announce Robertson's reassignment. David Unger, an assistant chief, was named acting chief temporarily.

Environmentalists in the Northwest generally welcomed the prospect that Thomas would take the reins of the agency most responsible for liquidating ancient forests. Whatever their opinion of Option 9, they understood that Thomas had shown real courage in presenting the Interagency Scientific Committee's path-breaking 1990 owl strategy, and consummate political skill in handling the fallout.

ANSWERING THE CALL

When the call finally came on November 16, 1993, it came over a loudspeaker at Chicago's O'Hare Airport, where Thomas and his wife, Margaret, were between planes. They were headed home after spending 20 frustrating days in Washington, D.C., waiting for his appointment as chief to be announced. Answering the page, Thomas called Lyons, who wanted to know whether the two could turn around and return to Washington. Agriculture Secretary Espy planned to make the announcement the next day.

But after three weeks on the road, Margaret Thomas was frail and exhausted. She had suffered a setback in her battle against colon cancer. There would be no Washington, D.C., press conference, Thomas told Lyons. It's time for us to go home. The next day, in a somber and reserved mood, he gave interviews and fielded questions in Portland.

It was in fact Margaret who had encouraged Thomas to take the job. In June, when Lyons first raised the possibility, he declined. His wife, he said, was dying of cancer. When he told her the news, Margaret Thomas recalled, "I looked at him and said, 'That's about the most stupid thing I've ever heard you say. We've been married 36 years and this is the first time you've made a career decision without me. What are you going to tell your sons?'" Thomas called Lyons back and told him he would think about it.

In his inaugural speech as chief-designate at Oregon State University a few days after the announcement of his appointment, Thomas revealed his weariness with the forest wars. He took aim again at the "professional gladiators" on both sides of the old-growth conflict—people who weren't interested in compromise because they were in the fight to win. He understood that they were part of the political system, he said. But they were not part of the approach he saw evolving in the management of public lands. He described that approach as "an attempt to preserve biodiversity through ecosystem management at the landscape scale." And people, he said, were an integral part of that landscape.

Thomas added that the public should not expect answers from scientists on contentious natural resource management issues. Science is a method, he said. Any side in a debate could find a scientist to point out weaknesses in the other side's assumptions or methodology. He added that scientists weren't used to being beaten up in the political arena. Many, he said, were now retiring from this "bruising game." If Thomas wished that he were one of them, he kept those feelings to himself.

In one of his first acts as chief, Thomas won plaudits from environmentalists when he sent a memo to all regional foresters and research station managers advising them that he expected them to tell the truth, obey the law, and practice ecosystem management.

But in his early weeks as chief, Thomas was distracted by his wife's worsening condition. In January, after packing up a lifetime of memories and saying goodbye to old friends, Margaret Thomas moved from the family home in La Grande to a suburban Washington townhouse to be with her husband. She died soon after. The new chief was left to mourn in the shark-infested political waters of Washington, D.C.

WINNING OVER THE RANK AND FILE

Lauri Hennessey, director of public affairs for the Oregon office of the Bureau of Land Management, recalls a meeting in Portland shortly before the April 1993 Forest Conference, at which Jim Lyons and Interior Department forest specialist Tom Tuchmann met with forest supervisors and BLM district managers in the Northwest. These young upstarts rubbed the old guard the wrong way, Hennessey said. "Lyons told them, 'I want you to know that I want you on board, I want you to be involved. But if you aren't, you can leave.'"

There were few questions. Tuchmann seemed pleased with the meeting. But Hennessey, who had learned her political street smarts as press aide to Senator Bob Packwood, buttonholed him after the meeting. "I said, 'Don't be bullshitted by what you heard in there. There's a lot of resistance.'"

From that day on, Hennessey was the official bearer of bad news. Still, she and Tuchmann hit it off, and in December of 1993, when he was named to head the administration's new Portland-based Office of Forestry and Economic Development, set up to oversee the forest plan's implementation, she agreed to serve as his press aide.

Deputy Forest Service Chief George Leonard, who was to be side-lined by Lyons later that year, bitterly resented the exclusion of forest supervisors and district rangers from development of the plan they would have to implement on the ground. Option 9 was front-loaded with requirements for watershed studies and environmental impact statements that had to be completed before the agencies could sell timber. Many managers considered these requirements onerous and unnecessary.

"The agency has to believe the plan is feasible in order to get behind it," Leonard said. Experienced forest managers could have warned the administration that it might take as much as three years after the plan was adopted to get timber sales moving again.

Lyons tells the story of a forest supervisor who remarked to Thomas soon after he became chief that his staff couldn't wait to get done with all the studies Option 9 required "so they can get on with their business." Thomas's response, Lyons said, was: "This *is* our business."

Though a number of forest managers saw Option 9 as too prescriptive and some felt it left them with little discretion, most biologists believed the environmental studies were necessary and long overdue. "To my mind, it meant line officers were going to have to be extraordinarily thoughtful, creative, and innovative to accomplish the mission that it established," said Cindy Deacon-Williams, a longtime Forest Service fisheries biologist.

"It's easy to cut trees."

Elaine Zielinski, Oregon director of the BLM, served on an interagency team charged with implementing Option 9. An early challenge, she said, was reconciling the very different cultures of the land management agencies—the Forest Service and BLM—and the regulatory agencies—the Fish and Wildlife Service and National Marine Fisheries Service. "The Forest Service and BLM are very can-do organizations," she said. "There's a certain production ethic. At first there was a feeling that under Option 9 timber sales were just a by-product, that if we get them, fine." Managers resisted that change in their traditional mission.

The plan's close association with the Clinton administration also made some managers gun shy. "If the plan had come from the ground up, they might have felt some ownership," Hennessey said. "But they felt it was the administration's plan, that someone might swoop down and take it away."

Still, by the spring of 1994, a paradigm shift was underway. At a meeting of the Applegate Partnership, in southwestern Oregon, Rogue River National Forest Supervisor Jim Gladen was asked by a timber industry representative when the Rogue would begin selling timber again. Gladen replied that Option 9's requirements for watershed studies made it impossible to predict.

"Timber is just one part of this plan," Gladen said. "Fish and recreation are important too. We're a different forest than we were a few years ago. You can argue the merits, but at least we know what we're supposed to be doing."

A NEW KIND OF PORK

In Portland, Tom Tuchmann and Lauri Hennessey were doing their best to smooth the rough spots in the implementation of Option 9. Hennessey said she got caught up in the experience. "I became a real believer. I was involved in this historically important change in forest management."

Tuchmann was responsible not only for implementing Option 9 but also for overseeing another major part of Clinton's Northwest Forest Plan, a program to help timber communities and workers through the economic transition. The administration had promised $27 million to put loggers and millworkers to work restoring damaged watersheds and $200 million in assistance to timber communities and businesses during the first year of Option 9's implementation.

Some members of the Northwest delegation quickly recognized watershed restoration money as a new kind of federal pork they could deliver to their districts. One of Hennessey's tasks was to cut through bureaucratic red tape to release money so members of Congress could announce economic development grants on trips home to their districts.

It was a heady time, and the high energy and optimism lasted until June of 1994, when U.S. District Judge William Dwyer dissolved the injunction blocking federal timber sales. "At that point, the Office of Forestry and Economic Development wasn't needed anymore," Hennessey said. In fact, some forest managers felt the office, a daily reminder of the Clinton administration's continuing oversight of their agencies, was in the way. They wanted the administration to give them back the management prerogative to implement the plan.

BLM Oregon Director Zielinski became a strong advocate for Option 9. She refused to refer to it as the Clinton Forest Plan. At the

BLM, it was the Northwest Forest Plan, period. Zielinski said the plan won early acceptance from many BLM forest managers because it was built on some of the same principles—key watersheds and reserves to protect old growth and stream corridors—as the agency's own draft management plans for the 1990s. Local BLM managers had been heavily involved in developing those plans. "We changed internally during that process," she said.

PULLING PUNCHES

Another goal of the administration's Northwest Forest Plan was to get federal agencies to work together more effectively on forest policy. In an effort to avoid new endangered species conflicts, the administration encouraged the Fish and Wildlife Service and the National Marine Fisheries Service to get involved in the early design of timber sales so they could head off potential problems. Inevitably there was pressure on both agencies not to wield the Endangered Species Act to stop potentially harmful logging practices.

This became evident in January of 1994, when the Fish and Wildlife Service proposed a rule for protecting owl habitat on heavily cutover private lands. Timberland owners in southern Oregon complained bitterly about the rule's impact on their ability to log their land. Weyerhaeuser Company officials went straight to the White House. Lines on maps were quickly redrawn to exempt most Weyerhaeuser holdings in Douglas and Coos Counties from the owl rule. Representative Peter DeFazio, an Oregon Democrat whose district included the two timber-dependent counties, cried foul. "Cozy relationships between multinational corporations and the Department of Interior should not govern forest policy in the Northwest," he said. Assistant Interior Secretary George Frampton was dispatched to the Northwest to do damage control.

The pressure to avoid new threatened and endangered species listings was intense. The bull trout, which had once thrived in the clear, cold waters of pristine streams all across the Northern Rockies and the Pacific Northwest, had become a victim of logging, road-building, livestock grazing, mining, irrigation, and dams—the gamut of human activities in the rural West. In February of 1994, federal scientists who had reviewed the trout's status reported that the fish were in imminent peril throughout their range. Yet in 1994 and again in 1995, the Fish and Wildlife Service, under pressure from political leaders in Idaho and Montana, declined to list the trout as a threatened species.

As during the Bush administration, the most controversial issues were being decided at the Interior Department level or at the White House. The difference was that in most cases the scientific findings no longer were suppressed. As David Klinger, a spokesman for the Fish and Wildlife Service, put it, "We're still stating our case. It's just that our case may not prevail."

REINVENTION RETREAT

Thomas's early efforts to put his own stamp on the Forest Service faltered. In December of 1994, as part of a broad initiative he called "Reinvention of the Forest Service," he proposed changing the boundaries of the Forest Service regions and eliminating some regional offices. Under the reorganization, the Portland office would gain jurisdiction over Alaska forests but lose the forests of eastern Oregon and eastern Washington to the regional office in Ogden, Utah. The proposal stirred instant opposition from Oregon's Senator Mark Hatfield and members of the Alaska delegation, who were used to dealing with the agency through the existing structure. It died a quick death.

There was unquestionably a need to reinvent the Forest Service. Steep reductions in timber sales and federal budgetary belt-tightening had forced the agency to downsize. Thousands of employees accepted a buy-out offer and took early retirement in 1994. In the new era of ecosystem management, fisheries biologists and landscape ecologists were in greater demand than engineers and timber sale planners. The agency needed a cultural transfusion.

Thomas's larger reinvention initiative, set out in a visionary but little-read document in December of 1994, was intended to reorganize the agency from top to bottom and change its entrenched timber culture. It called for such "transformational strategies" as team management at all levels of the agency and described a vision of a Forest Service that was the global leader in sustainable forestry practices. But Thomas's reinvention document attracted scant attention in the press or in the bureaucratic netherworld of the Forest Service, and it would soon be eclipsed by the politics of the Republican revolution.

A key element of reinvention was the agency's commitment to ecosystem management. But Clinton's Northwest Forest Plan, the prototype for this new paradigm, suffered a setback in March of 1994 when U.S. District Judge Thomas Penfield Jackson of the District of Columbia ruled in a lawsuit brought by the timber industry that the plan had been developed in violation of a federal open meetings law. Jackson listed 10 separate violations, from the makeup of the scientific team to its failure to hold open meetings and keep detailed minutes. The judge refused to overturn the plan because it was still in draft form and had not yet been adopted as official Forest Service policy. However, the ruling left the administration shaken.

One of the first casualties was the Applegate Partnership. In late June, paranoid administration officials told Forest Service and BLM employees they could no longer participate in the consensus-building group because it wasn't chartered as a federal advisory group. They were told the integrity of the forest plan itself was at stake.

A NEW HARD LINE

That same month, Thomas warned stunned forest activists at a lunch sponsored by the Natural Resources Council of America that unless timber began flowing from Northwest forests soon, Option 9 would be lost and the whole issue would end up in the lap of Congress. Roadless areas still open to logging under the plan would have to be entered as soon as possible, Thomas said, because the rest of the land Option 9 allocated to timber production had been so hammered by logging that it could not produce the timber yields the plan promised without serious environmental damage.

Efforts by environmentalists to undermine the plan were wearing thin, the new chief added. If those efforts continued, the administration would have no choice but to seek legislation to end the deadlock.

Thomas's halo slipped further in June of 1994, when an affidavit surfaced revealing that he had admitted ordering scientists to shred internal communications, including electronic mail messages, during preparation of the Northwest Forest Plan. The affidavit was made public by Andy Stahl, who had left the Sierra Club Legal Defense Fund to become executive director of the Association of Forest Service Employees for Environmental Ethics, the group founded by dissident Forest Service employee Jeff DeBonis. Stahl said that by failing to preserve the record of discussion, Thomas had destroyed evidence of dissent over the plan's scientific underpinnings.

Thomas retorted that he was guilty only of "shredding the garbage." Documents left for garbage collectors might have been retrieved and leaked before the process was finished, he said, scaring timber communities and allowing manipulation of timber markets.

Disillusionment grew in September of 1994, when environmentalists obtained a memo revealing that Thomas had quietly changed the agency's appeals process, giving managers discretion to reject appeals of timber sales and other projects out of hand if they concluded the appeals were based on procedural violations not "fundamental" to final decisions.

What many environmentalists failed to understand was Thomas's deep loyalty to the agency that had been his home for nearly three decades—a loyalty that blinded him to its many faults. As chief, Thomas saw his job as defending the Forest Service from its critics. Moreover, observers who were familiar with the internal politics of the agency said Thomas's reform efforts often were undermined by entrenched timber beasts in the chief's office, in the regional offices, and on the national forests, who kept the lines of communication open to sympathetic members of Congress. Chief Jack wasn't always kept in the loop.

Veteran forest activist James Monteith, who had known Thomas since 1974, was not surprised by the chief's new hard line. He had advised his fellow forest activists in the December 1993 issue of the advocacy journal *Forest Watch* that they should not expect to have things their way with Thomas. Though each of the scientific panels on which he served had made improvements in the status quo, he said, each had also made unnecessary compromises on protection of old-growth forests

"I believe he brings the necessary leadership, charisma, and integrity which that agency so desperately needs today, and in that regard he's the obvious choice," Monteith wrote. "But mark my words, Chief Jack is not nearly as green as he has been painted by many different people."

REINVENTION FROM THE GROUND UP

Though efforts to reform the Forest Service from the top down were running into rough water in Washington, D.C., by the mid-1990s real and fundamental change was occurring in the field, at least where motivated, solution-oriented managers were in charge. Jim Furnish, supervisor of the Siuslaw National Forest in the Oregon Coast Range, was one of those managers.

The Siuslaw has spotted owls and marbled murrelets and coho salmon. It is surrounded by heavily cut industry lands that were logged hard and repeatedly beginning in the 19th century. Lands too steep or remote for easy access became, by default, the Siuslaw National Forest. After World War II the Siuslaw became one of the high-volume forests, where ambitious career foresters cut their teeth.

In 1990, the Siuslaw sold 360 million board feet of timber. In 1991, after the Dwyer injunction hit home, it sold 12 million. By 1993, the numbers were in single digits. By 1994, Jim Furnish wasn't selling any timber on the Siuslaw.

"We had a big train that was moving down the track at a high rate of speed," Furnish said in 1994. "That train came to a halt in 1991. Now there's a lot of inertia. A lot of study has to happen before we can get the train moving again. When it does get moving, it will be much smaller. There's a public expectation that these coastal temperate rainforests will be managed differently."

Option 9 placed most of the Siuslaw in reserves—for old growth, owls, and murrelets. Very little land was allocated to timber production. The Northwest Forest Plan also required Furnish and his crew to pay more attention to coastal rivers and native fish runs, especially coho salmon. The Siuslaw has 8,000 miles of permanent, year-round streams; 1,200 of those stream miles harbor anadromous fish.

Even before Option 9 with its watershed protection strategy became final, Furnish and his team began looking for ways to protect salmon habitat on the Siuslaw. And even before Clinton's economic assistance program took effect, they were talking economic diversification with people in small coastal timber towns. Just having those discussions was a major departure from business as usual, said Alsea District Ranger Mike deLuz. "What we're looking at is that timber not be the sole driver in our conversations. Our discussions have been open and multidimensional."

Over six years, deLuz saw his staff shrink by more than 75 percent and his timber sale program plummet from 100 million board feet to zero. He said his crew now took as much pride in completing watershed studies as it had once taken in meeting timber targets.

The Siuslaw was also taking a look at its young forests. Thirty percent of the Siuslaw—200,000 acres—consisted of stands under 45 years of age that would take decades to reach maturity. Stewardship meant increasing structure and diversity in these plantations by planting maple and alder, cedar and hemlock. It meant turning a Douglas-fir plantation into a forest.

Low morale had been a problem at first, but that had passed, Furnish said. "Some people are really enthusiastic about the future. You have others who are really struggling. They don't like where we're headed. They yearn for the old days. There are some people who have chosen to leave the agency because they don't like this direction. We have made attitude adjustments to accommodate the new reality."

No one liked the red tape in Option 9, Furnish admitted. And he had received little direction from the top. "The chief's office has been largely insulated from what has been going on here," he said. In effect, he and his team had reinvented their agency from the bottom up.

Chapter Twenty-Seven

Ecosystems Forever

As the implications of the Northwest Forest Plan began to sink in, the action on forests moved east of the Cascades, where both the physical and the cultural climate were more extreme.

In early 1994, a small armada of federal land managers and scientists converged on a neat brick building in downtown Walla Walla, a college town surrounded by eastern Washington wheat fields. Their assignment was to write an ecosystem management plan for 30 million acres of federal land in eastern Oregon and eastern Washington.

With lawsuits looming over the federal government's failure to protect old-growth species east of the Cascades and wild salmon throughout the Columbia Basin, the Clinton administration had decided to put ecosystem management to its sternest test. It would take what it had learned west of the Cascades, in the owl forests, and apply it to federal lands in the Interior Northwest.

HEADING OFF GRIDLOCK

It was President Clinton himself who directed the Forest Service and Bureau of Land Management to develop "a scientifically sound and ecosystem-based strategy for the management of eastside forests" on July 1, 1993, the day he unveiled Option 9 for westside forests. It wasn't exactly a voluntary move.

Confronted with overwhelming evidence from its own biologists that it had failed to set aside enough old growth for wildlife east of the Cascades, in the summer of 1993 the Forest Service adopted temporary rules increasing protection for eastside old growth. The case for protecting these forests became more urgent in late 1993, when an independent panel of scientists commissioned by Congress called for a halt to all eastside logging and road-building within broad corridors along streams, and within entire watersheds critical to spawning salmon. The scientists also recommended a halt to road-building within roadless areas greater than 10,000 acres in size.

In March of 1994, to stave off federal court injunctions over protection of threatened Snake River chinook salmon and other sensitive fish stocks, the Forest Service and BLM adopted a set of temporary stream protection standards to reduce the impact of logging, road-building, and livestock grazing in areas where salmon spawned. Known as the PACFISH standards, these rules covering 15 national forests in four states east of the Cascades were nearly identical to the stream protection rules the administration had put in place on the westside forests with Option 9.

On both old growth and salmon, the administration needed to come up with permanent standards to avert new lawsuits and new injunctions. And it didn't have much time.

Assistant Agriculture Secretary Jim Lyons hoped ecosystem management would solve all the conflicts brewing in the Interior Northwest.

PUBLIC PARTICIPATION

Lyons determined not to make the same mistakes in Walla Walla that the administration had made on the west side. From the beginning, the eastside project unfolded in the glare of public scrutiny. The team's leaders held monthly public meetings, which were attended mainly by paid timber industry representatives, local government officials, and a few environmentalists.

Boise Cascade Corporation set up an office in the same brick building the ecosystem project had leased for its headquarters. The Boise-based timber giant, which depended on federal lands for 40 percent of its timber supply, hired the engineering firm CH2M-Hill to bird-dog every step of the process. It deployed two of its regional timber-land managers to keep close tabs on it as well. The close scrutiny from timber company executives and their contractors made some scientists jittery and prompted them to restrict access after the first few months.

The 100 counties of the basin had a prominent place at the table, where they looked after the interests of ranchers, miners, and timber companies. Planners were also supposed to take into account the views of 19 tribal governments that held land within the basin.

For many unpaid eastside activists, taking part in this new process was a thankless chore. For some, the trip to Walla Walla was a journey of six or eight hours. Nonetheless, in the early months a dedicated contingent made the monthly drive, trying to keep tabs on what was from the beginning a bewilderingly complicated and highly bureaucratic process. In August of 1994, with foundation support, they formed the Columbia Bioregion Campaign, with a paid coordinator, to press for an ecologically responsible management strategy.

EAST TO THE ROCKIES

In July of 1994, the administration's salmon woes deepened when a federal court blocked all activities on two national forests in northeastern Oregon that might pose a risk to migrating Snake River salmon. Similar challenges loomed upstream on six national forests in Idaho, where Snake River chinook and sockeye salmon spawned. Furious ranchers, who faced a moratorium on livestock grazing on the two forests, demanded that something be done. Then, in August, the National Marine

Fisheries Service upgraded the status of Snake River chinook from threatened to endangered after new numbers showed a precipitous decline.

The administration now recognized that if it hoped to extricate itself from salmon lawsuits, it could not stop practicing ecosystem management at the Idaho border. In August of 1994 the project was expanded to include all 60 million acres of Forest Service and BLM land in the Interior Columbia Basin—a 144-million-acre region stretching from the crest of the Cascades to the Continental Divide and including virtually all of Idaho, eastern Oregon, eastern Washington, western Montana, and small portions of Wyoming, Nevada, and Utah.

Steve Mealey, supervisor of the Boise National Forest, was appointed to head a new Boise, Idaho, office that would oversee planning for these federal lands in the Northern Rockies. For environmentalists in Idaho and Montana, Mealey's appointment was a red flag. They had given him the nickname "Butcher of the Boise" for his aggressive promotion of salvage logging.

FIRE SEASON

The expanded ecosystem project had several strikes against it going in. The first was its mind-boggling scope. Where to begin, what to study, and how much detail to include were all issues the Interior Columbia Basin Ecosystem Management Project had to grapple with. The question of scale soon overwhelmed the project.

Strike number two was the conservative political culture of the Columbia Basin, home to a thriving wise-use campaign and an emerging citizen militia movement. The Interior Basin was torn by conflicts not only over salmon and forests but over livestock grazing, open-pit mining, the reintroduction of wolves and grizzlies, the preservation of wildlands, and the role of the federal government in making decisions about all of the above. The basin's political leaders were among the most conservative in Congress. By 1994, the mood in the region had turned virulently antigovernment.

Strike three came in the late summer of 1994, when wildfire roared through drought-weakened forests in eastern Washington and Idaho. By the time fall rains extinguished the blazes, they had scorched 1.5 million acres in the Interior Basin. Even as the fires burned, politicians began clamoring for a massive timber salvage project to cut and remove the charred trees before they deteriorated and lost their commercial value.

At the August meeting of the eastside ecosystem team, environmentalists grilled Jeff Blackwood, director of the Walla Walla office, on the fire salvage issue. Already, one forest supervisor, Sam Gehr of the Okanogan National Forest in north-central Washington, had predicted that 30 million board feet of timber could be salvaged from his forest. Activists argued that it was premature to make such predictions while the ecosystem planning process still was in its early stages. Instead, they urged him to use the 1994 fires to educate the public about the role of fire in eastside forests. "When hot, dry conditions occur, eastside forests burn," they said in a letter to Blackwood. "These fires are a normal ecological event if viewed from a historical perspective."

Blackwood punted. He said the matter was out of his hands. The eastside ecosystem team, he said, "has no authority or expectation to jump into the middle of decisions on fire rehabilitation."

LOSING SIGHT OF THE PRIZE

In fact, it soon became obvious that the ecosystem planning team would not be involved in any of the critical management decisions on issues that could profoundly affect the basin's long-term ecological health. Instead, politics would drive those decisions.

On one level, the project was a gigantic research-gathering effort. Hundreds of scientists were preparing a scientific assessment that would serve as the foundation for management of the Interior Basin. This mega-inventory of natural processes and of plant, animal, and human communities was to cover everything from the role of fire to the invasion of exotic species, from the tree-munching habits of insects to the habitat needs of grizzlies, from the plight of timber communities to the availability of medical care.

From this massive report the teams in Walla Walla and Boise were supposed to develop separate planning documents laying out various alternatives for managing the basin. But the Walla Walla team became mired in the task of collecting information and lost in its own byzantine bureaucracy, which also threatened to confuse and overwhelm all but the most dedicated citizens. The project's scale, and its leaders' failure to keep focused on specific goals and objectives, eventually caused some scientists to question its relevance.

For Cindy Deacon-Williams, a fisheries biologist who was helping to direct the work of the Boise team under Steve Mealey, the problem developing in Walla Walla became apparent almost immediately after she joined the team in the fall of 1994. She believed in President Clinton's Northwest Forest Plan and hoped the new ecosystem project would expand on it. But she soon became convinced that the planners in Walla Walla had lost their way.

"The westside process was very strongly focused on solving very specific, clearly articulated problems," she said. "In the Interior Columbia Basin process it all went to mush real early. They lost sight of the fact that we were in fact trying to answer management policy questions."

Instead of concentrating on gathering the information they needed to develop strategies for protecting fish and wildlife, she said, project leaders got carried away with the logistics of gathering data. "What we lost was our lodestar," she said. "We were no longer anchored on the purpose for the activity."

After a year on the project, Deacon-Williams came to the conclusion that she could have a greater effect on public land management in the Columbia Basin from the outside. When an offer came from the Pacific Rivers Council to establish a Boise office, she jumped ship.

THE BIG WILD

Expanding the scope of the Columbia Basin project eastward drew the hard-core forest activists of Idaho and Montana into the process. They had earned their spurs fighting not only the timber industry but grazing, mining, and oil and gas interests and conservative western politicians. From the outset, they were skeptical that any project run by the Forest Service and BLM would result in increased protection for the large blocks of unprotected wild land remaining in the Northern Rockies.

Mike Bader, executive director of the Alliance for the Wild Rockies in Missoula, Montana, had his own vision for the future of those lands. He wrote that vision into the Northern Rockies Ecosystem Protection Act, a true ecosystem plan. Like the owl plan west of the Cascades, NREPA was a regionwide plan based on principles of landscape ecology. NREPA proposed to extend wilderness protection to more than 20 million acres of federal wildlands in five states, including all roadless areas bordering existing national parks and wilderness areas. Under the plan, broad connecting corridors would be managed to allow wildlife to move between the large reserves. Developed public lands would be managed to produce timber and forage at sustainable levels.

Bader's goal was to protect the last big chunks of wilderness outside Alaska as habitat for the gray wolf and the grizzly. In the contiguous 48 states, only the Northern Rockies and the North Cascades to the west had enough wild land to support the entire web of life, including these large predators at the top of the food chain. "Unfortunately, roading and development are fast invading the lands that lie between these protected blocks," biologist Lee H. Metzgar of the University of Montana wrote in testimony presented to two House subcommittees in support of NREPA in 1994.

But though the act had the support of prominent conservation biologists, and had attracted 20 House sponsors by the fall of 1994, it was not on the table in Boise.

In the forested mountains of central Idaho, a more confrontational campaign to save large blocks of wild land was underway. The Forest Service planned to build 145 miles of new roads into a 76,000-acre roadless area called Cove/Mallard and carve 200 clearcuts into its unprotected wilderness. Cove/Mallard was surrounded by three congressionally designated wilderness areas. Together, these and adjacent wildlands made up the 11-million-acre Greater Salmon–Selway Ecosystem, the largest tract of unlogged forest in the United States outside Alaska.

Cove/Mallard had a long and contentious history, dating from the early 1980s. Appeals and litigation had held off logging in the heart of the unprotected wilderness for a decade. But in November of 1991, the Forest Service began building roads into Cove/Mallard. The following summer Earth First! activists established a base camp near the timber town of Dixie, beginning a series of protests and acts of civil disobedience that made headlines across the nation. Those demonstrations continued in 1994.

The Greater Ecosystem Alliance, based in Bellingham, Washington, was working to protect the wildlands straddling the U.S.–Canada border on both sides of the Cascades. Gray wolves were moving down from Canada into the North Cascades on their own. Forests on the eastern slope of the mountains harbored lynx, a rare cat that had been proposed for listing under the Endangered Species Act. Mitch Friedman, founder of the Greater Ecosystem Alliance, had built an international coalition that favored establishment of an international North Cascades park to stop logging of unprotected wilderness, especially in British Columbia.

HOSTILE TERRITORY
Establishment of the park was an unpopular idea in northeastern Washington's Okanogan County, a stronghold of the wise-use movement. By the summer of 1994, ranchers and loggers in the county were in full battle dress over restrictions on logging and grazing on federal land. The extremist right-wing Militia of Montana had held two organizing meetings in the region.

Geraldine Payton, who lived in the tiny Okanogan County community of Chesaw, had received verbal death threats and intimidating messages for her support of the international park concept and other activities on behalf of the environment. So intense had the pressure become by the summer of 1994 that 40 activists in eastern Washington came together to discuss survival and coalition-building strategies with outside experts. "I admire my neighbors and like them," Payton said. "However, my neighbors have been radicalized by their trade press, which paints us all as radicals. They tell them we're trying to steal their children's future."

Okanogan County did not welcome the ecosystem project. In the spring of 1994, when planners came to the county to hold an informational meeting, John Shaver, a hot-headed timber worker, took over the meeting, tossed out the agenda, accused the Forest Service of pursuing a divide-and-conquer strategy, and proceeded to name every environmentalist in the room. "Until now they've been able to manipulate things and get their own way," Shaver said later. "I don't want them to get hurt, but I sure as hell want them to understand how they've hurt us."

Forest Service officials in Walla Walla and Washington, D.C., were shocked by the confrontational attitude in Okanogan County. It was becoming obvious that conflicts over federal land management in this hostile region would make the owl wars look like a Sunday walk in the woods.

Forest fires like the one that burned this area of Idaho's Boise National Forest in 1992 fueled a push by the timber industry and western Republicans in Congress to salvage "dead and dying" trees. Scientists warned that post-fire salvage logging operations like the Foothills sale pictured here, which cut trees on streambanks, often inflict additional harm on soils and streams.

PART SIX

BACKLASH

1994–95

“The handling of adversaries is perhaps the most difficult of all political skills to learn and is a significant test of
a movement's effectiveness.”

—Mark Dowie, *Losing Ground, 1995*

“There is no ecological need for immediate intervention
on the post-fire landscape.”

—Robert L. Beschta et al.,
"Wildfire and Salvage Logging," March 1995

“There is no such thing as biological waste in a forest.”

—Chris Maser, *"Salvage Logging: The Loss of
Ecological Reason and Moral Restraint," 1996*

THE 1994 WILDFIRES IN IDAHO and eastern Washington fueled
calls by the timber industry and western lawmakers for a massive salvage logging project to recover scorched trees from the forest and
reduce the risk of future fires. The Forest Service responded with a plan
to speed salvage sales by shortening environmental reviews.

In November 1994, Republicans won control of Congress and
launched an attack on the nation's environmental laws. Timber lobbyists and newly empowered Republican congressional leaders seized
the opportunity the fires had provided to draft a bill that opened
roadless areas and fragile forests across the nation to "salvage logging"

in the guise of restoring "forest health"—and to exempt those sales from federal environmental laws.

One cleverly written section of the measure ordered the Forest Service and Bureau of Land Management to release all timber sales in Northwest forests that had been withdrawn or delayed because of the damage they would inflict on fish and wildlife. Disregarding pleas from environmentalists, President Clinton inexplicably signed this "logging without laws" measure, in the process selling out Option 9, his own Northwest Forest Plan, and unleashing a brutal assault on forests across the nation.

Chapter Twenty-Eight

Dead and Dying

In late 1994, when Idaho forest activist Ron Mitchell saw the aftermath of the Foothills fire salvage sale along Little Rattlesnake Creek, he got mad. Then he got even.

Two years earlier, in the hot, dry August of 1992, a fierce wildfire ignited by lightning had scorched 257,600 acres of forest, brush, and rangeland east of Boise. In his zeal to recover marketable timber from the burn, Steve Mealey, then supervisor of the Boise National Forest, ordered the Foothills salvage sale and exempted it from citizen appeals.

As soon after logging as he could get access, Mitchell went in. He found hundreds of violations of the salvage plan. Logging had left slow-to-heal scars across the landscape. Roads roughly dug into hillsides for fire suppression bled soil into Little Rattlesnake Creek in the heart of the burn. Fresh-cut stumps marked areas where loggers had cut too close to streambanks. In some areas where the Forest Service had promised to reforest and to obliterate roads and helicopter landing pads, the work had not been done.

Frank Carroll, spokesman for the Boise National Forest, brushed off Mitchell's concerns. Though Carroll conceded that mistakes had been made on the Foothills sale, he insisted that they were in the acceptable range.

But Mitchell argued that the forests of the Northern Rockies needed to burn and mend on their own timetable, not one set by the Forest Service. Fire had been excluded from these dry hills for too long, he said. "Fire improves nutrients in streams and rejuvenates the soil. It releases seeds that need fire to bloom. In the Northern Rockies, fire is as essential as water."

With a small grant from the renegade group Save America's Forests, Mitchell published a report on the Foothills salvage sale, complete with photographs, and distributed it to the news media and selected members of Congress. The *Washington Post* and the *Seattle Post-Intelligencer* came to take a look. As congressional debate over wholesale salvage logging heated up in the aftermath of the 1994 fires, the Foothills sale became part of the debate.

"A SLASH-AND-GRAB JOB"

By 1994, the push from the timber industry to accelerate salvage logging across the forests of the Intermountain West had been building for four years. It began with the Forest Service's declaration of a forest health emergency in the wake of the spruce budworm outbreak in the Blue Mountains of northeastern Oregon. It spread north and east to other dry forests between the Cascades and the Rockies where drought, insects, cattle grazing, fire suppression, and overcutting had taken their toll.

A series of federal studies implicated past management practices in the weakened conditions of these forests. Scientists called for a combination of thinning, prescribed burns, and mechanical removal of dead wood to reduce the fire hazard posed by dead trees. The timber industry, however, was interested mainly in getting access to trees charred by fire or weakened by insects before they lost their commercial value. The Forest Service, which had a strong bias toward management, shared the enthusiasm for logging these forests back to health.

While Democrats controlled Congress, the pressure to speed salvage logging fell short. In 1992, U.S. Senator Slade Gorton, a Washington Republican, tried but failed to attach a measure to an appropriations bill directing the Forest Service and Bureau of Land Management to increase sales of insect-damaged timber even in areas inhabited by the spotted owl. Both of Oregon's U.S. senators, Republicans Mark Hatfield and Bob Packwood, jumped on the salvage bandwagon, as did Democratic U.S. Representative Les AuCoin. But Senator Brock Adams, a Washington Democrat, called the amendment "a slash-and-grab job" motivated by greed. Adams argued that the Forest Service already was selling salvage timber and that forcing it to sell more would delay other restoration work. Gorton's amendment failed.

The pressure continued in 1993 and 1994 as federal timber sales west of the Cascades remained frozen by federal courts. Some Oregon companies began turning to the forests of central Idaho, where logging remained wide open. The Forest Service was pushing new roads into Idaho roadless areas, and the Boise National Forest under Supervisor Steve Mealey had plenty of salvage timber to sell.

THE MEALEY MANTRA

Returning forests of the Intermountain West to their "historic range of variability" was Steve Mealey's mantra. His thesis, discounted by many fire ecologists, was that these ponderosa pine and mixed-conifer forests should be managed to return them to conditions that existed in the mid- to late 18th century, when low-intensity fires, many set by aboriginal people, regularly cleared the underbrush and thinned less fire-resistant conifer species to encourage game. Mealey proposed to do this mainly through intensive thinning of dense stands across the landscape. On the Boise National Forest, he also advocated intensive salvage of fire-damaged stands in projects such as the Foothills sale.

Mealey brought those biases with him when he was assigned in 1994 to direct preparation of an ecosystem plan for the federal lands in Idaho and western Montana. With wildfires still smoldering across the West, his message suddenly had broad appeal.

The voices of scientists who had studied cycles of insect infestations in the eastside forests, and who saw no true emergency, were largely ignored in the call for action. And the notion that even very hot, stand-replacing fires like those of 1994 might benefit forests by replenishing the soil and restoring a more natural mix of conifer species seemed almost unpatriotic. In the summer of 1994, fire was the enemy.

The forced evacuation of several eastern Washington and Idaho mountain communities in the path of the 1994 fires helped fan the fear of future wildfires. So did the deaths of 14 hotshot firefighters, who perished July 2 on a Colorado hillside as they fought to control a wind-whipped fire in dry piñon-juniper and Gambel oak. An investigation by the Occupational Safety and Health Administration later concluded that the Forest Service and BLM had committed "willful" safety violations by failing to alert firefighters to extremely dangerous conditions. Forest Service Chief Jack Ward Thomas took the deaths of the firefighters especially hard.

AN INTOLERABLE SITUATION

In late August of 1994, U.S. Senator Larry Craig, a conservative Idaho Republican and a good friend of the timber industry, presided over a Senate Agriculture subcommittee hearing in Boise to inquire about the Forest Service's plans for salvage logging in the aftermath of the fires. Chief Thomas testified at the Boise hearing that his agency "cannot, in my opinion, simply step back and wait for 'nature' to take its course."

"I do not believe that what has happened this fire season is acceptable as a solution to the problem," he said. "These fires at this scale and intensity are too hot, destructive, dangerous and too ecologically, economically, aesthetically, and socially damaging to be tolerable."

The only thing stopping the Forest Service from expediting salvage sales, Thomas said, was environmentalists' appeals and litigation. He knew some critics would question any approach that included cutting trees. But he vowed the Forest Service would not wait to begin restoring burned forests to some semblance of their historical condition through salvage logging, prescribed fire, and thinning of densely stocked stands. Immediately afterward, the Forest Service began preparing its Western Forest Health Initiative, a plan to do exactly that.

The timber industry followed up with its own large conference on salvage logging and forest health in Spokane, Washington, in early September, sponsored primarily by Boise Cascade Corporation. Soon after, the Intermountain Forestry Association, Boise Cascade, and other companies stepped up pressure on the Forest Service to give them access to fire-blackened stands throughout the Interior Northwest. They also pushed the agency to open insect-infested forests to extensive thinning, in the interest of reducing future fire danger and restoring "forest health."

Thomas's support for intensive forest thinning was no surprise. In the 1980s, he had endorsed a massive thinning operation on the Starkey Experimental Forest in northeastern Oregon. The Starkey was the site of Thomas's own pet research project, a long-term study to measure how Rocky Mountain elk responded to roads, cattle, and changes in forest habitat within a 3,600-acre fenced enclosure.

The Starkey had been particularly hard-hit by spruce budworm and pine bark beetle infestations. In 1988, it became the site of a massive salvage project designed to test various strategies for restoring diseased forests throughout the Blue Mountains. Over two years, half of the forested land enclosed by the fence was thinned. The jury was still out on whether the new forest that would grow up in its place would be more resistant to insects.

REWARDING ARSON

In western Oregon, a salvage debate of another kind was smoldering. The Willamette National Forest's plan to salvage timber blackened in a 1991 arson fire was on hold. Environmentalists had held off logging of the Warner Creek burn with appeals and lawsuits. They argued that it was dangerous public policy to reward arson by allowing logging in a spotted owl reserve that would have been off-limits to logging had it not burned. The Forest Service's own resource specialists had recommended only very light logging in the burn area, in instances where it might improve future owl habitat.

But Darrel Kenops, supervisor of the Willamette National Forest, was determined to salvage a significant amount of timber from the 9,000-acre burn. In 1992, he overruled his resource specialists and chose a plan that would allow far more extensive logging. Three years after the fire, however, the burned timber remained locked up in a court challenge.

EXTRAORDINARY MEASURES

On October 31, 1994, the Forest Service unveiled its promised Western Forest Health Initiative, which laid out its plan to move salvage sales through the system quickly. "Innovative and extraordinary measures are needed to restore forest health in stressed forests," the report began. But its definition of "forest health" was so vague and jargon-filled as to be meaningless: "A condition where biotic and abiotic influences do not threaten resource management objectives now or in the future."

The agency identified 330 salvage projects on national forests across the nation and predicted that salvage logging could produce 4.5 billion board feet of timber over the next 24 months.

On the Boise National Forest, where two wildfires burned through 102,000 acres in 1994, Steve Mealey had already directed preparation of the mammoth Boise River Project, a plan for logging 81,000 acres of fire-killed timber, including stands within roadless areas.

The timber industry suddenly saw its chance to push for more timber while buffing its image as a concerned steward of the public lands.

In late summer, the industry placed a large ad in 12 daily newspapers and spots on more than 30 radio stations in Washington, Idaho, and Montana blaming conservationists in part for the summer's fires in eastern Washington and central Idaho.

"The irresponsible actions of a few radicals have blocked even the most modest efforts to return to safe and healthy condition through thinning and selective logging," the ad accused. "Sadly, this year's tragic losses may be but a preview unless public land managers are immediately allowed to harvest dead and dying timber on our national forests."

AN EDUCATIONAL CHALLENGE

For eastside forest activists, the forest health issue posed a difficult public education challenge.

Environmentalists were placed on the defensive. They tried to counter the timber industry's ad campaign with logic. For instance, they pointed out that much of the 1994 Tyee Creek fire, which scorched 135,000 acres in the central Washington Cascades, burned in previously logged stands where eight years of drought had left insect-damaged trees vulnerable. They also accused the timber industry and its allies in Congress of deliberately preying on people's fear of devastating wildfires to stack the decks in favor of massive salvage logging.

"The timber industry is taking advantage of a void in public understanding," said Lisa Lombardi, a wildlife biologist and Moscow, Idaho, conservationist. "Fires are not like logging. Many species depend on snags and down logs. Those snags left on the land are the only remaining biomass" after fire sweeps through, she said.

In a January 1995 posting to Northern Rockies activists on the Econet Western Lands Gopher Service, Lombardi wrote: "This is a complex and contentious topic in our region, as you all know. Over the next few years, many things are going to be proposed under the guise of what is good for the health of our forests. One reason the issue is going to be difficult to deal with from a public education standpoint is that there truly are places where some intervention would be not only acceptable but also beneficial—in other words, there is no hard line, no yes/no; more like a 'yes, but . . . '"

Most foresters who argued that salvage logging was good for "forest health" were really talking about tree vigor, not the overall condition of the streams, soils, fish, wildlife, and vegetation that make up the forest ecosystem, Lombardi said.

Then she laid out the bottom line: "Are we in for some stand-replacing fires? Yes. Can some thinning be done in mismanaged stands? Yes, but it will have no effect on landscape-level fires. Should that be done over the landscape? No. Can we eliminate fire from these forests? No. . . . Unless we take every tree, trees will always burn."

But scientific arguments put forth in the debate over salvage logging seemed to carry little weight. Even Steve Mealey, a scientist by training, didn't let scientific accuracy get in the way of a good sound bite. After fire burned through the South Fork of Sheep Creek on the Boise National Forest, Mealey told a reporter for the newspaper *High Country News,* "We lost a unique, distinct, genetic population of bull trout."

When Forest Service fisheries biologist Cindy Deacon-Williams confronted him, pointing out that bull trout had never lived in that stream, she said Mealey replied that fish had indeed been lost, and that calling them bull trout would give the issue the attention the situation deserved. Mealey also predicted that "it would take millennia" before fish returned to Sheep Creek. But in fact, Deacon-Williams said, "It only took a month."

THE RUSH TO SALVAGE

In late October of 1994, when Congress passed the appropriations bill funding the Forest Service and BLM, a conference committee directed the agencies to "move expeditiously to restore and rehabilitate burned-over areas, and reduce excessive fuel loads in areas highly susceptible to wildfire."

Already, some Forest Service officials were rushing to offer salvage sales. On the Colville National Forest, the agency admitted it had marked trees for cutting within the Copper Butte Roadless Area before the close of public comment and that it had drastically overstated the size of the burn.

Evan Frost, an Okanogan County environmentalist, had walked the burn. He was incensed by the difference between rhetoric and reality. "The fire on Copper Butte did little damage to the old-growth structure and habitat value of this area," he said. "The way these trees were marked makes no sense at all. It looks as though a drunken sailor with a paint can went roaming through the forest."

Sara Folger of the Spokane-based Inland Empire Public Lands Council saw an ominous portent in the Forest Service's rush to salvage: "Any hope the public might have had that the Forest Service was capable of protecting forest ecosystems is gone."

Chapter Twenty-Nine

Contract on the Environment

On November 8, 1994, the world changed. Republicans took back the U.S. Senate and, for the first time since the Great Depression, gained control of the U.S. House of Representatives.

Within days of the stunning upset, rumors of plans to roll back 20 years of federal environmental legislation were coming from all directions. Leadership of congressional committees overseeing the nation's air, water, and public lands had passed from sympathetic Democrats to hostile Republicans. Friendly congressional staffers who had given environmental lobbyists access to the workings of House committees began getting layoff notices as House Speaker–designate Newt Gingrich announced deep cuts in congressional office budgets. Overnight, green Democrats like Senator Patrick Leahy of Vermont and Representative George Miller of California were out of the loop.

Environmentalists' most rabid adversaries in Congress were about to grab the reins of key natural resource committees. Republican Senator Frank Murkowski of Alaska would become chairman of the powerful Senate Energy and Natural Resources Committee. Republican Senator Larry Craig of Idaho would chair Murkowski's forestry subcommittee. Republican Senator Mark Hatfield of Oregon would take the reins of the powerful Senate Appropriations Committee. And Republican Representative Don Young would take over as chairman of the House Natural Resources Committee. In case anyone doubted his intent, Young promptly deleted the word "Natural" from the committee's name.

For national conservation groups, it was a nightmare from which there was no waking. By December, they were holding lengthy strategy sessions to figure out where they had gone wrong, what friends they had left, and how they could recast their message so that it connected with people's lives.

At the cramped offices of the Western Ancient Forest Campaign, the threat on everyone's mind was a bill that would exempt salvage logging from environmental laws.

Forest activists had reason to worry. In December, Murkowski and Craig asked Mark Rey, the timber industry's top lobbyist in D.C., to come to work for them. With Rey's help, the leadership's forestry agenda came together in a two-week period between mid-December and mid-January. At the top of the list was a bill to open the national forests to more logging.

A PREVIEW OF DISASTER

In late January of 1995, nearly 400 West Coast forest activists gathered in Ashland, Oregon, to get another sobering civics lesson from the D.C. lobbyists who were on the front lines in this fierce new battle. The message: Their foes in Congress and statehouses throughout the West had captured the populist high ground. Without serious political alliance building, environmental activists stood to lose everything they had fought for.

They were served up a preview of setbacks to come: Massive salvage logging throughout the West, possibly aided by an emergency congressional appropriation with language that would shield the sales from legal challenges. Proposals to turn over federal lands to the states. A moratorium on new endangered species listings. Raids on the Tongass National Forest and the Arctic National Wildlife Refuge.

Conservative Republicans sympathetic to the wise-use agenda had simply seized the initiative, said Roger Featherstone of the Endangered Species Coalition, a foundation-funded organization created to build national support for the Endangered Species Act. "The situation in Washington the past few years has built up a tremendous inertia," Featherstone said. "There's not been a lot of leadership from Congress, the administration, the agencies, or even the environmental groups themselves. We no longer have inertia. We have popped the ball out of the socket and it's rolling around."

If they hoped to have any credibility with the Republican majority, environmentalists would have to decide on a position and stick with it, Featherstone said. "To work with Republicans you have to have a measure of respect built up. You ask for what you want and you don't back off from that. We're backed into a corner and we have to fight our way out like a badger."

Steve Holmer of the Western Ancient Forest Campaign urged activists to be visible in Washington, D.C., and in the offices of their own congressional representatives, whether Democrat or Republican. "It's very important that we're bipartisan," he said. "We can't afford to write off one member. Make them realize there's a price to pay for a vote against the environment."

The conference's most discouraging words came from Tarso Ramos, a former labor organizer who headed the Wise Use Public Exposure Project in Portland. The wise-use movement's formidable power came in part from its populist call for political self-determination, especially in rural communities, Ramos said. Its support for private property rights had helped the movement expand into suburban areas as well.

The wise-use message fit the angst of the times, he said. People were fearful for their economic future and suspicious of government. "What's changed is that someone is going to organize these disaffected citizens, and for the most part that is not progressives or environmentalists."

He urged environmentalists to become more sophisticated about economic issues and to come up with their own proposals to keep rural areas alive: "Recognize the difference between timber companies and the people who work for them." "For most workers there's no option other than a job today versus no job today. You must take on these economic issues head-on. It's the only way the environmental movement stands a chance of surviving as a powerful political force in this country. If it stays isolated, the movement threatens to become an agent in its own destruction."

Even Brock Evans, vice president of the National Audubon Society, admitted that national conservation groups were under siege and trying to regroup. The hostility was so thick, he said, that Representative Young had told the major national conservation groups they would not be invited to testify before his House Resources Committee. "The tidal wave in Congress is a totally different structure than I've seen in my lifetime," Evans said. "The historian in me is fascinated; the lobbyist in me is scared."

Forest activists didn't have to wait long to see one of these prophecies borne out. On February 10, 1995, Senator Craig introduced the Federal Lands Forest Health Protection and Restoration Act. Under Craig's bill, salvage logging would be exempt from appeals in forests in which half or more of the trees were "dead or dying." Legal challenges of these sales would be limited. Citizens could petition to have forest tracts declared "emergency" areas. Forest managers would then have to justify the decision *not* to log.

At a March 1 hearing before Craig's subcommittee, Assistant Agriculture Secretary Jim Lyons expressed qualified support for the Craig bill, though he said the petition process was unnecessary.

At the same time, the House was busy designing a bill that would cut appropriations for programs already funded in the 1995 federal budget. It was Don Young who proposed dealing with the salvage issue by attaching it as a rider to the pending budget rescission bill. Soon after, the Craig bill was shelved. "We decided it didn't make sense to pursue it in both venues this year," Senate Energy Committee staffer Mark Rey said. Besides it was also far from clear that the Craig bill could win on the Senate floor.

DISREGARDING SCIENCE

At congressional hearings, scientists disputed whether a true forest health "crisis" even existed, let alone whether massive thinning and salvage logging were appropriate responses. But the message that fire and insect epidemics are nature's way of restoring balance to these stressed forests got lost in the din of timber industry rhetoric.

On February 10, 1995, the day the Craig bill was unveiled, Dr. Art Partridge of the University of Idaho recounted before a joint hearing of two House subcommittees his 30 years of research on forest diseases and forest insects in the Interior Northwest. He and other pathologists had recently evaluated the condition of 130,000 trees in more than 60 areas of Idaho, Montana, Oregon, Washington, and Wyoming. Their conclusion: There was no forest health crisis. Fewer than 2 trees out of 1,000 showed symptoms of a root disease that was a key indicator of serious forest health problems. In fact, the pathologists' tests revealed the lowest level of disease and insect activity in 28 years. Moreover, where past insect infestations had been severe, scientists had found high rates of recovery.

In March of 1995, a panel of eight prominent scientists issued a paper for the Pacific Rivers Council in which they argued that there was no ecological justification for salvage logging, that in fact burned-over forests must be treated with the greatest care to prevent mass erosion and damage to soils, streams, and fisheries. The only valid argument for post-fire salvage logging, the scientists said, was economic.

Yet, though environmentalists had mustered credible scientists for congressional hearings, they found themselves battling not only powerful members of Congress and a determined and cynical timber industry but a public largely ignorant of forest ecology.

In March 1995, Ron Mitchell of the Idaho Sporting Congress, who had documented salvage logging abuse on the Boise National Forest, went to Washington, D.C., to lobby against Craig's salvage bill. He made the rounds of 36 Senate offices, arguing that salvage logging was a budget buster and the forest health crisis a hoax. But he said Senate staffers were concerned that taking on the issue directly might cost western Democrats their seats. He said they told him, "The truth doesn't matter. Power does."

On March 30, 1995, Republican U.S. Senator Mark Hatfield of Oregon took to the Senate floor and pushed every button in arguing for expedited salvage logging. "There are those whose agenda is to prevent people from managing our forests altogether," he said. "They would rather let our dead and dying forests burn by catastrophic fire, endangering human life and long-term forest health, than harvest them to promote stability in natural forest ecosystems and communities dependent on a supply of timber from federal lands."

The drumbeat of the timber industry's ad campaign reinforced Hatfield's message. "Wildfire destroyed four million acres of America's forests last summer and killed dozens of people," said a Northwest Forest Resource Council newspaper ad that ran in April. "This year could be worse. Congress has asked federal resource managers to make our forests safer and healthier for fish, wildlife and people. Rehabilitation plans include immediately planting new trees, restoring watersheds and leaving snags for birds and wildlife while allowing the careful and speedy salvage of dead and dying trees before they rot, lose their value and spark further forest fires."

Who could be against a bill that would do all that?

THE UNHOLY TRINITY

The Contract for America, Newt Gingrich's manifesto for the Republican freshman class, hadn't mentioned the word "environment." What it had promised was regulatory reform. Three tenets of that manifesto, dubbed the "unholy trinity" by Beltway environmental lobbyists, were the early focus of the 104th Congress.

Unfunded mandates legislation prohibited the federal government from passing along the costs of new regulations to the states without full funding for compliance. It sailed through Congress and was signed by President Clinton.

"Takings" legislation required the federal government to pay private property owners when government rules decreased the value of their property. Takings became embroiled in bitter debate as its supporters told largely apocryphal tales of federal bureaucrats running roughshod over the rights of ordinary citizens and as environmentalists worked hard to debunk the anecdotes.

The third member of the trinity was a bill requiring impossibly complex risk assessments and cost-benefit analyses before new federal laws and rules could be enacted. Corporate lobbyists from virtually every polluting industry favored this bill, which like takings legislation would make it prohibitively expensive for federal agencies to enforce rules on the books. Both regulatory reform and takings eventually fell by the wayside in 1995.

But these were just the opening salvos. When Congress convened, Republican leaders quickly made it clear that they would use all the arrows in their legislative quiver to undo environmental safeguards: self-standing bills, rewrites of the Endangered Species Act and Clean Water Act, deep cuts in appropriations, and attachments to appropriations riders and omnibus spending bills. Conservation groups found themselves inundated.

ALASKA'S TURN

The three-member Republican Alaska delegation flexed its new muscle shamelessly. A team of federal and state biologists had recently warned that continued logging of the Tongass National Forest at current rates threatened the survival of nearly a dozen species. Senator Ted Stevens of Alaska inserted language in an appropriations bill forbidding the Forest Service to take any action implementing the findings. Senator Murkowski floated a bill to turn over large sections of the Tongass National Forest to so-called "landless Natives" who had not qualified for timberland allotments under a 1971 law. He was forced to abandon the bill after it drew strong opposition from fishermen, Southeast Alaska communities, and a number of Alaska Natives, who had seen their hunting grounds and salmon streams ruined by logging.

Don Young, Alaska's only representative in the House, set up several task forces headed by his own hand-picked chairmen to bypass the existing subcommittee structure. He appointed Representative Richard

Pombo of California to chair a task force that would undertake a rewrite of the Endangered Species Act. Young wanted a bill that would put economic arguments against saving endangered species on an equal footing with ecological arguments in favor of saving them. Pombo, who represented a Central Valley district with numerous simmering endangered species conflicts, stacked his task force with western conservatives.

One of the worst fears of Northwest forest activists—that they might save the forests but lose the Endangered Species Act—seemed about to be realized.

STACKING THE DECK

In April 1995, Congress took its first shot at the ESA when it attached a rider to a Defense supplemental appropriations bill placing a temporary moratorium on new endangered species listings. That same month, Pombo's task force held field hearings in several states. The first three—in Louisiana, Texas, and North Carolina—featured speakers invited to air grievances against the act. In Louisiana, a shrimper complained about having to equip his boat with a turtle exclusion device to save endangered sea turtles. In Texas, a rancher protested the curtailment of pumping from the Edwards Aquifer to protect an endangered fish. In North Carolina, a landowner griped about the reintroduction of endangered red wolves. Task force members were wined and dined by the wealthy constituents they had invited to testify. Several disgusted Democrats on the panel boycotted the hearings.

On April 24, the task force held a hearing in Vancouver, Washington. The speakers' roster was stacked with critics of the act: a mill owner, a resident of a timber town, an aluminum worker, a rancher, a miner, and three irrigators. Representatives of fishing groups, who supported a strong Endangered Species Act, were added to the panel only after fishermen flooded Pombo's office with phone calls. The U.S. Fish and Wildlife Service and the National Marine Fisheries Service, the two agencies charged with enforcing the act, were nowhere in sight.

But attempts to build a case for gutting the act backfired in the Northwest, where polls showed 60 percent of residents favored retaining the law. Environmentalists, tapping into a nationwide network, succeeded in exposing the hearing as a sham and turning some of the testimony to their advantage.

"Pushing species to the brink of extinction and beyond not only wastes future economic opportunities but helps destroy those industries we already have, such as the Pacific salmon industry," testified Glen Spain, regional director for the Pacific Coast Federation of Fishermen's Associations. "Without a strong Endangered Species Act, there will never be salmon recovery in the Northwest, and the approximately 85,000 jobs which the salmon resource could potentially generate in this region would be gone forever."

Stan Shaufler, a former sawmill owner, testified that he had come to realize that the overcutting of old-growth forests had to stop. "The old-growth logs I milled represented centuries of growth," Shaufler said. "The logging of the national forests was a disgrace at the rates instituted and maintained by our expert forest managers."

Some environmentalists struck a conciliatory note, conceding that the act could do a better job of involving local people in developing conservation plans for threatened and endangered species.

Nevertheless, Pombo's committee went back to Washington and wrote a bill gutting the act. On the Senate side, Slade Gorton, a Washington Republican, unveiled a bill giving the secretary of interior unilateral authority to decide the fate of imperiled species. Gorton freely acknowledged that the bill was written by Washington, D.C., lawyers representing timber, mining, ranching, and utility interests.

RUNNING OUT OF PATIENCE

Though Interior Secretary Bruce Babbitt had praised the Endangered Species Act as the nation's strongest and most important environmental law, his voice was largely absent from the debate for much of 1995. He tried to defuse opposition by publicizing the act's successes and by negotiating with private landowners to adopt voluntary habitat conservation plans.

By April, when President Clinton still had not dug in his heels against the Republican attack on the environment, national groups went public with their frustration, saying they now believed they could not count on the president to veto bills rolling back environmental protection. "I think the American people have to demonstrate this is their air, their water, their communities," said Carl Pope, executive director of the Sierra Club. "And they have to demonstrate they are not going to let anybody—whether it is Bill Clinton, the U.S. House, or the U.S. Senate—mess with it." That same month, more than a dozen national groups launched a $2 million media campaign to alert voters to the GOP assault on the nation's environmental laws.

Young activists join hands and face off against authorities to protest logging of old-growth stands in the Breitenbush area of the Oregon Cascades in 1986. Breitenbush, the site of a new age community and resort in the heart of timber country on the Willamette National Forest, became a crucible of conflict over logging in the 1980s. © Gary Braasch

Below: *Roy Keene of the Public Forestry Foundation (at right) leads a group of conservationists on a tour of the Shasta Costa area, site of a planned experiment in "new forestry," in July of 1990.*

Demonstrators rally in Portland during a January 1992 evidentiary hearing held by the Bush administration to gather information for the God Squad, a Cabinet-level body authorized to grant exemptions from the Endangered Species Act.

Dressed up as denizens of the old-growth forest, activists en route to lobby members of Congress in Washington, D.C., in 1992 deliver their message at Chicago's O'Hare International Airport.

Environmentalists rally in support of the Endangered Species Act outside a Vancouver, Washington, motel in April of 1994, while a Republican House task force charged with weakening the act holds a field hearing inside.

Andy Kerr, executive director of the Oregon Natural Resources Council (in jacket and tie) and Mike Roselle, an Earth First! activist (at right), submit to arrest outside the office of U.S. Senator Mark Hatfield in July of 1995 to protest the enactment of the timber salvage rider and the suspension of federal environmental laws.

Opposite: *Environmentalists gather in the rain at Pioneer Courthouse Square as President Clinton and Vice President Gore convene a Northwest Forest Conference in Portland on April 2, 1993.* © Elizabeth Feryl

Wearing suits and ties, mainstream environmentalists (from left: Jim Jontz of the Western Ancient Forest Campaign, Brock Evans of National Audubon, and Charlie Ogle of the Sierra Club) join a protest march into a closure area surrounding the Sugarloaf timber sale in the Siskiyou National Forest on October 30, 1995. © Elizabeth Feryl

© Sky Shiviah

A forest activist from the environmental group Umpqua Watersheds communes with a newly fallen giant on the Umpqua National Forest, where ancient forests began to fall within a few months after the timber salvage rider became law.

Jim Jontz, director of the Western Ancient Forest Campaign, is dragged away by Forest Service officials during a protest rally at the North Umpqua Ranger Station near Roseburg, Oregon, in January of 1996.

Demonstrators from all walks of life join an April 1996 rally at the site of the Enola Hill timber sale on the Mount Hood National Forest, an area considered sacred by some Native American people.

Chapter Thirty

Logging without Laws

As the 104th Congress and its "Contract with America" grabbed headlines in the spring of 1995, timber industry lobbyists huddled with congressional staffers on Capitol Hill to craft a bill that would open the national forests to virtually unrestricted logging for at least one more year. They decided to promote their bill as an effort to restore sick forests. With so much else going on, this "forest health" bill largely escaped scrutiny outside a small circle of lobbyists, western lawmakers, and committee staff members.

ANY TREE IN THE FOREST

The bill that finally emerged from a conference committee, attached to a massive budget-cutting measure, directed the agriculture secretary and the secretary of interior to immediately implement a two-year timber salvage program on national forests and BLM land. Its broad language, borrowed from the Forest Service's own regulations governing salvage logging, called for removing "disease- or insect-infested trees, dead, damaged, or down trees, or trees affected by fire or imminently susceptible to fire or insect attack," as well as "associated trees or trees lacking the characteristics of a healthy and viable ecosystem." The bottom line, as sponsors and industry lobbyists intended, was to give the agencies a blank check to cut any tree in the forest under the guise of "salvage."

The bill exempted all such sales from all administrative appeals and from the requirements of all applicable environmental laws. No legislated timber sale target was necessary; the Clinton administration, through its Western Forest Health Initiative, already had committed to selling 4.5 billion board feet of timber in salvage sales over the next two years.

This so-called "salvage rider" applied to all Forest Service and BLM lands in the nation, though it had particular relevance for ecologically stressed forests of the Intermountain West. However, it quickly became a Christmas tree for timber industry add-ons that had nothing to do with "forest health"—and that applied specifically to the spotted owl forests of western Oregon, western Washington, and northern California.

SNEAK ATTACK

House Republicans added a section that directed the Forest Service and BLM to promptly award all timber sales released by the 1989 Rider from Hell, regardless of environmental consequences. A number of those sales had been put on hold or canceled because of their impact on owls, marbled murrelets, salmon, and other sensitive species. The new language required that these old sales be logged according to their original specifications and at the original price.

On the Senate side, Washington Republican Slade Gorton added language insulating all new sales offered under President Clinton's Northwest Forest Plan from legal challenges. That language was never debated on the floor of either the House or the Senate.

Gorton described the provisions affecting westside forests differently to different audiences. In a speech on the Senate floor, he told colleagues its purpose was to release timber sales held up by "gridlock over the marbled murrelet"—roughly 300 million board feet of timber in all. A number of senators voted for it with that understanding.

But a careful reading revealed that the provision in fact said something quite different. It said the agencies must release all unawarded timber sales on federal lands *subject to* the 1989 rider—in other words, all unawarded timber sales in Oregon and Washington. The clever wording was worth millions of dollars to federal timber purchasers in the two states who had never given up on logging these sales from the bad old days.

Federal timber sale managers in the Northwest understood immediately that the rider threatened the integrity of the Northwest Forest Plan. On March 11, 1995, the head of the BLM timber sale program for western Oregon wrote a memo to BLM State Director Elaine Zielinski stating his dismay over the rider's implications.

"BLM would suffer a severe setback in the implementation of the Northwest Forest Plan," Lyndon Werner wrote. "We support the need to improve forest health and expedite the salvage of diseased, infested, or dead/dying timber; however, we are opposed to this amendment. . . . We believe (the sales) should occur in compliance with existing laws and land management plans. We plan to only put sales in appropriate locations, and analyze and mitigate the impacts. We are not going to sacrifice quality on the ground to meet sale targets. That would be irresponsible land stewardship."

The Forest Service's regional timber sale office in Portland quickly grasped the impacts as well. Timber sale planners sent off to Washington, D.C., a long list of environmentally damaging timber sales that would have to go forward if the language became law.

But if the agencies got it, Clinton's advisors apparently did not. Whether they failed to read the language carefully or chose to misinterpret it, they would soon regret the oversight.

Ironically, the timber industry was not clamoring for salvage timber. In May, the Boise National Forest auctioned the first Boise River salvage sales. To the agency's chagrin, some of the sales drew no bids in a market already glutted with salvage timber. Forest officials were forced to redesign the sales, lower the minimum bid, and reduce their estimate of how much money the sales would produce for the federal treasury. The pattern soon would be repeated in other forests.

CLINTON'S FIRST VETO

The Budget Rescission Act of 1995 passed the House and Senate with the salvage rider intact and was sent to President Clinton's desk in early June. Among other add-ons, it contained money for California flood relief and aid to victims of the Oklahoma City bombing.

In a blitz organized by the Western Ancient Forest Campaign, environmentalists across the nation swamped the White House with more than 30,000 calls, faxes, and letters urging Clinton to veto the rider. More than 600 pieces of wood carrying the message "Veto Salvage Logging—Salvage Your Presidency" arrived at the White House. The *Washington Post, Los Angeles Times,* and *USA Today* editorialized against the measure. Even groups not usually involved with forest issues, including the Native American Rights Fund and Physicians for Social Responsibility, weighed in against suspending the nation's environmental laws.

It worked. On June 7 Clinton, exercising his veto power for the first time in his presidency, vetoed the Rescissions Bill. In his veto statement, he specifically objected to "the very bad environmental provision . . . which says that no environmental laws will apply for the next three years to any cutting of so-called salvage timber in our forests, and we'll just have the taxpayers pay for whatever damage occurs to the environment."

Environmentalists lavished praise on the president for his decision. "President Clinton seems to have discovered a renewed affinity for environmental protection," the *Headwaters Journal* exulted in its summer 1995 issue. "If we want the President to follow through with more action, we need to let him know that we like what we hear and see."

ROUND TWO

But to the rider's supporters, Clinton's veto was merely round one. Even as environmentalists rejoiced, back-room negotiations between Congress and the administration over the salvage rider were underway. Republican Senator Mark Hatfield of Oregon, who chaired the powerful Senate Appropriations Committee, engaged in political hardball, reportedly threatening to attach the rider to every appropriations bill—a move that would force Clinton to veto each bill or let the government shut down. At the same time, Hatfield promised the president that under the rider, his agencies still would have the latitude to follow environmental laws and regulations except for those suspending appeals and legal challenges.

On June 13, speaking to an audience of pro-timber activists, Hatfield predicted that the rider would become law. A day earlier, Representative Charles Taylor of North Carolina, sponsor of the House version, had promised them that "the timber salvage bill will be intact in the new rescission bill."

On June 28, as rumors of a deal in the making swirled on Capitol Hill, Democratic Senator Patrick Leahy of Vermont circulated a Dear Colleague letter asking pointedly why the proposed salvage rider was needed now. "The reality is that the Forest Service cannot get bids on all the sales it has offered," Leahy wrote. He cited economic reports revealing that Oregon and Washington had in fact gained 4,000 forest products jobs in the previous two years, and new evidence that public forests in the West were healthier than private timberlands. "Now, when the data shows that the industry is doing well, the public forests are relatively healthy, timber supply appears sufficient, and jobs are on the rise, why should Congress suspend environmental laws?" he asked.

There was no answer. Instead, the next day the White House released a statement saying President Clinton had reached agreement with Congress on the budget-cutting bill. Clinton said he still did not support the salvage rider, but that the conference committee had agreed to language that preserved the Forest Service's ability to comply with its forest plans. "Furthermore," he said, "Chairman Hatfield insists that the timber salvage provisions provide complete discretion for the administration to implement these provisions according to our best judgment. I take Senator Hatfield at his word."

It was to prove a hollow promise.

On July 6, the day after the House voted on the budget bill, Representative Peter DeFazio, an Oregon Democrat, got his first look at the rider. He denounced it in a scorching press release. "The salvage rider would allow logging along wild and scenic rivers and in sensitive riparian and roadless areas, with no restrictions based on slope or soil conditions," he warned. "Its definition of salvage is so broad that it opens the door to wholesale logging in the region's remaining old-growth forests and roadless areas."

DeFazio said he wasn't impressed by the administration's promise that federal agencies would follow the law. "The Clinton administration says 'Trust us.' But I don't trust any federal agency with the kind of unlimited power granted by this salvage amendment."

Clinton's top environmental advisors, including Vice President Al Gore, Assistant Interior Secretary George Frampton, Assistant Agriculture Secretary Jim Lyons, and Katie McGinty, now director of the Council on Environmental Quality, argued vehemently against the rider. They warned Leon Panetta, Clinton's chief of staff, that it could sink his Northwest Forest Plan, on which the president had staked his environmental record.

McGinty, Frampton, and Lyons refused to divulge the precise content of their conversations with the president. But McGinty did say, "Congress had a gun to his head on that bill. When you're talking about Oklahoma City and the terrible tragedies in California and the emergency money that needed to get there, that's no way to have to put a choice to the president that either you attend to the emergencies or you sell out the fundamental environmental protection."

On July 27, Clinton signed the Budget Rescission Act into law—timber salvage rider and all. The final version of the rider was essentially unchanged from the version he had vetoed in June.

On July 28, leaders of the nation's major environmental groups gathered outside the White House for a "21-chainsaw salute" to draw attention to Clinton's retreat. "Actions speak louder than words," said an angry Kevin Kirchner of the Sierra Club Legal Defense Fund. "And your action in signing the 'logging without laws' legislation yesterday speaks volumes to the American people about your lack of commitment to the environment and environmental protection in this country." Kirchner called on Clinton to issue an executive order instructing the Forest Service and other agencies to obey the nation's environmental laws despite the rider.

In one swift stroke, the rider took away every tool environmentalists had to stop environmentally destructive logging. It prohibited appeals of all salvage sales everywhere in the national forest system and all sales of healthy trees offered under the Northwest Forest Plan. It declared that all such sales would be "deemed to satisfy the requirements" of every federal environmental law and treaty. It overrode all existing federal court orders. And there was more to come.

SENATORIAL SCIENCE

The day Clinton signed the bill, before the ink was dry, its Republican sponsors—Senators Slade Gorton, Frank Murkowski, and Larry Craig and Representatives Charles Taylor, Pat Roberts, and Don Young—sent a letter to Agriculture Secretary Dan Glickman and Interior Secretary Bruce Babbitt. The letter punctured any illusion that the administration might be able to have it both ways in Northwest forests.

The sponsors stressed that the rider was intended to apply to all unawarded timber sales in western Oregon and western Washington, not just sales delayed to protect the marbled murrelet. The only sales exempt, they said, would be those in which murrelets were "known to be nesting" when logging was scheduled. Even then, eggshells or other physical evidence of nesting would have to be produced. This requirement flew in the face of a protocol developed by biologists who had studied the murrelet's nesting behavior. Because murrelets don't actually build nests, but lay their eggs in mossy depressions of tree limbs that are difficult to locate, biologists developed a set of standards that used sightings of the birds in or near old-growth stands to determine whether they were likely nesting nearby.

That Republican lawmakers would substitute their judgment for that of the experts wasn't as bizarre as it appeared. The unawarded murrelet sales in the coastal forests of the Siskiyou, Siuslaw, Olympic, and Mount Baker–Snoqualmie National Forests contained some of the most valuable mature and old-growth timber west of the Cascades. From the timber industry's viewpoint, logging the murrelet sales was akin to taking part in the last buffalo hunt.

From a biologist's perspective, the 4,600 acres of coastal old growth at stake represented a critical chunk of all murrelet habitat remaining in Oregon, Washington, and California. Two-thirds of the acreage at risk was on Oregon's Siuslaw National Forest. Logging those 3,000 acres would destroy nearly a quarter of all murrelet habitat remaining on the forest, as Supervisor Jim Furnish warned in a letter to his bosses three days before Clinton signed the rider into law.

The rider's sponsors didn't limit their attention to birds. In the summer of 1995, the National Marine Fisheries Service was considering a petition to protect several sharply declining runs of coastal coho salmon under the Endangered Species Act. In their letter to Babbitt and Glickman, the sponsors asserted that timber sales in areas critical to coho salmon would fall under the rider's provisions. They warned that "the agencies may not in any way delay the award, release, or completion" of timber sales even if coho were listed, and even if NMFS concluded that sales posed a high risk to the fish.

The timber industry immediately went to court to enforce this broad interpretation of the rider. It filed its lawsuit in the federal district court for western Oregon, in Eugene, where U.S. District Judge Michael Hogan presided. It was a shrewd move. Hogan soon made it clear that he agreed with the industry's interpretation in virtually every respect.

STREET GANG ASSAULT

On August 1, 1995, President Clinton directed his department heads to begin implementing the timber rider "in an environmentally sound manner." On August 9, the administration released a detailed memorandum to field managers, explaining how they could do that within existing laws.

The next day, at a Senate subcommittee hearing, Senator Larry Craig of Idaho went on the attack. He charged that the memo completely undermined Congress' intent, which was to give federal agencies unfettered discretion to sell salvage timber sales without the impediments of environmental laws. "It's a formula for gridlock," Craig told Assistant Agriculture Secretary Jim Lyons. "I suggest you toss it in the wastebasket."

"If we have to cut off your funds, we'll cut off your funds," Senator Frank Murkowski of Alaska chimed in. "Gentlemen, we're going to get your attention."

Lyons, caught squarely between his principles and administration politics, defended the memo. But he added that he remained committed to producing 4.5 billion board feet of salvage timber from national forests during the life of the rider.

It wasn't enough to placate the timber industry. On September 14, industry lawyers asked Hogan to hold Lyons and Tom Tuchmann, the administration's forest plan pointman, in contempt of court for failing to release timber in forests used by the marbled murrelet. Hogan denied the motion.

On September 19, the full Senate, led by Republican Senator Ted Stevens of Alaska, turned up the heat when it adopted an amendment to an appropriations bill removing the Forest Service from Lyons's jurisdiction. "I consider it to be just a modest shot across the bow," Stevens said. "We want the laws that Congress passes to be observed."

The amendment was later withdrawn. But Kevin Kirchner of the Sierra Club Legal Defense Fund, a Capitol Hill veteran, called what happened to Lyons on the Senate floor "the most vicious thing I've ever seen in 14 years. The Senate is supposed to be the greatest deliberative body in the world, but this looked like a street gang assault."

A COOPERATIVE JUDGE

On September 7, 1995, Judge Hogan issued the first in a series of rulings siding with the timber industry when he dismissed challenges to the Warner Creek salvage sale in an area burned by arsonists four years earlier. Hogan said the sale clearly fell under the provisions of the Rescission Act and must go forward. The next day, a blockade went up on the logging road above Oakridge, Oregon. A group of Earth First! activists vowed to stay as long as necessary. It was the opening volley in what would become an impassioned return to direct action in the woods.

Hogan followed up with a September 13 ruling that the rider did indeed apply to all unawarded timber sales in Oregon and Washington. He ordered the government to release an additional 250 million board of feet of timber. That day Mick Garvin, a 37-year-old contract forest worker, locked himself to a metal fire door buried in the logging road that led to the Warner Creek sale.

Hogan's decision jolted forest activists out of their numbed state. They faced the prospect of losing everything they had fought for. But they had few weapons to fight the logging. These odious sales resurrected from the past could not be challenged in court under the usual environmental laws. Nevertheless, the Sierra Club Legal Defense Fund took up the challenge and filed a blizzard of lawsuits challenging the timber industry's interpretation.

On October 2, Tim Ream and Shannon Wilson set up tents on the steps of the federal courthouse in Eugene and began a liquids-only fast to protest the measure Northwest environmentalists were now calling "logging without laws."

"Our remaining forests are threatened by a back-room congressional trick to sell precious public assets at fire sale prices," Ream, a 33-year-old former Environmental Protection Agency employee, told the *Eugene Register-Guard* newspaper eight days into the fast. He called for public hearings on logging of old-growth forests and a separate vote on the measure in Congress so the issue could be debated in the open, for all to see.

Sleeping in tents, and braving rain, cold, catcalls, and traffic noise, Ream and Wilson spent their days explaining to anyone who asked the purpose of their fast. Wilson dropped out after losing 20 pounds in 18 days. Ream remained. His quiet presence tugged at the conscience of the community, and forced other environmentalists to contemplate what they were willing to do to right this wrong.

REPACKAGING THE FOREST

Beyond the owl region, in forests east of the Cascades and across the nation, the Forest Service wasted no time ratcheting up timber sales under the rider's broad definition of "salvage." In northeastern Washington, the Okanogan National Forest offered two large salvage sales that required entering Washington's largest unprotected roadless area, a region providing critical habitat for an imperiled population of rare forest-dwelling lynx. In eastern Oregon, the heavily logged and roaded Malheur National Forest offered a series of sales in roadless areas that provided spawning habitat for wild salmon and steelhead and essential cover for Rocky Mountain elk.

In the Northern Rockies, forest managers saw the opportunity to enter large roadless areas that had been closed to logging because of appeals, lawsuits, and restrictions in forest plans. In Idaho, old sales were revived in areas where logging threatened to wipe out salmon runs and increase flooding. In New Mexico, the Gila National Forest offered a fire salvage sale in a roadless forest occupied by the threatened Mexican spotted owl—a forest that ignited the same day the salvage logging rider was signed into law. Arson was suspected.

In the Great Lakes region and in forests of the Southeastern Coastal Plan, the Forest Service offered salvage sales of healthy trees in rare forest ecosystems touched only lightly by windstorms. One huge sale on the Conecuh National Forest, successfully challenged by Alabama environmentalists, proposed to log healthy stands of rare longleaf pine. Another sale, in the Chippewa National Forest of Minnesota, cut remnant white pine, a species nearly eliminated from the Great Lakes by timber barons in the 19th century.

In central Idaho, the Boise and Payette National Forests auctioned the Thunderbolt sale, one of the most controversial sales in the history of the Forest Service. Thunderbolt, which was in the works before the salvage rider took effect, called for logging in the watershed of the South Fork of the Salmon River, the most productive salmon spawning habitat in Idaho. After reviewing the plan, the National Marine Fisheries Service sent up a red flag, warning that Thunderbolt could jeopardize endangered Snake River chinook salmon.

But throughout most of 1995, Forest Service Chief Jack Ward Thomas put heavy pressure on the fisheries service not to issue a formal jeopardy opinion on Thunderbolt. NMFS Director Rollie Schmitten finally backed off, and the sale was auctioned to Boise Cascade.

Nothing slowed the rush to salvage. Late fall rainstorms in central Idaho triggered massive landslides on unstable mountainsides even as new roads and timber sales were being laid out under the salvage rider.

On the Clearwater National Forest, 28 roads were closed after heavy rains triggered more than 200 slides. On the Boise National Forest, a massive landslide downstream from an area where salvage logging was underway blew out a logging road and triggered a huge mudslide that sent roiling brown water into downtown Boise 55 miles away.

Jennifer Ferenstein of the Alliance for the Wild Rockies in Missoula, Montana, saw a disturbing new attitude among Forest Service officials as they realized that under the rider they were under no obligation to follow environmental laws. "On some forests, they're saying, 'We're going to do what we want.' They're realizing there's not much we can do anyway, that the pubic process has no power. The people who want to sell timber can ride roughshod over everyone else."

"In the debate over 'forest health,' biological truth has been overwhelmed by political manipulation," wrote Sara Folger of the Inland Empire Public Lands Council. "The greatest timber propaganda blitz ever perpetrated on the American public is now underway."

OPTION 9 REVISITED

As the furor over the rider accelerated, the Forest Service and BLM auctioned the first big old-growth sales under Option 9. The administration was eager to move these sales to market so it could blunt accusations from impatient congressional critics.

But when Jeff Dose, a fisheries biologist on the Umpqua National Forest, reviewed five sales his own forest was preparing to auction, he tried to put on the brakes. The sales, in the Oregon Cascades, had been prepared without involvement by fish biologists. Taken together, they called for removing 630 acres of old-growth forest surrounding the headwaters of the North Fork of the Umpqua River, a premier fly-fishing river known throughout the West for its sea-run cutthroat trout. Cutthroat trout numbers had dwindled from tens of thousands in the 1950s to less than 100 in the 1990s. The National Marine Fisheries Service was considering a petition to protect the trout under the Endangered Species Act.

Dose warned in writing that the cumulative impact of the five sales would be devastating and might violate the aquatic conservation strategy in Option 9. The upper reaches of the North Umpqua had been logged so heavily that further logging and road-building on the scale the agency was proposing could deal the trout a lethal blow, Dose said. His advice was ignored; the sales were auctioned.

On September 1, 1995, the Oregon Natural Resources Council and Umpqua Watersheds, a Roseburg group, sued to stop the North Umpqua sales. They argued that the Forest Service had violated the National Environmental Policy Act by offering the sales against the advice of its own biologist. The lawsuit was a deliberate test of the salvage rider. Lawyers wanted to find out whether sales offered under Option 9 would be held to any standard at all. If not, said Patti Goldman of the Sierra Club Legal Defense Fund, "then there are no environmental standards for any logging in the forests of the Pacific Northwest."

Judge Hogan wasn't long in delivering an opinion: On December 5 he ruled, in effect, that any sale the federal agencies called an Option 9 sale was covered by the rider and was exempt from legal challenge. President Clinton's forest plan was beginning to unravel in full public view.

On October 25 a three-judge panel of the 9th U.S. Court of Appeals upheld Hogan's ruling requiring the release of all unawarded sales in Oregon and Washington. The administration had run out of legal remedies. "We fought this to the bitter end and this is the bitter end," said Peter Coppelman of the U.S. Department of Justice. "The damage will be done."

By November, the Clinton Justice Department had taken control of the westside timber sale process. In weekly conference calls to Portland from Washington, D.C., Justice Department attorneys directed the Forest Service and BLM to search their pantries for every sale that might fall under the rider under the court's broad interpretation.

WAR FROM PEACE

As late as October 1995, Katie McGinty, Clinton's lead advisor on environmental issues, still maintained that the administration could comply with the rider without compromising the environment. But McGinty admitted, "It's very difficult. Congress's objective is simply to cut timber, to cut it as quickly as possible and as much as possible. It's very hard for us to maintain our commitment to cutting timber, for example, but not, for example, killing fish."

Tom Tuchmann, the man in charge of implementing the Northwest Forest Plan from Portland, insisted the rider would have minimal impact. "What we're talking about is 600 million board feet of the last of the old sales," he said. "It's less than 1 percent of all late-successional and old-growth habitat. I don't think this legislation has to tear the heart and soul out of the forest plan."

"I won't argue the ecological point, but politically he's got his head stuck in the sand," said Adam Berger of the Sierra Club Legal Defense Fund. "These sales have a long history. Environmentalists have worked for years to stop them. The administration has miscalculated their political significance."

The irony, Berger said, was that the rider might undo the president's hard-won forest plan. "We had a resolution to the timber debate in the Northwest," he said. "It didn't mean everyone was happy and it didn't mean there weren't still issues, but it did signal an end to the great debate. Now this rider has reopened the whole conflict. Congress has snatched civil war from the jaws of peace."

Sentries from Cascadia Forest Defenders stand guard at the Warner Creek logging road blockade in the Willamette National Forest. Activists kept vigil at their encampment throughout the winter of 1995-96, thwarting the Forest Service's attempt to begin salvaging trees scorched by a 1991 arson fire in a northern spotted owl reserve.

PART SEVEN

RENEWAL

1995–96

“Civil disobedience . . . asserts that we are the public, and that as the public we will be actors in history, not an audience to it. Direct action takes back history from the corridors of power and gives it to the public gathered in public places.”

—REBECCA SOLNIT, *Savage Dreams, 1994*

“Environmentalism or conservation or preservation, or whatever it should be called, is not a fact, and never has been. It is a job.”

—WALLACE STEGNER, *"A Capsule History
of Conservation," 1990*

“We have so much to work with, and will only have ourselves to blame if we fail.”

—MITCH FRIEDMAN, *January 1996*

THE TOPPLING OF THE FIRST ancient forests sentenced to destruction under the rider reverberated across the Pacific Northwest. As the full implications of "logging without laws" became clear, and as court rulings steadily expanded the rider's scope, this new attack rekindled the desperate passion that had driven the forest protection campaign for 20 years. Forest activists took to the woods. Rallies, marches, and civil disobedience actions sprouted in the Oregon Coast Range and the Siskiyous and quickly spread throughout western

Oregon and north to Washington's Olympic Peninsula. Not only Earth First! activists but mainstream conservationists crossed the line to protest the destruction unleashed by Congress and the Clinton administration. It soon became clear that under the salvage rider no forest, regardless of its condition, was safe.

Forest activists across the nation and across the political spectrum joined forces to oppose this assault on the forests. Confronted with a threat they could not counter with law or science, they were forced to invent new tactics, welcome new voices, find new courage, and engage the political system directly.

From the dark winter of 1995–96, a more inclusive, more politically astute, and newly empowered ancient forest campaign was born.

Chapter Thirty-One

Sugarloaf

For more than a decade, environmentalists in the Siskiyou country of southwestern Oregon fought to stop logging on Grayback Mountain. In September of 1995 they lost that battle.

Grayback Mountain, at 7,000 feet the highest peak in the Siskiyous, lay within the Kangaroo Roadless Area, which anchored a narrow corridor of pristine wild country connecting the heart of the Siskiyous to the Klamath River, 20 miles to the south in California. Classic old-growth forests blanketed the mountain's lower slopes. Yet despite its ecological value, the 100,000-acre roadless area had been left out of the 1984 Wilderness Act.

In the late 1980s the environmental group Headwaters documented repeated reforestation failures in nearby high-elevation areas of the Siskiyous due to poor soils and extreme temperatures. Nevertheless, the Siskiyou National Forest management plan for the 1990s designated part of Grayback Mountain for logging.

HISTORY OF A TIMBER SALE

The original Sugarloaf timber sale called for building nearly 11 miles of logging roads and cutting 424 acres on Grayback Mountain. Headwaters and other groups appealed the sale. In 1989 U.S. District Judge William Dwyer blocked all national forest timber sales in spotted owl habitat. Sugarloaf was released by the Rider from Hell, but a citizen timber review board declined to recommend that the sale be logged.

In 1990, as part of its embrace of "new forestry," the Forest Service announced that Sugarloaf would be redesigned. Instead of clearcutting the mountainside, loggers would make a number of partial cuts over a larger area of the mountainside. Road construction would be kept to a minimum; trees would be removed by helicopter. About 1,000 large old trees more than 250 years old, including Douglas-fir, white fir, and Shasta red fir, would be cut. The agency justified this unusual prescription as a way to restore "forest health."

In September of 1990 Sugarloaf was auctioned. Boise Cascade Company offered the high bid.

Environmentalists throughout the Siskiyou region banded together to halt the Sugarloaf sale. They filed legal appeals. They built strong state-level support for protecting the area. Oregon Governor Barbara Roberts and the Oregon Democratic Party urged the Forest Service to cancel the sale. When President Clinton's Northwest Forest Plan included Grayback Mountain within a key watershed and an old-growth reserve, the forest defenders thought the mountain was safe.

However, language inserted in the final version of the document that adopted the Northwest Forest Plan allowed Sugarloaf and 10 other sales released by the Rider from Hell to go forward.

Prominent scientists denounced the agency's "forest health" rationale for cutting big trees at Sugarloaf. After David Perry, a professor of forestry at Oregon State University, reviewed the plan, he wrote a scathing letter to Assistant Agriculture Secretary Jim Lyons, taking strong exception to the claim that the project would "perpetuate old-growth structure" and "enhance vigor" in the forest.

"In my opinion the sale as marked will do neither, and in fact is likely to degrade owl habitat and make the stand more vulnerable to wildfire," wrote Perry, an expert on fire ecology in August 1994. "Removing older trees will open the stand to wind and heat, hence dry it out."

Perry added, "Cutting healthy old trees under the guise of improving forest health will only fuel the cynicism among scientists and environmentalists about Forest Service motives. Presently that cynicism is getting in the way of real measures to improve forest health, and it sure as hell doesn't need more fuel."

The decision to cut Sugarloaf ultimately was made by Lyons in Washington, D.C.

THE TRESPASSERS

When the trees began to fall on Grayback Mountain, only Jerry Hurley's contract cutters were there to witness it. The Forest Service had sealed off 35 square miles of forest and Boise Cascade had posted around-the-clock guards at the access roads.

On September 11, three days after logging began, 19 protesters crossed into the closure area and were promptly arrested. "We're here to raise public awareness that the timber corporations have taken over public land," said Steve Marsden, executive director of the Siskiyou Regional Education Project, one of the protest's leaders.

That was the beginning.

The following day, officials from the Siskiyou National Forest conducted a media tour of the Sugarloaf sale and told the press they had found sabotaged equipment, a tree perch, and 30 tree spikes, probably left over from a 1992 protest. Boise Cascade logging supervisor Ken Wienke said his loggers had heard people hiking inside the closed area. "We've had several different things left inside units that weren't there the day before," he said. Loggers in camp had been awakened one morning by the beating of a drum.

On September 15, more than 50 Ashland High School students walk out of school to protest the Sugarloaf sale in front of Boise Cascade's Medford office.

On September 16, more people entered the Sugarloaf closure; more were arrested.

On September 19, 60 people protested the sale in front of Siskiyou National Forest headquarters in Grants Pass.

On September 23, Lou Gold led a peaceful walk into the closure area, to a place he had claimed as a traditional prayer spot during a summer vigil on Grayback Mountain.

By early October, when the rains came, forest activists had established a base camp in a soggy meadow at the edge of the forest. Some of them came from the nearby counterculture community of Williams. Others had read about the Sugarloaf sale in *Earth First! Journal* and had traveled to the site from out of state.

On October 9, activists from the base camp staged another trespass action. This time 56 were arrested. But the local news media ignored the event. Dispirited forest activists concluded that the outside world had lost interest in the destruction of ancient forests.

THE RATIONALE

By October 9, the biggest trees were on the ground, bucked into 15-foot sections and waiting for the big helicopters that would pluck them from the mountainside and lift them above the forest canopy on the first leg of their journey to the Boise Cascade mill in Medford.

On a tour of the Sugarloaf sale when the cutting was nearly done, Illinois Valley District Ranger Mary Zuchslag offered the Forest Service line in defending the project: these trees were infested with mistletoe, that area was prone to a root fungus. She even defended the narrow forested border left along a stream, inadequate by 1995 standards.

It would have been more honest for the Forest Service to admit that Sugarloaf was being logged under orders from Congress to provide timber volume. In a moment of candor, as she rested on a 30-inch-diameter log, Zuchslag confessed as much. "A lot of this is a values argument," she said. "We think we have to argue from science. But there is a value in human economics and there is value of wild areas, roadless areas, and big trees. It's got to be okay for us to care about those values."

Still, if the choice on whether to log Sugarloaf had been hers alone to make, she said, "I probably would have done it, given the legal advice we got."

By then it wasn't just about Sugarloaf anymore. The full import of the salvage rider was beginning to hit home in the Northwest.

THE WARRIORS

A steady rain pelted the tents and teepees at the base camp two days after the October 9 demonstration. Wind whipped the blue tarp covering the makeshift kitchen, where bedraggled young men and women peeled potatoes for the evening meal. Several camp residents were late returning from their arraignments at the Josephine County Courthouse in Grants Pass, 40 minutes away. They were among the 56 arrested for standing 150 feet inside the closure area.

Inside a smoke-filled teepee, the edgy sense of risk was palpable. Angela Beigenwald, the 19-year-old who appeared to be in charge of the base, was dressed in camouflage pants and jacket. She introduced herself as Fawn. Her partner, a young man who wore his long blond hair in dreadlocks, gave his name as Llama.

Fawn claimed that backcountry people had repeatedly penetrated the perimeter of the closure area under cover of darkness to monitor the progress of logging. They had eluded the "camo-freddies," federal agents trained to locate marijuana plots on the national forests and hunt down trespassers in the woods. In fact, a kind of clandestine guerrilla war was being waged deep in the forest, pitting self-appointed forest monitors against federal agents. "They know we can get in. They can't stop us," Fawn said.

Fawn and Llama were no strangers to direct action. The previous winter they and a few others had holed up in a snow cave high in the mountains of central Idaho so they could alert other environmentalists when the Forest Service began pushing a new logging road into a roadless area called Cove/Mallard. Because it had delayed the Forest Service project, Fawn considered the Cove/Mallard campaign a success. "It took them two and a half years just to get the logging road finished," she said. "We've slowed them down considerably."

Raised in Silverdale, Washington, Fawn claimed to have been an activist since the age of 12. She had met Llama on the campus of Evergreen State College, a center of environmental activism in Olympia, Washington. Together they had perfected techniques of civil disobedience detailed in *Earth First! Journal* and Earth First! founder Dave Foreman's book *Ecodefense*. They had conducted nonviolence and civil disobedience workshops throughout the Northwest. Fawn's first arrest was in Olympia, where she took part in a civil disobedience action at the office of the multinational timber company MacMillan-Bloedel, locking herself to the axle of a paddy wagon with a bicycle U-lock.

She was fearless. She saw the campaign she was involved in as a religious war—a war, she said, to decide whether the government had the power to "remove the spiritual, sacred land and habitat of feral humans . . . " Her hope was that many of the activists drawn to the Sugarloaf campaign would stay on in the area and buy land.

Asked whether the base camp was harboring tree spikers, Fawn considered her response carefully as the others watched in silence. Finally she said, "There is born out of necessity a division between people who sneak around at night and spike trees and burn bulldozers, and those who engage in public activism and civil disobedience.

Anyone engaged in a public campaign does not engage in monkey-wrenching or tree spiking."

The reason was obvious, she said. "We have public actions. Everyone knows where to find us." But she was careful not to condemn those tactics: "I would be very surprised if Sugarloaf was not spiked. There are a lot of people who feel that public activism is a sham, that it does no good."

THE PURPOSE OF CIVIL DISOBEDIENCE

At the Josephine County courthouse that same rainy afternoon, a deputy district attorney offered two dozen protesters a deal: plead no contest and agree to stay out of the closed area, and in 60 days, at sentencing, the second-degree trespassing charges pending against them would be reduced to violations. They'd get off with fines and fees of $75 and no criminal record. Some of the trespassers, those with jobs and homes elsewhere, accepted the deal on the spot. Others rejected the plea bargain. One young man said he wanted to address the court. But the overworked judge, who had a courtroom full of tree huggers, probation violators, and marijuana dealers to process, told him to save his statement for the sentencing.

For the protesters, the adrenaline rush of the action and the mass arrest was beginning to fade as the wheels of the criminal justice system cranked up. And for organizers, the action had been a disappointment. It had attracted almost no press coverage. Because most of the demonstrators wore their countercultural identity on their backs, it was easy for the mainstream media to dismiss them.

Not all the arrestees wore dreadlocks, overalls, and bulky Ecuadorian sweaters, however. Gary Schrodt, a businessman from Ashland, stood out in a silk shirt, pleated trousers, and graying, stylishly cut hair. "My purpose in going up there was to be part of what I hoped would be a large number of middle-class people willing to risk going to jail," Schrodt said. "These young people have no credibility with the media."

Brad Courier, a balding part-time Unitarian minister with a wry sense of humor, had helped organize a "mourning for the trees" to protest the loss of democratic processes. At the October 9 Sugarloaf action, several elderly members of his congregation had read it in unison.

Courier too had dressed up to get arrested. He hadn't particularly enjoyed the experience. "It was a big hassle. You have to go to court at least twice. It seems silly, really. We have to do it, and they have to do it too—the judge and the jailers have to go through this process. On the other hand, what else can we do? We don't have access to the courts."

At 68, Dot Fisher-Smith was a veteran of 30 years of antinuclear civil disobedience actions. She had done jail time on at least a dozen occasions. A Buddhist, she lived with her husband three and a half miles up a dirt road in the Siskiyou foothills above Ashland, in a cedar house shaded by oaks and pines. She had taken part in Lou Gold's spirit walk into the closure area, though she had not yet been arrested at Sugarloaf.

Effective civil disobedience, she said, was about more than getting arrested. It was about solidarity, about commitment, about putting your bodies in the way of the criminal justice system to make a clear and unambiguous statement. "If you're going to commit civil disobedience, the best thing you can do is to give yourself over to it. You make your statement with your body. If you say, 'I have a job, I'll pay my fine,' you're saying 'This isn't important to me.' If you go to jail, you're still in the woods. For as long as you're in jail, it makes an impact. You're saying, 'I did it willingly, I did it on purpose, and I'm willing to accept the consequences.'"

THE VETERANS

Longtime activists in the counterculture outpost of Takelma took the defeat at Grayback Mountain hard. Steve Marsden had worked 12 years, since the 1983 Bald Mountain Road blockade, to save the roadless areas of the Siskiyous. At his office in the converted health clinic that serves as headquarters for the Siskiyou Project, two days after his second arrest for trespassing inside the Sugarloaf closure, he was unshaven, red-eyed, and burned out. He had decided to leave his job and spend some time in the desert.

"Never as an activist have I put so much pressure on a timber sale," he said. "I got the governor and the Democratic Party of Oregon to oppose it, along with most of the local business community. But the Forest Service acts on behalf of the industry. They act to produce volume."

Asked if he had been up to see the logging at Sugarloaf, he was silent for a moment. No, he said. He didn't think he could bring himself to go up there. Asked whether this was a major defeat, Marsden was silent again. "It's not a defeat," he finally said with a sigh. "It's a long-term campaign. Unless we have legal protection, we have no protection."

George Shook, an artist, musician, and longtime Earth First! activist, lived above Takelma in a rustic house surrounded by national forest land. Shook had a degree in forestry from Syracuse University. He said the logging at Sugarloaf made no sense ecologically. But Shook's larger concern was with the buzzwords the Forest Service had adopted to justify logging roadless areas of the Siskiyous. "Forest health, ecosystem management, these things have no specificity, no meaning," he said. "The agencies cannot be held accountable, because there is no right or wrong."

Lou Gold, the former political science professor who had done more than anyone to publicize the botanical and ecological treasures of the Siskiyous, had come down from Bald Mountain, shaved his beard, and cut his gray ponytail. Strangely, his shorn curly gray locks gave him a more radical appearance. He had decided to try a new tack. "I'm going with the grand proposal. Let's transfer the national forests to the administration of the National Park Service. My bottom line is public preservation and restoration of the land and renewal of the human spirit."

Gold admitted this was a long shot—a campaign that could carry him through the rest of his life. But he said the past two years, in which he had come close to walking away from the environmental movement, had taught him a painful lesson: "Never try to reform an entrenched agency. Start a new one. The error we made was to spend 13 years trying to reform the Forest Service, starting with the Bald Mountain Road blockade."

THE NEXT GENERATION

Down the road in Takelma, Prema and Lila Heller, part of a new generation of forest activists, felt no such pessimism. To them, the issue seemed simple: No more ancient forests must be logged. For them, the gains of 20 years represented the status quo.

The solemn-eyed sisters, students at Illinois Valley High, had prevailed on their parents to take them to the October 9 Sugarloaf demonstration. After several hours, they had decided to join others in occupying the closure area. With their affinity group, Prema, 15, and Lila, 17, sat in a tight circle and offered each other encouragement as they waited to see what would happen next. They didn't wait long: Forest Service law enforcement officials arrived and warned that anyone who didn't leave would be arrested in five minutes. The girls were cuffed in plastic handcuffs and forced to sit for six hours in the cold without water or a bathroom break as night fell and the air turned chill. Prema had swollen hands from the too-tight cuffs.

At their high school, which serves a largely blue-collar community, Prema and Lila found themselves heroes briefly after their arrest. It hadn't always been the case. "Most people I've talked to just listen to what they've been told," Lila said, eating her lunch in the school parking lot on her first day back. "They don't understand about the forest. Anyone who cares about the environment is a hippie. Sugarloaf isn't mentioned in school at all." Now, however, her U.S. government teacher had asked her to talk to the class about her experience.

"There's a lot of stereotyping that students in our generation don't care," Lila said. "We wanted to show we do care. There's hardly any virgin forest left. We'll never see these trees again and our children won't see them. It makes you wonder if you want to bring a child into the world."

"It's everyone who is affected," Prema added. "I was so sad when we were sitting in the circle, wondering why this was necessary. We all breathe the air, we all drink the water. This is our *home.*"

THE ORGANIZERS

In September 1995, while attending a meeting sponsored by the Oregon Natural Resources Council at Breitenbush Resort, Susan Prince and her cousin Catherine Lucas took a break from high-level environmental strategizing to visit the Warner Creek logging road blockade high in the Oregon Cascades.

The two Bend, Oregon, women found a few determined activists fortifying their camp against the day the Forest Service moved in. The Warner Creek protesters had dug two deep trenches in the road, erected two teepees, and set up a field kitchen. Boulders in the road spelled out "Warner Creek Sucks." An Earth First! banner was draped over the steel gate the Forest Service had installed to block public access. The protesters had vowed to wait out the Forest Service and the timber sale purchaser, Thomas Creek Lumber Company, even if that meant staying all winter. The Forest Service, armed with Judge Hogan's ruling that the sale must go forward under the salvage rider, was equally adamant that logging would proceed.

Prince and Lucas were shaken by what they saw. "We sat on the top of a hill and I thought, 'This is ridiculous,'" Prince recalled. "What we needed up on that hill were the people at Breitenbush. We needed the middle-aged, mainstream, gray-haired Eddie Bauer folks. But up until then, they hadn't been willing to cross that line."

Prince left Lucas at the blockade for a week while she returned to Breitenbush to raise awareness about the Warner Creek action. After returning to Bend, the two decided to hold a gathering for the purpose of developing a strategy to defeat the rider. But they needed money. They turned to Carl Ross and Mark Winstein at Save America's Forests, who put them in touch with funders at the Foundation for Deep Ecology.

THE PITCH FOR REPEAL

On a frenetic October afternoon, in the cluttered two-story crash pad near Capitol Hill that serves as headquarters for Save America's Forests, the phones were ringing off the hooks. Ross and Winstein had managed to get 130 signatures from all over the country on a letter that asked President Clinton not to sign the 1996 appropriations bill funding the Forest Service and Bureau of Land Management unless Congress gave him language repealing the salvage rider.

The previous day, October 24, Winstein had presented Clinton's top environmental advisor, Katie McGinty, with the repeal letter. But McGinty told him it was too late. The 1996 appropriations bills were in conference committee. Adding new language now would mean sending the bills back to both chambers for approval. Five days later, however, the White House issued a press release saying Clinton might ask Congress to modify the rider to prevent the logging of a few westside old-growth sales. It was a seed planted, the first glimmer of hope.

Save America's Forests was the first group to call on President Clinton for a repeal of the rider. The idea quickly caught fire.

ALERTING THE TROOPS

In the bleak days of early fall 1995, the Western Ancient Forest Campaign was on the ropes. Loss of foundation funding had forced the layoff of regional coordinators and part-time forest monitors. A grant from the Lazar Foundation allowed the two remaining staff members to keep attending congressional hearings and strategy sessions and publishing a monthly newsletter that kept activists informed about the steady assault on the forests.

Jim Jontz had agreed to become the campaign's new executive director. But the former Democratic congressman from Indiana, who had lost a reelection bid after introducing the Ancient Forest Protection Act, was finishing a stormy tenure as director of the Endangered Species Coalition. He was immersed in building a nationwide network of grassroots support for saving the Endangered Species Act. He had not been paying close attention to the latest forest controversy out in the Northwest.

Brock Evans, vice president of the National Audubon Society, had just been offered an early retirement deal by John Flicker, the new president of Audubon. He had decided to accept it. In September, Paul Engelmeyer, a forest activist and local Audubon member on the Oregon Coast, invited Evans to come to Oregon and have a look at a timber sale in the headwaters of Tenmile Creek. The sale was upstream from a forest preserve National Audubon had purchased to preserve a critical piece of the Oregon Coast's last intact watershed. The sale had been withdrawn by the Forest Service, but the salvage logging rider had resurrected it. Engelmeyer told Evans that forest activists would be resorting to direct action to protest this sale and other imminent forest destruction wrought by the rider.

Evans was shocked by this firsthand look at the rider's impact. "I came back and sent out e-mail messages and said, 'People are going to go back out in the woods. What is our policy on civil disobedience and direct action?' But then I determined that I had to go out there and bear personal witness. I didn't care what National Audubon said."

After he announced his decision, Evans got a call from National Audubon's lawyer, who advised him he could not participate as an Audubon employee or at Audubon expense. He agreed. "I knew the press would identify me as vice president of Audubon anyway," he said. When his colleagues found out that Evans would be paying his own way, some of them were outraged. "They were asking, 'What kind of an outfit are we?'"

MOBILIZATION

On a brilliant weekend in mid-October, forest activists from across the Northwest converged at Blue Pool Campground south of Oakridge. Both Jontz and Evans attended the gathering organized by Susan Prince and Catherine Lucas. During the weekend of forest tours and strategy sessions, the group settled on a massive demonstration at the edge of the Sugarloaf closure on October 30 to draw attention to the salvage rider. At a follow-up meeting in Eugene, a new organization, Witness Against Lawless Logging, was born. Its goal was to draw attention to the carnage occurring in the forests as a result of the salvage rider, and to build public support for its total repeal.

This time it all came together, and in just 10 days.

On October 30, 300 people rallied and 90 were arrested after they entered the closure area—the largest number ever arrested in an Oregon logging protest. The names of those arrested spanned the spectrum of environmental politics: Steve Marsden and Lou Gold. Brock Evans and Jim Jontz. Sierra Club member Charlie Ogle and Earth First! founder Mike Roselle. Lila and Prema Heller and Dot Fisher-Smith. Cable News Network sent a television crew, which spent three days reporting from the scene.

By then, trucks had been hauling logs out of the forest to the Medford mill for 10 days. "There is nothing we can do now to stop Sugarloaf," Jontz said. "But we can insist Congress stop the assault on our environmental laws."

Evans told reporters he was wearing the same suit he had worn to the White House the day he spoke to the president about the rider. "I'm hoping that my being here and bearing witness and being arrested will encourage my thousands of colleagues who wear coats and ties to be counted too," he said. When he returned to Washington, D.C., his colleagues gave him a hero's welcome.

For the first time in a long while, it seemed the ancient forest campaign might bind its wounds and regain its momentum.

Chapter Thirty-Two

Full Circle

The Republican leaders' reign was as brief as it was brutal. Their strident attack on the nation's environmental laws in particular drew a strong backlash. By the end of 1995, the campaign against the environment was in full retreat.

The tide began to turn in October 1995, when a leaked memo revealed that the Republican leadership in the House was girding for a backlash in the hinterland over its extreme anti-environmental positions. The House Republican Conference advised GOP members to "go over the heads of the elitist environmental movement" with constituents by planting trees, adopting a highway, or touring a recycling plant—and being sure to invite the press.

"Your constituents will give you more credit for showing up on a Saturday to help clean up the local park or beach than they will give a press release from some Washington-based special interest group," the memo promised.

The Clinton administration was delighted. Both Vice President Al Gore and Carol Browner, director of the Environmental Protection Administration, mentioned the memo prominently in speeches to environmental journalists at a conference in Boston later that week.

On October 22, 1995, Interior Secretary Bruce Babbitt let loose with an op-ed piece in the *Washington Post* that accused Republicans of pulling a fast one on the American public. "There aren't any voters out there saying we have too many parks or our water is too clean," Babbitt wrote. "Yet without public debate, Republicans have engaged a quiet agenda to dismantle environmental and public resource protection. Their program is being rushed through Congress at a dizzying speed, which is troubling, for in the frenzied blur, few people outside the committee chambers know how, much less why, it is being carried out at all."

Moderate Republicans who did not share the views of their freshman colleagues began to speak up. "The old bipartisan coalition to protect the environment is slowly coming back," Representative Bill Richardson, a New Mexico Democrat, told Knight-Ridder News.

It was apparent by then that the House Republicans' Endangered Species Act rewrite, which called for effectively dismantling the law, was destined for a quiet death. Republican House Speaker Newt Gingrich declined to schedule it for a floor vote. Instead, he appointed a task force to study the act.

Republican leaders were forced to admit they had played their hand badly on an issue that had unexpectedly deep public support. "I'll be real straight with you—we have lost the debate on the environment," Republican whip Tom DeLay of Texas told the *Wall Street Journal* in late December. "I can count votes. There really has not been a leadership environmental strategy. There was a regulatory-reform strategy that deteriorated into an environmental issue, and it cost us."

Environmental groups implored President Clinton to veto the 1996 Interior appropriations bill, which was loaded with anti-environmental riders. Among other things it called for slashing funding for the Interior Columbia Basin study, getting rid of temporary fish protection standards, continuing a moratorium on endangered species listings, and ordering an increase in logging on the Tongass National Forests.

In December, Clinton did veto it. And this time, his veto stuck. In the winter of 1995–96, Congress and the administration reached a budget impasse that led to a series of government shutdowns. Efforts by Congress to attach some of the environmental rollbacks to continuing resolutions that would keep the government in business failed when Clinton threatened to veto them as well.

President Clinton had rediscovered the saliency of the environmental issue. National public opinion polls showed the American public supported strong environmental protection laws. In speeches, Clinton made it clear that the environment would be a major theme in his 1996 reelection campaign.

But the tide wasn't turning fast enough to save ancient forests. Eleven months after the Republican Revolution of 1995 began, "logging without laws" remained its only enduring legacy.

LOCAL KNOWLEDGE

As the Forest Service and the BLM cranked up their rusty timber sale machinery to comply with the salvage rider, forest activists channeled their anger into documenting the irreversible destruction that was occurring in the forest. All the passion, on-the-ground knowledge, and expertise of the grassroots groups was now needed, desperately.

Some forest defenders mourned the loss of ancient forests with public rituals. On the day after Thanksgiving 1995, in the Olympic National Forest, Alex Bradley, founder of the Quilcene Ancient Forest Coalition in Port Townsend, Washington, and 20 friends gathered beneath 250-year-old hemlocks and cedars. They collected rocks, branches, and leaves and made small shrines beside a nameless creek where it cascaded down a steep slope on its way to the Dosewallips River. Then they held hands in the rain and sent their respects to the doomed forest. "Logging without laws" was about to return clearcutting to the Olympics.

On December 16, 1995, Tim Ream concluded his 75-day fast outside the federal courthouse in Eugene, Oregon. The night before he broke bread, two dozen tents sprouted on the courthouse steps as his supporters sang and burned candles. "Only Massive Public Outcry Will Save Old Growth Forests," a hand-painted sign in their midst declared.

Ream, 35 pounds lighter than when he began, looked gaunt but joyful as he hugged his girlfriend and talked to friends. The previous week, during the final days of his fast, he had traveled to Washington, D.C., to meet with congressional staffers on Capitol Hill. He believed now that there was a chance President Clinton would support modifying the rider, if only to save his Northwest Forest Plan.

For Ream, the fast had been a life-transforming experience. "Whenever I needed energy, it was there," he said. Two strangers had put his journal entries on the Internet; he had received messages from an attorney in Ireland and a Peace Corps volunteer in Swaziland.

Meanwhile, in the Oregon Cascades, the Warner Creek blockade continued under 10 feet of snow. By January 1996, it had grown to include a drawbridge over a deep trench and a fortress wall built of small logs set vertically in the ground. It didn't look as if the scorched timber at Warner Creek would be logged anytime soon.

On the North Fork of the Elk River, where the Oregon Coast Range meets the Siskiyous, loggers began cutting in mid-January 1996 above one of the most productive coho salmon streams on the Pacific coast. Jim Rogers, founder of Friends of Elk River, had worked 20 years to protect these wild forests. In a note to Siskiyou National Forest Supervisor Mike Lunn after he returned from viewing the logging, Rogers wrote, "The sadness I feel, and the rage at the injustice and stupidity of it all, is profound."

On January 22, 69-year-old Helen Engle, a member of the board of directors of National Audubon, led a sit-in at the office of U.S. Representative Norm Dicks in Tacoma, Washington. Twenty-eight protesters in suits and ties demanded that Dicks, a Democrat, work to repeal the rider, which had returned clearcutting to the Olympic National Forest. Fifteen protesters were arrested by federal marshals after they refused to leave at day's end. "We really believed when we signed on to the Clinton Forest Plan that the war would be over," Engle said. "We just feel that we've been cheated."

Engle had asked for time on the Audubon board's December 9, 1995, agenda to explain what was going on out in the woods of the Pacific Northwest. "I told them, 'If you pick up the newspaper one day and read that Helen Engle, National Audubon Society board member, got arrested, you shouldn't be dismayed,'" she said. "There's a little patch of old growth in the Wynoochee Valley, near my childhood home, that I guess I would stand in the road to stop."

Afterward, the board passed a resolution expressing "concern and moral support to the chapters in their activities to challenge logging in the Northwest."

THE WORST LAW EVER

With each federal court ruling by Judge Michael Hogan over the fall, winter, and spring of 1995–96, the reach of the rider grew. As reports of environmentally damaging timber sales proliferated, some Democrats in Congress spoke out.

In early December, Senator Patrick Leahy of Vermont and eight House members filed a brief with the 9th U.S. Circuit Court of Appeals stating that sponsors of the rider had deliberately misrepresented the measure's intent during debates on the House and Senate floors. Nevertheless, the 9th Circuit Court of Appeals eventually upheld Hogan's interpretation of the law.

Editorial pages across the country attacked the rider. In early December, *Washington Post* columnist Jessica Mathews called it "arguably the worst piece of public lands legislation ever."

On December 7, Representative Elizabeth Furse, a progressive Oregon Democrat with roots in the peace movement, introduced a bill with 40 co-sponsors to repeal the rider and reinstate all applicable environmental laws and regulations. By March of 1996, the list of sponsors had grown to nearly 120.

The rider's Republican sponsors, including Republican Senator Mark Hatfield of Oregon, now saw that damage control would be necessary. They entered into negotiations with the White House to "fix" the rider so that some environmentally damaging sales west of the Cascades could be canceled. But with newfound solidarity, westside activists made common cause with their allies on the other side of the Cascades and across the country, who were battling equally destructive timber sales offered under the guise of "salvage." They insisted that they would accept only full repeal, not a partial fix to solve problems in one region of the country.

UMPQUA WATERSHEDS

Oregon's Douglas County was timber country both economically and culturally. The few forest defenders who lived there kept their activism low-key until the fall of 1995, when four old sales released by the salvage rider and five new sales offered under Option 9 hit the Umpqua National Forest and the Roseburg District of the BLM with a double whammy. All of the sales posed high risk to sensitive fish runs. The National Marine Fisheries Service warned that some of them would jeopardize both cutthroat trout and coastal coho salmon.

In the first week of January 1996, Tim Lewis and Sky Shiviah, two photographer-activists from Eugene, showed up unannounced at the office of a small Roseburg group called Umpqua Watersheds. Francis Eatherington and Ken Carloni agreed to take them into the Cascades to see areas scheduled for logging. When they got there they discovered that logging already was underway. The photographers captured images of the giants toppling. The result was a powerful video, *Last Chance for the Umpqua*. Umpqua Watersheds contributed $400 to produce copies of the video, which were distributed widely.

Shiviah and photographer Trygve Steen, a professor of biology at Portland State University, used still photos from the Umpqua logging operations to put together an evocative multimedia slide show. In early 1996 Tim Ream, still recovering from his fast, took the show on the road, driving 10,000 miles cross-country to spread the word about the salvage rider's impact to people in Cleveland, Boulder, and Washington, D.C.

On January 18, 1996, buses carried activists from Portland and Eugene to the North Umpqua Ranger Station east of Roseburg, where they joined Douglas County activists for the first logging protest and civil disobedience action ever held in the county. "We salute you for protecting your home in very hostile circumstances," said Jim Jontz, director of the Western Ancient Forest Campaign, who had flown west for the protest. "We're witnessing a tragedy. What we're seeing are the consequences of a concerted effort by a few wealthy timber industry people and their friends in Congress. The timber lobbyists are nowhere near the scene of the crime." Twenty protesters marched onto the porch of the district ranger's office and were cited for violating a closure.

In late March of 1995, loggers began moving into a stand of enormous ancient Douglas-firs in the first timber sale on the Umpqua National Forest. Protesters filtered into the woods to try to disrupt the logging. On March 20, Trygve Steen visited the site of the First sale to document the age of the trees and took a core sample of one behemoth, which revealed it to be at least 850 years old. When local activists learned the age of the stand, they demanded that the Forest Service swap the giants for trees elsewhere. The issue quickly reached the White House.

Roseburg Forest Products president Allyn Ford, who held the contract to log the stand, agreed to discuss a trade with the Clinton administration. But the talks bogged down over the administration's concern about where replacement timber would be found. In the meantime, logging of the big firs appeared imminent. On April 1, Steen, desperate to stop the cutting, picked up the phone and called Ford to appeal to him directly. He said he was concerned that trees of such great age and ecological significance might be lost over the next few days while negotiations were underway to save them. He asked Ford to pull his loggers out of the area. To his amazement, Ford agreed. On April 7, the trade went through, and trees older than the Magna Carta were saved from the chainsaw.

COMMUNICATING

Constant communication became critical as the campaign against the rider picked up steam. Grassroots activists from Roseburg to Missoula created electronic home pages to spread the word. In Port Orford, Oregon, Jim Britell spent the fall of 1995 designing a system of compatible computer hardware and software that could link forest activists in an instant communications network across the nation. In late November, the Western Ancient Forest Campaign set up an electronic "Logging Without Laws" bulletin board to spread the word about the worst of the sales moving forward, and to keep activists posted on efforts to get the rider repealed.

On January 22, 1996, the campaign released a report to Congress highlighting 10 sales from all regions of the country put forward as salvage sales to promote "forest health." In each case, local activists had obtained documentation that the forest health rationale was a ruse. Some sales were composed entirely of healthy trees; others had been offered as regular sales of healthy trees but then repackaged with a component of diseased trees and renamed "salvage."

Save America's Forests published its own definitive special issue on the rider's origins and impacts, which was highlighted in the Western Ancient Forest Campaign's electronic bulletin board. Spurred by grassroots activists, the feuding groups in Washington, D.C., were now working together against an imminent threat.

In Missoula, the Alliance for the Wild Rockies established a home page on the World Wide Web to describe environmentally damaging sales in the Northern Rockies that were being put forward under the rider.

Francis Eatherington of Umpqua Watersheds began communicating her feelings about the loss of irreplaceable old forests via a World Wide Web page she called "In Memory of Yellow Creek." Named for an old-growth timber sale on the Roseburg BLM District, it featured digitized photographs of the forest before it was logged and, eventually, after logging. She got responses from as far away as Tampa, Florida, and Portland, Maine. One person who saw the web page called her and wept.

NEW VOICES

Calls for repeal of the salvage rider multiplied. The Confederated Tribes of the Umatilla Indian Reservation in northeastern Oregon and the Klamath Tribe, in southern Oregon, said the logging unleashed by the rider threatened their traditional hunting, fishing, and food-gathering areas. In March, 1996, the Klamath Tribe sued to halt eight old sales within its traditional territory that had been revived by the rider.

Jennifer Belcher, Washington state's commissioner of public lands, denounced the rider for undermining a first-of-its-kind habitat conservation plan her office had prepared to govern management of Washington state trust lands. The Portland City Council passed a resolution calling for the rider's repeal because of its potential impact on the Bull Run Watershed in the Mount Hood National Forest, the source of Portland's drinking water.

In early February of 1996, 400 forest activists braved icy roads to make the pilgrimage to Ashland for the annual Western Ancient Forest Conference—a record attendance. The new wave of civil disobedience was the number-one topic of conversation. Former Earth First! activist Mitch Friedman had a provocative message for a new generation of Earth

First!ers: Update your tactics or stand aside. The movement was on the cusp of a new era, he said. It could not afford to alienate mainstream people who were now ready to stand up for the forests.

Since his own evolution into the mainstream, Friedman said, he had looked forward to the day he could return to civil disobedience. "I dreamed of the day when the scientist and the little old lady would sit in the logging road and the Earth First!ers would sit on the side quietly applauding, ducking the roving eye of the cameras." "I see that opportunity this year. I see anger and passion when I talk to my friends in Audubon and the community groups. They are saying, 'I'm ready to get out on the front lines!' The organizing opportunities are monumental this year, largely because of the clearcut rider."

Friedman was working with these mainstream activists, helping them think about what kind of direct action would convey their message. But when Earth First! activists in western Washington insisted on getting involved, some of those mainstream people backed off. If the movement hoped to reach out to new constituencies, he said, it was going to have to shed its proprietary attitude, empower people to convey their own messages about saving the Earth, and get out of the way.

"The commercial fisher wants to deliver a fish message. The racial minority wants to deliver an environmental justice message. The children want to deliver the future generation message. The Auduboner wants to deliver the bird message. The senior wants to deliver the responsibility message. And they all have their own way of doing so. Working with other groups is not a matter of convincing them to get behind the Earth First! banner. It's a matter of convincing yourself to get behind a common banner, and one that everyone can share."

If activists could do that, Friedman said, the possibilities were limitless. "This year we have great issues to organize around. And we have energy greater than we had even at the height of the ancient forest wars. We have so much to work with, and will only have ourselves to blame if we fail."

MOTHER NATURE SPEAKS

In February of 1996, the worst floods in 32 years hit Oregon and Washington, ripping out logging roads, triggering massive landslides, and dumping soil, debris, and giant conifers into streams. It was a classic rain-on-snow event: a heavy snowstorm followed by warm temperatures that melted the snowpack and heavy rains that filled streambanks to overflowing. Swollen rivers, heavy with runoff from freshly logged mountainsides and failed logging roads, swept trucks, dock pilings, and backyard decks downstream. The turbulent brown waters of the Willamette River threatened bridge supports and lapped at the Portland seawall. Heavy turbidity threatened Portland's drinking supply from the Bull Run watershed on Mount Hood, and Salem residents were forced to boil their drinking water from the Santiam River. In the days following the flood, the impacts of logging and road-building in the steep mountains of the Northwest were driven home in a way that every city-dweller could understand.

Forest activist Andy Stahl flew over the Siuslaw National Forest in the Oregon Coast Range during the flooding and counted 183 landslides; 114 were in clearcuts and 38 were on logging roads. A follow-up aerial survey of more than 80 watersheds in the Oregon and Washington Cascades and the Oregon Coast Range, commissioned by the Pacific Rivers Council, documented 650 landslides and confirmed that slides were far more prevalent on logged-over land. In late February, the Forest Service released its own study of new landslides that had occurred during the flooding in the Clackamas River drainage of the Mount Hood National Forest. Of the 254 slides surveyed, 72 percent had occurred in logged or roaded areas.

Yet immediately after the waters subsided, logging in some flood-ravaged areas resumed.

A NEW REALITY

As protests continued to flower across the Northwest, a paradigm shift, subtle but unmistakable, was occurring in the forest debate. By the spring of 1996, it was no longer environmentally acceptable to log ancient forests.

On February 24, 1996, President Clinton spoke at a community college in suburban Seattle as more than 1,000 people rallied in downtown Seattle to demand that he repeal the rider. Clinton admitted that he had made a serious mistake in allowing the rider to become law. Sometimes, he said, "good things have bad consequences." Three days later, the White House quietly issued Clinton's six-point plan for working with Congress to undo the damage. "We are losing ancient forests," the statement said. "We are losing valuable fish runs. Wild places that people in the Northwest and across America want to protect are being lost forever."

By then, however, most environmentalists had stopped expecting Clinton to save the forests. They were focusing on reaching Congress and the American people with their message of environmental destruction.

Andy Kerr, executive director of the Oregon Natural Resources Council, had resigned himself to the loss of some ancient forests. They were casualties, he said, in the high-stakes political battle the movement was now engaged in. "Even though we'll lose some, we won't lose as much as we've gained," Kerr said. "And the environment will be a huge political issue in 1996. Every so often we have to refight these battles. How many wars did Ho Chi Minh fight to win Viet Nam?"

James Monteith had not given up on his 20-year vision of winning protection for all of Oregon's roadless forests, though by 1996 there were far fewer of them to save. His organization, Save the West, had spent thousands of dollars in legal fees in an ultimately unsuccessful legal challenge of President Clinton's Northwest Forest Plan. Yet

Monteith made it clear that he was in this fight for the duration: "It's adapting to a changing situation and still trying to save what's left."

Nearly a quarter-century earlier, during what seemed like a hopeless fight to keep dams out of Hells Canyon, Brock Evans, another aging warrior of the forest preservation movement, had described the effort that would be needed to save wild places. It would require, he said, "endless pressure, endlessly applied."

Full Circle

In the spring of 1996 the hard truth of those words once again reverberated across the scarred mountainsides of the Pacific Northwest as ancient forests fell.

Epilogue

As the summer of 1996 began, seismic political shifts in the Northwest signaled that the orgy of clearcutting resulting from the salvage logging rider would be the timber industry's last.

Earlier in the year Democratic U.S. Representative Ron Wyden of Oregon had won the U.S. Senate seat vacated by the resignation of Republican Bob Packwood. Wyden, an environmental moderate, won with strategic help and endorsements from the Sierra Club and ONRC Action, the new political lobbying arm of the Oregon Natural Resources Council. Soon after, Republican Senator Mark Hatfield announced that he would leave the Senate in early 1997, ending his 30-year reign as the timber industry's most powerful friend in Congress. Summer polls showed Democratic political newcomer Tom Bruggere leading Republican conservative Gordon Smith in the race to succeed Hatfield, raising the possibility that, for the first time since 1967, Oregon might soon be represented by two environmentally moderate Democrats in the U.S. Senate. In Washington too the conservative tide of 1994 was ebbing; in the House at least three conservative GOP freshmen faced serious reelection challenges.

The campaign to repeal "logging without laws" faltered in April, when Republican House leaders refused to allow a vote on Oregon Democratic Representative Elizabeth Furse's repeal bill. Timber companies warned the public to expect a summer of frenetic logging as they rushed to cut timber sales before the rider expired. In response, forest activists stepped up their direct action campaigns. In Washington, D.C., environmental lobbyists turned their attention to defeating a bill sponsored by Republican U.S. Senator Larry Craig of Idaho, which threatened to incorporate the worst features of the temporary salvage rider in permanent legislation.

In the face of veto threats from President Clinton, Western Republicans in Congress were forced to drop environment-killing riders from 1997 appropriations bills. A bill co-sponsored by Furse, which would have cut off funding to implement the salvage logging rider, came within two votes of passage. Among those voting for it were several Republicans. "This shows the anti-environmental forces still control the House—but just barely," remarked Marty Hayden of the Sierra Club Legal Defense Fund.

Also in April, a federal appeals court upheld President Clinton's

Northwest Forest Plan, ending challenges to its legality. However, the Forest Service's own 1997 budget revealed that the administration would be unable to produce as much timber as the plan called for anytime soon. The agency also reported that recreational use of national forests was at an all-time high.

In May, after expiration of a one-year congressional moratorium on new listings, the U.S. Fish and Wildlife Service and the National Marine Fisheries Service were back in the endangered species business—though NMFS announced that it would delay long-overdue and politically volatile decisions on whether to protect steelhead and coho salmon under the Endangered Species Act.

Oregon marked a significant milestone in mid-1996 when the state's burgeoning electronic technology sector overtook timber as its leading industry. A report by a panel of economists led by Thomas Power, chairman of the University of Montana economics department, delivered good news for the region as a whole: The economists found that between 1988 and 1994, despite declines in the timber and aerospace industries, overall employment in Oregon, Washington, Idaho, and Montana had grown by 18 percent, two and a half times the national average. No longer a timber colony, dependent on liquidating the last of an irreplaceable resource, the Northwest at the close of the 20th century has built a mature, diversified economy. Even many rural communities have found new life.

There were stunning developments within the ranks of the environmental movement as well. In April, the membership of the venerable Sierra Club voted 2-to-1 to advocate an end to commercial logging in national forests—a view sharply at odds with that of the club's leadership. Chad Hanson of Eugene, Oregon, co-founder of the John Muir Sierrans, which led the insurgency, said he hoped the club's new stance would help bridge the gap between grassroots activists and the national conservation groups.

In May, Andy Kerr announced that he would step down as executive director of ONRC, leaving the organization he had come to personify after 20 years. During his two-year tenure as director, Kerr moved the organization boldly into the realm of electoral politics, establishing a political lobbying arm and two political action committees to influence federal and state campaigns. Kerr's name had come to symbolize the angry polarization of the forest issue in the Northwest. More recently, his political pragmatism—ONRC had endorsed political newcomer Bruggere over Harry Lonsdale and Jerry Rust, two loyal advocates of forest protection, in the U.S. Senate race to replace Hatfield—had alienated some of his compatriots. Yet his legacy as the uncompromising voice of the movement during the high-stakes years of the early 1990s seemed secure.

The floods of February 1996 had opened the eyes of ordinary citizens to the effects of logging and road-building in municipal watersheds. Residents of Salem, Oregon's capital, forced to boil water after the flood because of heavy sedimentation in the North Santiam River watershed, were especially sensitive. In June, Salem officials publicly opposed a huge new timber sale in the North Santiam, forcing the Forest Service to put the project on hold.

Across the Northwest, new people and new energy continued to flow into the forest protection movement. In just eight months, the activist network Witness Against Lawless Logging, born in response to the salvage logging rider, had established a strong communications link and a visible presence in the woods. Protests and civil disobedience actions widened. On April 21, in observance of Earth Day, WALL sponsored simultaneous rallies to protest logging at Enola Hill on the Mount Hood National Forest, a site used for vision quests by some Native Americans, and at Tobe West in the Oregon Coast Range, where trees had fallen in stands believed to be occupied by marbled murrelets. The rallies drew at least 1,000 people from all walks of life and attracted coverage by the CBS's "60 Minutes." By June, civil disobedience actions had occurred at about a dozen sites in Oregon and Washington, and the number of arrests associated with nonviolent protests over "logging without laws" had climbed to 600.

In early July, activists blockaded roads leading to the China Left timber sale in southwestern Oregon and the Jack timber sale, part of the Cove/Mallard project, in central Idaho. At the Warner Creek blockade in the Oregon Cascades, where forest defenders had held down the fort all winter, activists from across the country were practicing tree-sitting and other nonviolent resistance tactics to prepare for an imminent showdown with the Forest Service over salvage logging in the Warner Creek burn.

In Bellingham, Washington, 24 students from the Western Endangered Species Alliance volunteered their summer to getting the rider repealed. Members of local Audubon chapters in Washington and Oregon signed up for training to become certified marbled murrelet surveyors so they could comb the woods for signs of the nesting seabirds. It was direct action of another kind; every murrelet nest they found might save an ancient forest.

As the Forest Service scrambled to meet top-down timber quotas by offering massive salvage sales in roadless areas harboring grizzly, lynx and endangered salmon, scattered demonstrations sprouted in more hostile territory—eastern Oregon, northeastern Washington, northern Idaho, western Montana.

Sympathetic members of Congress stepped up their efforts to halt the worst of the sales. In early June, a deal brokered by Democratic Representative Peter DeFazio of Oregon saved the roadless forests in the North Fork of the Elk River drainage on Oregon's South Coast.

On June 14, good news arrived: the 9th Circuit Court of Appeals in San Francisco, overturning a decision by U.S. District Judge Michael Hogan, ruled that in the absence of clear direction from Congress, the

Forest Service and BLM must use scientific criteria to determine where marbled murrelets were nesting. The ruling instantly saved 4,000 acres of coastal old-growth forest. "The district court erred . . . in substituting its own judgment on a question requiring highly specialized or scientific expertise," the three-judge panel scolded. The ruling also saved four hotly contested old-growth sales on the Umpqua and Siskiyou national forests. The environmental group Umpqua Watersheds took to the woods on the summer solstice to celebrate the reprieve for ancient forests.

On July 2, as President Clinton sought to mend fences with environmentalists in preparation for his 1996 reelection campaign, there was more good news. U.S. Agriculture Secretary Dan Glickman, acknowledging that the Forest Service had suffered a severe loss of credibility over its implementation of the salvage rider, announced strict new guidelines. The new rules sharply restricted logging in roadless areas under the rider and the cutting of healthy trees as part of "forest health" treatments. The Forest Service immediately withdrew some of its largest and most controversial roadless area sales. The new restrictions were expected to reduce 1996 timber sale levels by 12 percent in Oregon and Washington alone.

Three weeks later, protesters bracing for a showdown at the Warner Creek road blockade learned that the Clinton administration, apparently seeking to avoid an ugly election-year confrontation in the woods, had temporarily withdrawn one large timber sale in the Warner Creek area to comply with Glickman's directive. White House officials were negotiating with the purchaser to cancel another sale entirely. "Taken together, delaying the South Warner timber sale and canceling the North Warner contract would be a huge victory for environmentalists, most likely signaling the Forest Service's abandonment of efforts to log in the fire-burned area," reported Lance Robertson of the *Eugene Register-Guard*. The victory was a testament to the raw physical courage and commitment of activists who had refused to back down.

The fresh clearcuts on mountainsides and the monster logs rolling down the highways in the summer of 1996 testified to the price the environment had paid for "logging without laws." But the cynical raid on the forests had forced the environmental movement to develop new political muscle in a hurry.

Only a crusade led by the young and audacious could have stopped the timber juggernaut in the 1970s. Only a legal and political campaign could have won tenuous protection for ancient forests in the 1980s and 1990s. But only a mature, broad-based movement will sustain those gains into the 21st century.

The challenge, as forest activists had learned the hard way, was to build political support for these forests not only in the halls of Congress, or in the federal courthouse, but in the hearts and souls of the American people.

Chronology

1946   The Forest Service creates the Shelton Sustained Yield Unit, giving the Simpson Timber Company in Shelton, Washington, a 99-year monopoly on timber from the Shelton District of the Olympic National Forest.

1957   Congress signs the first of two 50-year contracts with Alaska pulp mills, guaranteeing them heavily subsidized timber from Alaska's Tongass National Forest.

1964   Congress passes the Wilderness Act, creating a national wilderness preservation system and conferring permanent protection on 9.1 million acres of national forest land.

1967   Brock Evans becomes Northwest regional representative of the Sierra Club and meets with a group of conservationists committed to saving an Oregon old-growth valley named French Pete.

1968   Wildlife biology student Eric Forsman begins studying the northern spotted owl.

1969   Congress passes the National Environmental Policy Act, requiring federal agencies to inform the public of the environmental impact of major federal projects.

1970   Earth Day ushers in the modern environmental movement. Oregon State University initiates a research project to study the characteristics of old-growth Douglas-fir forests.

1973   Congress passes the Endangered Species Act, committing the federal government to prevent the extinction of native plants and animals and their habitat.

1974   The Oregon Wilderness Coalition is born in Eugene, Oregon.

1976   Congress passes the National Forest Management Act, which requires the Forest Service to prepare management plans for each national forest and to conduct wilderness suitability inventories of all roadless national forest lands.

   The Beuter Report, prepared by forestry professors at Oregon State University, predicts that private companies will experience a gap in timber supplies beginning in the 1990s unless cutting is accelerated on public lands.

1978   Congress passes the Endangered American Wilderness Act, conferring permanent protection on French Pete.

   Timber sales on national forests in Oregon and Washington reach an all-time high of 5.344 billion board feet.

1979   A seminal conference on old-growth forests is held at Lewis & Clark College in Portland.

The state of California sues the Forest Service to prevent the development of 47 roadless areas the agency has excluded from its wilderness recommendations.

1980   Mount St. Helens erupts.

Ronald Reagan is elected president, ushering in 12 years of conservative Republican control of federal land management.

Biologist Eric Forsman begins conducting radio telemetry studies on northern spotted owls and discovers their range is much larger than he had realized.

1981   John Crowell, Reagan's assistant agriculture secretary, says he believes the cut on national forests can be doubled without adverse environmental effects.

1982   The Northwest timber industry is flattened by the worst downturn since the Great Depression.

Congress creates the Mount St. Helens National Volcanic Area.

1983   Earth First! activists blockade Bald Mountain Road to halt penetration of the North Kalmiopsis Roadless Area in the Siskiyou National Forest.

In a lawsuit brought by the Oregon Wilderness Coalition (now the Oregon Natural Resources Council), a federal judge blocks entry into roadless national forest land in Oregon for logging until Congress makes final determinations about which areas will be protected as wilderness.

Supervisors of major timber-producing national forests in the Northwest meet with Forest Service Chief Max Peterson to warn him that the cut will have to drop drastically under new forest management plans.

1984   Congress passes Oregon, Washington, and California wilderness bills, setting aside millions of roadless acres, most of it high-elevation forests, rocks, and ice. Millions more acres are released from consideration and opened to "multiple-use management."

Environmentalists appeal the Forest Service's first regional guide for the northern spotted owl.

Senator Mark Hatfield and Representative Les AuCoin of Oregon push through the Timber Contract Modification Act, which lets timber companies get out of high-priced timber contracts and keeps some marginally profitable mills in business for several more years.

1985   Congress passes the first in a series of appropriation bill "riders," overriding a federal injunction in a lawsuit brought by the National Wildlife Federation over logging on unstable slopes in the Oregon Coast Range.

1986   Loggers for Willamette Industries cut down Millenium Grove, believed to contain the oldest Douglas-fir stands in Oregon.

1987   The Sierra Club Legal Defense Fund opens an office in Seattle and begins a litigation campaign to protect old-growth forests.

1988 George Bush, campaigning to succeed Ronald Reagan, promises he will be "the environmental president."

A federal judge rules that a decision by the Fish and Wildlife Service not to initiate a study of the status of the northern spotted owl is "arbitrary and capricious."

1989 U.S. District Judge William Dwyer blocks most national forest timber sales in western Oregon and western Washington until the Forest Service adopts a scientifically credible plan for protecting the owl.

Scientists from throughout the Northwest meet in Portland under tight security for the first-ever old-growth forest wildlife symposium.

The Fish and Wildlife Service proposes listing of the northern spotted owl as a threatened species.

Yellow Ribbon rallies erupt in timber towns throughout the Northwest.

The Oregon congressional delegation holds a timber summit in Salem and follows up with passage of a measure releasing more than 1 billion board feet of timber from the Dwyer injunction.

The Wilderness Society opens an office in Portland.

1990 The Interagency Scientific Committee, headed by Forest Service wildlife biologist Jack Ward Thomas, releases its strategy for conservation of the spotted owl.

The owl is listed as a threatened species throughout its range due to destruction of its habitat. Tension mounts at hearings across the Northwest.

California forest activists stage Redwood Summer, a series of protest actions to draw attention to the imminent logging of the last old-growth redwoods on private land.

1991 Interior Secretary Manual Lujan announces that he will convene the "God Squad" to determine whether the economic costs of protecting the owl are too high.

The American Fisheries Society releases a report declaring that 214 Pacific salmon runs are in decline, due in part to logging and road-building in sensitive watersheds.

A panel of scientists known as the Gang of Four develops a range of proposals for legislation to protect owls, salmon, and other old-growth species.

1992 The God Squad hearings turn into an expensive debacle.

Lujan rejects an owl recovery plan written by his own handpicked team.

Satellite images gathered by NASA show that forest fragmentation is far more severe in the Mount Hood National Forest than in the Brazilian tropical rainforest.

George Bush blows it at the Rio Earth Summit.

Bill Clinton selects Al Gore as his running mate.

The U.S. Fish and Wildlife Service lists the marbled murrelet as a threatened species.

Clinton is elected; he promises to hold a forest summit within the first 100 days of his administration.

1993 Clinton convenes the Northwest Forest Conference and promises to produce a balanced plan for the management of the old-growth forest ecosystem within 60 days.

A team of scientists develops Option 9. The compromise plan reduces logging and increases protection for sensitive watersheds, but also allows about one-third of the remaining old growth to be cut and sanctions salvage logging and thinning even in old-growth reserves.

Forest activists petition for protection of all remaining old growth east of the Cascades.

Jack Ward Thomas becomes chief of the Forest Service.

1994 The Clinton administration launches an ecosystem planning process for forests of the Interior Northwest.

Fires sweep through eastern Washington and Idaho. Pressure builds for a massive salvage logging program to restore "forest health."

Republicans win control of Congress.

1995 Republicans unleash the Contract with America and a broad assault on the nation's environmental laws.

President Clinton first vetoes and then signs a budget bill containing a "salvage rider" that exempts virtually any timber sale on federal land from environmental laws.

Demonstrations protesting the "logging without laws" rider erupt throughout the West.

1996 The Sierra Club membership votes by a 2-to-1 ratio to oppose commercial logging on federal land.

As ancient forests fall, new recruits join the campaign to stop the destruction.

Reading List

Andruss, Van, Christopher Plant, Judith Plant, and Eleanor Wright. *Home! A Bioregional Reader.* Philadelphia: New Society Publishers, 1990.

Barker, Rocky. *Saving All the Parts.* Washington, D.C.: Island Press, 1993.

Cone, Joseph. *A Common Fate: Endangered Salmon and the People of the Pacific Northwest.* New York: Henry Holt, 1995.

Davis, John, ed. *The Earth First! Reader: Ten Years of Radical Environmentalism.* Layton, Utah: Gibbs Smith, 1991.

Dietrich, William. *The Final Forest.* New York: Simon & Schuster, 1992.

Dowie, Mark. *Losing Ground: American Environmentalism at the Close of the Twentieth Century.* Cambridge: Massachusetts Institute of Technology Press, 1995.

Egan, Timothy. *The Good Rain.* New York: Knopf, 1990.

Ervin, Keith. *Fragile Majesty.* Seattle: The Mountaineers Books, 1989.

Foreman, Dave, and Howie Wolk. *The Big Outside.* New York: Harmony Books, 1992.

Gottlieb, Robert. *Forcing the Spring: The Transformation of the American Environmental Movement.* Washington, D.C.: Island Press, 1993.

Helvarg, David. *The War against the Greens.* San Francisco: Sierra Club Books, 1994.

Langston, Nancy. *Forest Dreams, Forest Nightmares: The Paradox of Old Growth in the Inland West.* Seattle: University of Washington Press, 1995.

Lash, Jonathan, Katherine Gillman, and David Sheridan. *Season of Spoils: The Story of the Reagan Administration's Attack on the Environment.* New York: Pantheon Books, 1984.

Leopold, Aldo. *A Sand County Almanac.* Oxford: Oxford University Press, 1949.

Lien, Carsten. *Olympic Battleground: The Power Politics of Timber Preservation.* San Francisco: Sierra Club Books, 1991.

Manes, Christopher. *Green Rage: Radical Environmentalism and the Unmaking of Civilization.* Boston: Little, Brown, 1990.

Manning, Richard. *Last Stand: Logging, Journalism, and the Case for Humility.* Layton, Utah: Gibbs Smith, 1991.

Maser, Chris. *Forest Primeval: The Natural History of an Ancient Forest.* Toronto: Stoddart Publishing, 1991.

————. *The Redesigned Forest*. San Pedro, Calif.: R & E Miles, 1988.

May, Elizabeth. *Paradise Won: The Struggle for South Moresby*. Toronto: McClelland & Stewart, 1990.

Nash, Roderick. *Wilderness and the American Mind*. New Haven, Conn.: Yale University Press, 1967.

Norse, Elliott, ed. *Ancient Forests of the Pacific Northwest*. Washington, D.C.: Island Press and The Wilderness Society, 1990.

Noss, Reed R., and Allen Y. Cooperrider. *Saving Nature's Legacy*. Washington, D.C.: Island Press, 1994.

O'Toole, Randal. *Reforming the Forest Service*. Washington, D.C.: Island Press, 1988.

Pyle, Robert Michael. *Wintergreen: Listening to the Land's Heart*. Boston: Houghton Mifflin, 1986.

Robbins, William G. *Hard Times in Paradise: Coos Bay, Oregon, 1850–1986*. Seattle: University of Washington Press, 1988.

Roth, Dennis. *The Wilderness Movement and the National Forests*. College Station, Tex.: Intaglio Press, 1984.

————. *The Wilderness Movement and the National Forests: 1980–1984*. Washington, D.C.: USDA Forest Service, 1988.

Seideman, David. *Showdown at Opal Creek*. New York: Carroll & Graf, 1993.

Snow, Donald, ed. *Voices from the Environmental Movement*. Washington, D.C.: Island Press, 1992.

Snyder, Gary. *The Practice of the Wild*. San Francisco: North Point Press, 1990.

Sullivan, William. *Listening for Coyote*. New York: Henry Holt, 1988.

Udall, Stewart L. *The Quiet Crisis*. New York: Holt, Rinehart & Winston, 1964.

Wallace, David Rains. *The Klamath Knot*. San Francisco: Sierra Club Books, 1983.

Wilkinson, Charles F. *Crossing the Next Meridian: Land, Water, and the Future of the West*. Washington, D.C.: Island Press, 1992.

Wood, Wendell. *A Walking Guide to Oregon's Ancient Forests*. Portland, Oregon: Natural Resources Council, 1991.

Zakin, Susan. *Coyotes and Town Dogs: Earth First! and the Environmental Movement*. New York: Viking, 1993.

Index

Numbers in italics refer to photographs

About the Author

The granddaughter of an Aberdeen, Washington, logger, Kathie Durbin grew up in Eugene, Oregon, the epicenter of the old-growth wars. A journalist with over 20 years of experience, she has received numerous awards for her coverage of education, social issues, and the environment. Her work has been published in *High Country News, National Wildlife, Amicus Journal, Audubon* magazine, *Defenders of Wildlife, The Seattle Weekly,* and *Willamette Week.*

She began tracking the Pacific Northwest's ancient forest conflict in 1989 while working as an environmental reporter for *The Oregonian.* Since then she has logged tens of thousands of miles on land and in the air touring forests from Southeast Alaska to northern California, met hundreds of grassroots activists, and covered all the key events in the struggle. Currently a contributing editor and columnist for the monthly newspaper *Cascadia Times,* she lives with her husband and their golden retriever, Fiona, in Portland.

Charles F. Wilkinson, the Moses Lasky Professor of Law at the University of Colorado, has written widely on the American West. His 10 books include *Federal Public Land and Resources Law* (with Coggins and Leshy); *Land and Resources Planning in the National Forests* (with Anderson); *The Eagle Bird: Mapping a New West;* and *Crossing the Next Meridian: Land, Water, and the Future of the West.*

THE MOUNTAINEERS, founded in 1906, is a nonprofit outdoor activity and conservation club, whose mission is "to explore, study, preserve, and enjoy the natural beauty of the outdoors . . . " Based in Seattle, Washington, the club is now the third-largest such organization in the United States, with 15,000 members and five branches throughout Washington State.

The Mountaineers sponsors both classes and year-round outdoor activities in the Pacific Northwest, which include hiking, mountain climbing, ski-touring, snowshoeing, bicycling, camping, kayaking and canoeing, nature study, sailing, and adventure travel. The club's conservation division supports environmental causes through educational activities, sponsoring legislation, and presenting informational programs. All club activities are led by skilled, experienced volunteers, who are dedicated to promoting safe and responsible enjoyment and preservation of the outdoors.

If you would like to participate in these organized outdoor activities or the club's programs, consider a membership in The Mountaineers. For information and an application, write or call The Mountaineers, Club Headquarters, 300 Third Avenue West, Seattle, WA 98119; (206) 284-6310.

The Mountaineers Books, an active, nonprofit publishing program of the club, produces guidebooks, instructional texts, historical works, natural history guides, and works on environmental conservation. All books produced by The Mountaineers are aimed at fulfilling the club's mission.

Send or call for our catalog of more than 300 outdoor titles:

 The Mountaineers Books
1001 SW Klickitat Way, Suite 201
Seattle, WA 98134
1-800-553-4453, e-mail: Mbooks@mountaineers.org